100% Student Success

GWENN WILSON, MA

THIRD EDITION

CENGAGE Learning

Australia • Brazil • Japan • Korea • Mexico • Singapore • Spain • United Kingdom • United States

CENGAGE
Learning·

100% Student Success,
Third Edition
Gwenn Wilson

Product Director: Annie Todd

Senior Product Manager: Shani Fisher

Senior Content Developer: Judith Fifer

Associate Content Developer:
Danielle Warchol

Content Coordinator: Rebecca Donahue

Product Assistant: Kayla A Gagne

Media Developer: Amy Gibbons

Production Management, and Composition:
Manoj Kumar, MPS Limited

Production Manager: Elena Montillo

Senior Art Director: Pam Galbreath

Manufacturing Planner: Sandee Milewski

Rights Acquisition Specialist:
Shalice Shah-Caldwell
Marketing Brand Manager:
Jennifer Levanduski
Senior Marketing Manager: Lydia LeStar

Photo Researcher: PreMedia Global

Text Researcher: PreMedia Global

Interior and Cover Design: Suzanne Nelson,
essence of 7

Cover Image: Ryan McGinnis/Flickr/
Getty Images

For product information and technology assistance, contact us at
Cengage Learning Customer & Sales Support, 1-800-354-9706

For permission to use material from this text or product,
submit all requests online at **www.cengage.com/permissions**
Further permissions questions can be emailed to
permissionrequest@cengage.com

Library of Congress Control Number: 2013949661

ISBN-13: 978-1-285-19450-9

ISBN-10: 1-285-19450-0

Cengage Learning
200 First Stamford Place, 4th Floor
Stamford, CT 06902
USA

Cengage Learning is a leading provider of customized learning solutions with office locations around the globe, including Singapore, the United Kingdom, Australia, Mexico, Brazil, and Japan. Locate your local office at:
www.cengage.com/global

Cengage Learning products are represented in Canada by Nelson Education, Ltd.

To learn more about Cengage Learning Solutions, visit **www.cengage.com**

Purchase any of our products at your local college store or at our preferred online store **www.cengagebrain.com**

Printed in the United States of America
1 2 3 4 5 6 7 17 16 15 14 13

Table of Contents

COMMON CONCERNS OF THE
ADULT COLLEGE STUDENT 45

PART 2   SHAPING AND COMMUNICATING YOUR IDEAS / 71

4   LEARNING STRATEGIES 73

5   COMMUNICATION SKILLS FOR STUDENT SUCCESS 101

6 CRITICAL THINKING AND PROBLEM SOLVING 125

PART 3   HARNESSING INFORMATION / 147

 7   INFORMATION LITERACY FOR THE 21ST CENTURY 149

Preface

HOW WILL THIS TEXT HELP YOU?

Thank you for choosing *100% Student Success*, third edition. As a text that promotes student achievement, this book is special and different from many others covering the same topic. In addition to addressing the practical student tasks such as note-taking and reading strategies, the text also encourages students to develop skills such as self-reflection and lifelong learning that will serve them well beyond college. The book also addresses practical concerns of adult students, such as financial management and balancing life responsibilities with school.

Students today represent a variety of age groups, backgrounds, learning styles, and personal situations. Many 21st century students are returning to school for retraining in a new profession. In addition, technology has greatly expanded the information and resources available to students. The third edition of *100% Student Success* addresses and appeals to diverse student needs in the following ways:

- The book is written in a conversational tone that speaks to the student in a direct, straightforward manner.
- Recommended activities are diverse and appeal to a variety of learning styles.
- Key suggestions for successfully applying the concepts presented in the book allow students to make immediate and practical use of the information.
- Applied case studies provide students with common scenarios that illustrate typical concerns of today's students.
- Suggestions for using current technology appeal to students who are tech savvy and provide students who are less so the opportunity to learn new technologies.

▶ Suggestions for materials to include in a professional learning portfolio provide students with the opportunity to develop a record of their academic and professional accomplishments.

▶ A helpful web site provides resources that students can print and collect in their professional development portfolio.

A new edition includes new and updated material as well as changes that improve the flow and delivery of the content. The third edition of *100% Student Success* has been changed to better serve the needs of students.

HOW TO USE THIS BOOK

100% Student Success is written to actively involve you in developing positive and productive personal and professional skills. The following features will help guide you through the material and provide opportunities for you to practice what you've learned:

▶ **BE IN THE KNOW:** A new feature to the third edition of *100% Student Success*, Be in the Know provides vignettes of real-world situations as they relate to the chapter content. The intent of this feature is to help students focus on the subject at hand and show them how they can learn from the provided examples in these content areas.

▶ **LEARNING OBJECTIVES:** Learning objectives outline the information in each chapter. Use them to identify the important points and to understand what you are supposed to learn. Learning objectives can also be used as a tool to measure what you have mastered and what you still need to work on. You are encouraged to use the learning objectives as a guide and expand on them according to your goals and interests.

▶ **CASE IN POINT:** Within each chapter, a scenario ("Case in Point") illustrates an issue commonly faced by college students and reflects the chapter contents. Use the questions following each scenario to stimulate your critical thinking and analytical skills. Discuss the questions with classmates. You are encouraged to think of your own ideas regarding how to apply concepts and to raise additional questions.

▶ **SELF-ASSESSMENT QUESTIONS:** Self-assessment questions ask you to reflect on and evaluate your personal development. This section is intended to increase your self-awareness and ability to understand your decisions and actions. Self-assessment questions are also included on the companion web site so that you can print and respond to them and include them in your professional portfolio (discussed below).

▶ **CRITICAL THINKING QUESTIONS:** Critical thinking questions challenge you to examine ideas and to thoughtfully apply concepts presented in the text. These questions encourage the development of thinking skills that are crucial for efficient performance in school and in the workplace.

▶ **APPLY IT!** After many sections of the text, you will find activities that help you apply to real-life situations the concepts discussed in the section. Your instructor may assign these as part of the course requirements. If they are not formally assigned, it will be helpful to complete them for your own development. There are three types of activities available:

- **Individual activities** are directed at your personal development.

- **Group activities** typically include projects that are more successfully completed with the addition of several perspectives or broad research. A team effort adds to the success of these learning projects.

- **Internet activities** are intended to help you develop online skills. For example, you may research a topic or participate in an online discussion thread.

You may find it helpful to combine the activity types. For example, an individual project may require Internet research. Some individual activities can be adapted to group activities, and vice versa. Use the activities as guides and modify them in ways that best support your learning. Activity sheets are available on the companion web site, and you are encouraged to print these and include them in your portfolio.

▶ **SUCCESS STEPS:** Success Steps are included throughout the text and provide concise steps for achieving various goals. They are offered as a summary of each process. Details of each step are discussed fully in the body of the text. Use Success Steps to actively apply what you learn to practical situations. These are intended to give you a "hands-on" experience.

▶ **CHECK YOUR UNDERSTANDING:** Check Your Understanding, found on the companion web site, provides an opportunity for you to assess the effectiveness of your learning and to set goals to expand your knowledge in a given area.

▶ **SUGGESTED ITEMS FOR LEARNING PORTFOLIO:** A portfolio is a collection of the work that you have done. A *learning portfolio* is used to track your progress through school and a *professional portfolio* showcases your professional accomplishments. A developmental portfolio typically contains documents that illustrate your development over time. A professional portfolio contains finished projects and work that represents your best efforts and achievements. Throughout *100% Student Success* there are suggestions to include completed activities in your portfolio. The items suggested for your portfolio are simply that—suggestions. You are encouraged to tailor your portfolio to your needs and goals by including items you find relevant to your situation.

As you read and complete the activities in *100% Student Success,* keep your long-term goals in mind and think about how you can apply these concepts to your everyday activities. Application is the key—and the more you practice, the more proficient you will become in using and communicating information.

Visit the companion web site for this textbook by going to **www.cengagebrain.com**, where you will find additional resources to help support your success in college.

WHAT IS NEW IN THE THIRD EDITION?

Instructors who have previously used *100% Student Success* in their classrooms will find the following changes throughout the textbook:

▶ The text has been divided into four different parts to reflect common learning areas, and various chapters have been reordered within those parts.

• Part I: Starting Out, contains the first three chapters from the previous edition: Chapter 1: Strategies for College

Success; Chapter 2; Human Behavior; and Chapter 3: Common Concerns of the Adult College Student.

- Part II: Shaping and Communicating Your Ideas, includes Chapter 4: Learning Strategies; Chapter 5: Communication Skills for Student Success (formerly Chapter 10); and Chapter 6: Critical Thinking and Problem Solving (formerly Chapter 5).

- Part III: Harnessing Information, houses Chapter 7: Information Literacy for the 21st Century (formerly Chapter 9), and Chapter 8: Legal and Ethical Issues in the Academic Environment (formerly Chapter 6).

- Part IV: Success Strategies for Personal Well-Being, contains Chapter 9: Financial Considerations for School Success (formerly Chapter 8), and Chapter 10: Nutrition and Fitness Strategies for the Successful Student (formerly Chapter 7).

▶ A new feature, Be in the Know, has been added to the beginning of each chapter.

▶ Cases in Point have been moved within each chapter and have been changed to encourage student participation and discussion.

▶ Resource Boxes have been removed from various chapters.

The following list includes changes by chapter to assist instructors in transitioning to the third edition of *100% Student Success*.

CHAPTER 1:

▶ The "Importance of Education" section has been updated to apply Web 3.0 tools to education and business.

▶ The "Financial Considerations" section has been updated to include the top financial mistakes many young people make and what they can do to avoid making those mistakes.

CHAPTER 5:

▶ A new section, "Social Networking and Social Media," has been added to discuss the positives and negatives that this new type of communication has on the ability to learn.

CHAPTER 7:

▶ The section "Information Literacy in the 21st Century: An Overview" has been renamed "Introduction to Information Literacy in the Digital Age."

▶ A new section, "Defining Digital Literacy," has been added to address the relationship between digital literacy and information literacy.

▶ A new section, "Working with Your Librarian," has been added to focus on the importance of librarians as the need for information moves into the digital age.

CHAPTER 8:

▶ The section on plagiarism has been expanded to discuss strategies to avoid plagiarism.

CHAPTER 9:

▶ A new section, "Seeking Financial Advice," replaces the section, "Sound, Individualized Financial Advice."

▶ A new section, "Saving While in College," addresses ways in which students can save money on food, transportation, and entertainment while in college.

▶ A new section, "Saving for the Future," replaces the section "Planning Finances Beyond College" and talks specifically about retirement planning.

CHAPTER 10:

▶ The "MyPyramid" section has been removed and updated with the "MyPlate" federal government initiative to reflect current nutritional recommendations.

ANCILLARY MATERIALS

100% Student Success has a companion web site for students. Visit **www.cengagebrain.com** to access the web site. Available materials include additional resources to help your students be successful in college.

An Instructor Companion Site includes an Instructor's Manual, PowerPoint slides, and a Test Bank. The instructor resources can be accessed at **login.cengage.com**. A WebTutor Toolbox is available for this textbook, to be used with WebCT or Blackboard.

If you're looking for more ways to assess your students, Cengage Learning has additional resources to consider:

▶ College Success Factors Index 2.0

▶ Noel-Levitz College Student Inventory

▶ The *Myers-Briggs Type Indicator ® (MBTI ®) Instrument* *

You can also package this textbook with the College Success Planner to assist students in making the best use of their time both on and off campus.

An additional service available with this textbook is support from TeamUP Faculty Program Consultants. For more than a decade, our consultants have helped faculty reach and engage first-year students by offering peer-to-peer consulting on curriculum and assessment, faculty training, and workshops. Consultants are available to help you establish or improve our student success program and provide training on the implementation of our textbooks and technology. To connect with your TeamUP Faculty Program Consultant, call 1-800-528-8323 or visit **www.cengage.com/teamup**.

For more in-depth information on any of these items, talk with your sales rep or visit **www.cengagebrain.com**.

*MBTI and Myers-Briggs Type Indicator are registered trademarks of Consulting Psychologists Press, Inc.

part 1

Starting Out

Part I of *100% Student Success* addresses some of the common issues faced by students who are new to the college environment.

Chapter 1: Strategies for College Success focuses on the many factors that contribute to success in college. The purpose of Chapter 1 is to lay a foundation for you to build strong skills that will serve you throughout your academic career.

Personality and human behavior play a significant role in one's success in school and other venues. **Chapter 2: Human Behavior** highlights how our needs motivate us, and why these basic needs must be addressed in order to achieve success in school. Self-image and self-esteem, which spring from feeling that our needs are met, play a role in both achievement and success.

What are some of the concerns of the college student in the 21st century? Depending on your current situation, you may find various challenges in the college environment. **Chapter 3: Common Concerns of the Adult College Student** will help you identify specific concerns and provide suggested resources for addressing them.

Strategies for College Success

LEARNING OBJECTIVES

By the end of this chapter, you will achieve the following objectives:

- Explain the importance of goal setting.
- Explain how technology has affected the need for continuing education.
- Explain what it means to be a responsible student.
- Describe how effective communication can affect the classroom experience.
- Describe the impact that attitude and motivation can have on your academic experience.
- Demonstrate the ability to set goals and identify the steps to achieve those goals.
- Explain and demonstrate an understanding of time management.
- List top financial mistakes that many young people make.

1

BE IN THE KNOW

Getting the Most Out of Every Class

Whether you're pursuing an Associate or a Bachelor degree in your field of study, you only have a finite amount of classroom time with your instructors and fellow students. To make the most of those interactions, follow the guidelines below to maximize your learning.

- **Get to know your instructor.** Aside from actual classroom face time, make an effort to get to class a few minutes early or stay a few minutes late to ask questions, to get clarification on course materials, or to get noticed. Instructors genuinely like interacting with their students, and they welcome the curiosity and passion students show for the subject matter. And don't forget about posted office hours. Here's your opportunity to spend quality time with your instructor and get help as you need it. Remember, an instructor who has a favorable impression of you may be able to recommend you for an internship, or even a job.

- **Participate in study groups.** Study groups, if not turned into an excuse for a social gathering, can have a positive effect on your coursework. Not only do study groups provide support for members, they provide personal accountability for participation. If you are struggling with the course content, assignments, or tests, chances are your fellow students are as well. Show up at the appointed hour and be prepared to work.

- **Use all the resources available to you.** This includes your school's library or Learning Resource Center and its staff, your instructor's web site (here you may find PowerPoint presentations that support class lectures, articles that pertain to course content, and the like), your textbook's student companion web site, if available, and on-campus tutoring support.

- **Take meaningful notes.** Don't write down everything the instructor says. For one thing, you will never be able to keep up with all of the information presented. Instead, listen for key words and concepts as they pertain to the subject matter. Link new information with what you already know about the topic. Review your notes right after class and rewrite passages for greater clarification if necessary. Most importantly, use a method of note-taking that works best for you, even if this means trying a couple of different approaches until you settle on one tactic.

1

- **Plan, organize, strategize.** As you will learn in this text, getting yourself and keeping yourself organized and on top of your workload is incredibly important. Have a strategy for completing your coursework for the semester, organize yourself and your materials to support that, and plan your days accordingly to accomplish your assignments.

- **Go to class, really.** How much money are you paying per credit hour? This isn't high school where you *have* to go to class. Sure, instructors take attendance and count that toward your final grade, but no one is forcing you to attend class. Once you enter the workforce you will be expected to be accountable for your actions on many different levels. Get in the habit now about being disciplined about your attendance, and carry that habit to the workplace.

STRATEGIES FOR COLLEGE SUCCESS: AN OVERVIEW

For some individuals, beginning a college course can be a daunting ordeal; for others, it is a challenging and exciting adventure. Regardless of one's feelings related to starting school, all individuals typically have a strong desire for success. Arriving at success can be more challenging for some than for others. Most (if not all) individuals encounter roadblocks in their lives that can divert them from their goals. This textbook offers you information to help you take the responsibility to make your college experience an enjoyable journey, as well as to maximize your opportunities for successful program completion.

Chapter 1 provides a general overview of elements that are important to college success. It is intended to supply a big picture of the many considerations important to you as a college student. Subsequent chapters will provide more detailed strategies and information about these areas.

THE IMPORTANCE OF EDUCATION

Technology continues to advance, forcing society to develop methods that facilitate adaptation to change. One of the biggest changes that has affected society over the last few years is the increasing use and

1

sophistication of technology in the form of cloud computing, Wi-Fi, Web 2.0 and emerging Web 3.0 tools, and mobile computing devices, to name a few. These developments, which have resulted in modifications in the way business is accomplished and communication occurs, have required industries to rapidly adapt and to be ready for ongoing change.

As these industries are affected by change, so are employees. New jobs are created and old job descriptions are revised to meet new business demands and incorporate new technologies. Individuals who are willing and able to learn new technologies are most likely to be successful.

A degree in higher education offers many benefits. Not only does higher education enable people to gain skills and grow intellectually, it also challenges individuals to broaden their understanding of the world around them. Employers continue to seek individuals who embrace changing technologies and demonstrate an appreciation of ethnic and cultural diversity, competency in effective communication, and the ability to set goals and achieve them. Completing a college education is a unique opportunity to learn the technical skills and develop the characteristics needed to acquire a job and continue your personal growth in the ever-changing 21st century work environment.

TAKING RESPONSIBILITY FOR YOUR EDUCATION

Embracing your academic experience requires taking responsibility for what you learn. Taking responsibility begins with self-reflection and assessment of your goals, attitudes, and motivation.

SELF-REFLECTION

Self-reflection is the process of making an assessment of your thoughts, actions, consequences of your behavior, and, based on your assessment, determining how you can modify your thoughts and actions to optimize your professional and personal growth. As you proceed through your first year of school, ask yourself these types of self-reflection questions as they pertain to your academic accomplishments to date:

▶ What has been my best experience at school so far? The worst?

▶ Have my college experiences been what I expected?

▶ What outside activities (internships, volunteering, clubs, organizations) can I do that will enhance my learning experiences?

1

▶ Have I set realistic and attainable goals for myself? Am I on track with those goals?

▶ What truly motivates me?

▶ Am I in the right program of study?

Effective self-reflection requires honesty and the ability to prioritize engaging in the process. Honest self-reflection supports goal setting and motivation by giving direction through self-awareness. Use self-reflection to your advantage both in your personal and professional life.

GOAL SETTING

Goal setting is an important part of succeeding in college. By setting goals, you accomplish the following:

▶ You set a "road map" for where you want to go.

▶ You are able to select the most appropriate method(s) for reaching your goal.

▶ You are able to more easily gauge your progress toward your goal.

▶ You are able to make adjustments to your goal and methods as needed.

▶ You know when you have reached your goal and can appreciate your accomplishment.

success steps for setting goals

The following success steps are based on suggestions made by Mind Tools (2010) for effective goal setting and achievement.

• Set goals based on something that is important to you and something that you desire. Consider significant others in your life, but ultimately, your goals should be what you want.

• State goals positively. For example, "I will study every night for two hours before doing other tasks" is more positive than "I won't do other tasks in the evening before studying."

continued

1

continued

- Be as detailed and specific as possible when writing your goals. A goal should tell you what you will achieve, describe the conditions under which you will achieve the goal, and provide a timeframe during which the goal will be achieved. In addition, goals should be measurable so that you meet a standard. For example, "I will study [what will be achieved] for two hours [measurable element] every weekday night [another measurable element] with no interruptions [conditions] throughout the fall semester [timeframe]."

- Set your goals high enough to be challenging, but make them reasonable enough to be achievable.

- State your goals in writing. Written goals serve as a reminder and motivator and provide a guide to your success. Telling others about your goals may also contribute to goal achievement.

- Focus on personal performance. Outcomes can be affected by circumstances that are beyond your control. You can manage and control your own performance. For example, a salesperson has control over a goal to make 10 sales calls in a week. Conversely, he or she has no control over others' decisions to buy. Therefore, a goal to make 10 sales is considered an outcome and not a performance goal, as the salesperson has control over the number of calls made in a week, but not the number of sales, which are based on others' decisions.

Breaking long-term goals into shorter-term goals allows you to see progress toward the longer-term goal. For example, completing a course successfully might be your long-term goal. By plotting out a schedule for completion of assignments over the term, each assignment becomes a short-term goal. Completion of each assignment brings you closer to achieving your long-term goal. Your progress is more obvious and rewarding when you recognize the accomplishment of smaller steps.

Another important aspect of goal setting is its cyclic nature. Achieving goals or steps toward them usually makes you aware of new areas for growth and learning, setting the stage for new goals. When you review your progress toward a goal, determine new goals that you can set for continued growth and development. Goal setting is an ongoing process that should continue as part of your lifelong learning.

When setting goals, make sure your goals represent short-term and long-term educational and professional plans. Once you have set your goals, make a serious effort to achieve each one. Upon successful completion of a goal, remember to recognize and reward your accomplishments in addition to being aware of opportunities for setting new goals.

Consider the diagram in Figure 1-1, which represents the process of goal setting and its relationship to your professional growth.

ATTITUDE AND MOTIVATION

Your attitude toward succeeding can directly impact your academic and overall life experiences. As in many other areas of life, school will have its ups and downs, and there will be times when you will encounter difficulties. Do not let problems become a roadblock to your success. Individuals who are able to use difficulties as opportunities to learn and develop solutions will be valued in the classroom and later as professionals. Motivation is discussed in Chapter 2; barriers commonly faced by adult learners and methods of addressing them are covered in Chapter 3.

Learning to remain motivated during difficult situations is a valuable lesson that will make a difference to your success in school, in your career, and in other life circumstances.

SELF-ASSESSMENT QUESTIONS

- What is your attitude toward learning?
- What motivates you to learn?
- Reflect on your motivation to do well in class. What do you really want from your education?
- How can you use your motivators to help you reach your education goals?
- What other methods might you personally find helpful for addressing difficulties in school?

? CRITICAL THINKING QUESTION

▶ Upon the successful completion of a goal, how might you recognize and reward your accomplishments?

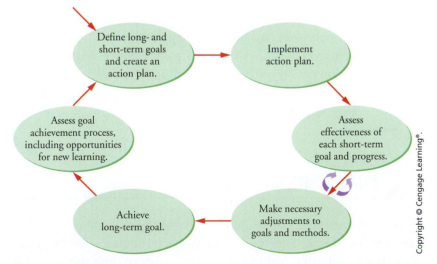

Copyright © Cengage Learning®.

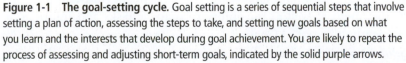

Figure 1-1   The goal-setting cycle. Goal setting is a series of sequential steps that involve setting a plan of action, assessing the steps to take, and setting new goals based on what you learn and the interests that develop during goal achievement. You are likely to repeat the process of assessing and adjusting short-term goals, indicated by the solid purple arrows.

success steps for maintaining motivation

Consider the following steps for maintaining your motivation:

- Clearly identify your motivators.
- Ensure that your motivators are realistic. For example, if you identify a reward for yourself, make sure it is something you can realistically do or afford.
- Keep your motivators "top of mind" so that they remain visible and you are aware of them.

Motivation can be a significant factor in the ability to learn. Motivated individuals tend to solve problems and seek out methods that will help them overcome and achieve in difficult areas.

GETTING THE MOST OUT OF EVERY CLASS

Getting the most from every class has specific benefits, including acquiring the most education for your investment of time and money, preparing to the best of your ability for your future career, and achieving self-improvement. Fully participating in and being actively involved in your classes allows you to gain a better perspective on and appreciation for others' beliefs and ideas. The diversity of today's workforce requires that you develop an understanding and acceptance of a wide range of cultures, beliefs, lifestyles, and other unique aspects of individuals.

ORGANIZATION

Becoming organized can be quite challenging for some people. The meaning of "being organized" can vary considerably among individuals. Organization includes the components of time and materials management as well as the ability to manage tasks and information efficiently. The rest of Chapter 1 and the remaining chapters in *100% Student Success* address these elements in greater detail. For now, consider how these components contribute to your organizational skills and which elements might be important for you to improve.

The first step toward improving organizational abilities is understanding your need to improve and determining where improvement is needed. Organization can impact function at home, in school, and at work. In addition, organization is a key factor in learning. The brain processes well-organized information more effectively than information that is presented in random order. Your ability to organize information will directly affect your mastery of course information. To get the most out of each of your classes, try implementing the following organizational steps.

success steps for developing organizational skills

- Assess your current organizational skills and then develop an action plan to improve where needed.

- Use the Internet as a resource to develop your organizational skills. Conduct a search using the terms "organizational skills" and "organizational methods" and select resources that are relevant to your needs.

- Begin to work on organizing your classroom activities. Work toward organizing your notes, tests, activities, study area, times for studying and completing homework, and so forth. Select filing and archiving systems that work for you.

- Develop charts, diagrams, flow charts, tables, lists, and other tools that can help in organizing the information you are trying to learn.

- Don't procrastinate. Disorganization sometimes stems from not following through in a timely manner, as tasks and materials tend to pile up. Take the necessary time to complete assignments and projects thoroughly and well. Procrastination results in the need to rush, and rushing can actually create disorganization.

- Complete assignments on or ahead of an established schedule so that you have time to think them through in a well-organized fashion as well as review them.

SELF-ASSESSMENT QUESTIONS

- What are your expectations regarding your classes?
- What do you want and hope to get out of each of your classes?
- What specific things can you do to make sure you get the most out of every class?

? CRITICAL THINKING QUESTION

▶ How might you come to understand and accept the wide range of cultures, beliefs, lifestyles, and other aspects of individuals with whom you interact at school?

SELF-ASSESSMENT QUESTIONS

- How effective are your organizational skills?
- How can you improve your organizational skills?
- What organizational strategies work well for you? How can they be applied to organizing for school?

? CRITICAL THINKING QUESTION

▶ What items might you include in an action plan to improve your organizational skills as they specifically relate to school?

TIME MANAGEMENT

Many students have very full lives. Besides the time spent in school, time is often split between work and taking care of parents, children, spouses, and the home. In addition, extracurricular activities that support personal and professional interests must often be factored into the schedule. Finding time to accomplish all the tasks related to each of these responsibilities can be overwhelming. Accomplishing all of these tasks successfully requires effective time management skills.

Good time management starts with assessing what must typically be accomplished for each day and the time available to complete each task. Consider the following suggestions for effective time management.

success steps for effective time management

- Focus on one thing at a time. Multitasking can dilute your attention and may not be as efficient as concentrating on one task at a time. Complex tasks require concentrated attention.

- Prioritize your tasks. There will be times when all tasks simply cannot be completed in the amount of time that you have available. In those cases, prioritizing and completing the most pressing tasks first is necessary.

- Assess the amount of time each task requires. Schedule the task when you have the appropriate amount of time for it, and reserve the time for that task. Determine the tasks and task components that are essential and eliminate nonessential elements.

- Don't procrastinate unenjoyable tasks. Get them done in a timely manner and reward yourself for the accomplishment. One suggestion is to complete less enjoyable tasks first to get them out of the way. Your motivation to complete them is getting to the more enjoyable tasks.

1

- Make a realistic daily schedule and to-do list based on the amount of time needed for each task. Print out the list each day and refer to it as needed to stay focused on what must be completed. Periodically check your progress and adjust the schedule as needed. Identify specific times for phone calls, meetings, and other duties. If a task is not completed, move it to your list for the following day.

- Establish a weekly game plan. Determine projects and goals on a weekly basis and then break them down into daily tasks.

- Determine your most productive time of day. Use that time to complete the most important tasks. Routine tasks should be accomplished during lower-energy periods.

Time management practices and time concepts vary considerably across cultures. Your time concepts and management methods may reflect your culture or how you were raised. Likewise, other individuals that you encounter in school and in the workplace may also have their unique perspectives. To function effectively in school and in the workplace, it is important to understand these differences and how they interface with school and workplace demands. If you recognize time management practices in a colleague that seem to contradict Western expectations, consider that the differences might be cultural. Consider how to address scheduling and time-related issues with tact and respect.

A variety of tools are available for time and life management, including both paper and electronic planning systems. Examples of paper planning systems include daily, weekly, and monthly calendars in a variety of bound and desk calendar formats. Electronic solutions include smart phones and software programs that are compatible with various computer operating systems. All time management tools accomplish the same task. The one you choose will depend on your preference for paper or electronic formats and the features that best serve your needs.

apply it

Find printable activities on the companion web site for this book, accessed through www.cengagebrain.com.

Web Research

GOAL: *To research time management tools offered online.*

STEP 1: Conduct an Internet search using "electronic time management tools" as your search term. Explore the types of tools that are available.

STEP 2: Explore the time management tools that you find as a result of your search. Assess and compare the benefits and shortcomings of each based on your personal needs and preferences. Make a decision regarding which would best support your time management efforts.

STEP 3: Write a brief report on your evaluation. Explain and give reasons for your choice of tools. Be prepared to share this information with your classmates.

STEP 4: Consider placing this evaluation in your Learning Portfolio.

apply it

Find printable activities on the companion web site for this book, accessed through www.cengagebrain.com.

Analysis of Paper Planning Systems

GOAL: *To analyze types of paper planning systems.*

STEP 1: As a group, compile a list of paper planning systems.

STEP 2: Assign a planning system to each group member so duplication does not occur. Visit an office superstore or other office supplier and review the various paper planning systems. Review your assigned paper planning system and record relevant information about it, including price, binding systems, features, and other information.

STEP 3: Bring your information back to the group and conduct a comparison of the various types of paper systems available. Discuss the advantages and disadvantages of each system.

STEP 4: Write a brief analysis of each system and your comparison and share your report with the class.

COMMUNICATION

Communicating effectively is a requirement of most professions. Classroom and academic activities provide an excellent venue for developing and practicing communication skills. Effective communication is another factor in getting the most from each course and learning effectively. Effective communication enhances your performance in a variety of classroom activities, including the following:

Active participation will help enhance your learning experience in each class.

▶ **Group activities and discussions.** Students working in groups depend on each other for clear communication. The success of group activities requires that participants follow through on required tasks and communicate their progress and concerns with other group members. Group discussion is successful when all participants are willing to share their views as well as respect the views of others. Active participation in group discussion contributes to the learning process and typically increases the relevance and interest of the activity by providing a variety of perspectives and ideas.

▶ **Reflection and critical thinking questions.** Employers seek individuals who have skills in problem solving and critical thinking. Students who develop these skills and are able to effectively and logically communicate their thought processes are likely to be desirable employees.

▶ **Instructor and student interactions.** The ability to communicate questions and concerns to the instructor in an effective manner adds to your ability to benefit from course material. Appropriately addressing issues regarding your learning experience is critical to your satisfaction with school and will contribute to your ability to assertively address issues in the workplace.

▶ **Individual presentations.** Assignments requiring group and individual presentations provide the opportunity to develop skills in communicating with an audience. Giving thoughtful, organized presentations and participating as an active listener to other students' presentations adds to effective communication skills.

▶ **Electronic resources.** Technology today makes possible communication in a variety of formats. E-mail, social media, blogs, podcasts, and webinars are just some of the examples available for communication in the classroom and in the workplace. Being a student in the 21st century requires competency in using a variety of communication resources and staying abreast of the rapid changes in media choices. Being knowledgeable about current technologies contributes to being an effective student and employee.

Communication is another area that can be significantly influenced by cross-cultural diversity. Western culture values assertiveness, asking questions, and stating individual ideas and opinions. Individuals who have been raised with other communication values and practices may not respond comfortably to expectations in Western classrooms or work situations. For example, individuals from certain cultures may find it disrespectful to disagree with the instructor or supervisor, who is viewed as an authority figure. In Western culture, a lack of assertiveness is frequently viewed in a negative light. In other cultures, a lack of assertiveness is respectful of authority. It is important to be aware of and sensitive to diverse communication practices. There are situations in which individuals may need coaching in developing the skills that will support their success in the Western work environment.

Getting the most out of your college courses also requires you to use the available communication tools to keep you informed about class and institutional requirements. Understanding how to use these tools will help you meet expectations, keep track of deadlines, and prepare effectively for class. Consider the following tools, which play a significant role in the classroom communication and with which you are probably familiar:

▶ **The syllabus.** The syllabus communicates what you should expect to learn and the grading requirements of the class. It should contain clearly stated objectives that can be used as a guide for what will be taught in the course. It is up to you to communicate to the instructor if you are unclear about any parts of the syllabus or if you are not achieving course objectives.

▶ **Grades.** Grades communicate whether you are accomplishing the required tasks and achieving an understanding of the material. It is your responsibility to keep track of your grades and know where you stand in each class. If your grades are below expectations, it is important for you and the instructor to agree on a course of action in as timely a manner as possible. It is your responsibility to approach the instructor if you have concerns. If you disagree with an instructor regarding a grade, clear and assertive (rather than aggressive) communication and negotiation skills become important. Briefly, assertive communication means that you state your point in a conversational tone, express your perspective and feelings as opposed to blaming another person, and demonstrate respect for the other point of view. Approaching the situation with an open mind and in a spirit of negotiation is also helpful. Assertive communication often results in increased respect between student and instructor and a clearer understanding of expectations for future assignments.

▶ **Classroom and school policies and procedures.** Written policies and procedures communicate to students the expectations of instructors and school officials. You must review these policies and procedures and clarify what is unclear, as you are responsible for following the policies and procedures that affect you. Written communication in the form of deadlines, policies, and postings from school administration and instructors provides information that is critical to your success. For example, published deadlines for dropping courses without adverse consequences are important in the event that you have to drop a course. Pay attention to institutional and classroom bulletins and notices. The student is responsible for knowing and adhering to published policies and deadlines.

1

CASE IN POINT: DON'T TAKE CREDIT FOR THIS

Read the scenario below. Then, in groups or as a class, discuss the questions at the end.

Lauren Bishop is an incoming freshman at a college one state away from where she grew up. This is her first time away from home without the daily guidance of her parents.

While still in high school, Lauren worked part-time at a local gourmet shop assisting customers and stocking merchandise. Although her earnings were relatively small, Lauren's parents insisted that she open a checking account at the local bank so that she could learn "the ropes" of managing her money and how to use a debit card. While she is at school, Lauren's parents are going to use that checking account to give Lauren a monthly budgeted amount to fund items that are not paid for by other means.

During freshman orientation on campus, Lauren noticed a hub of activity at the student union where vendors were peddling a variety of services, among them several credit card companies offering such incentives as a free T-shirt, a Frisbee, or 10 percent off their first purchase, simply by filling out a credit card application. Enticed by that 10-percent discount and the notion of being an "adult" with a "real" credit card, Lauren filled out the application and waited for her card to arrive in the mail.

When the credit card arrived in her dorm mailbox a short time later, she immediately went to the local mall to purchase a sweater like the ones so many young women on campus were wearing that fall. She figured that she could pay her credit card bill from her checking account when the statement arrived 30 days later and not tell her parents about it.

Unfortunately for Lauren, when the card statement arrived, she did not have enough money in her checking account to cover the cost of the sweater. In addition, the credit card company had tacked on a $25 annual fee that Lauren had not anticipated. Lauren decided that the best thing to do would be to pay the minimum amount required that month while hoping she would have sufficient funds next month to bring the balance to zero.

▶ How dependent are you on others for your financial well-being?

▶ How well do you think you manage your personal finances?

▶ Do you take full responsibility for your financial situation?

1

▶ How do you decide if a purchase is something you need or want?

▶ How do you rate yourself when it comes to understanding the use of credit cards?

▶ What steps can you take to gain greater control over your finances?

FINANCIAL CONSIDERATIONS

Lack of financial planning can negatively affect your schooling and your future. Many young adults fall into a "trap" of common financial mistakes because they do not understand how to effectively manage their money. Certainly everyone makes financial mistakes at one or more points in their lives, but the trick is to keep those mistakes at a minimum, and, even more important, to learn from them. This is a significant facet of your financial education and one that you are wise to learn from sooner rather than later.

The following list includes top financial mistakes that many young people make and what you can do to avoid making those mistakes from the start:

▶ **Purchasing items you don't need and paying extra for them in interest.** If you purchase an item with credit and only pay the minimum monthly amount due guarantees that you will incur finance charges in the coming month (and perhaps for many months to follow). So how do you avoid this situation? Consider the following:

- Really assess if you "need" the item versus "want" the item. Try not to bow to peer pressure or to reward yourself if things are going well or not so well. Impulse buying can make you feel good for the moment, but it won't make you feel so great when that credit card statement comes calling. Waiting a day or two, or even just a few hours, before you purchase (and be mindful of how quick and easy it is to shop online) may prevent you from making a costly decision that you will come to regret.

- Research major purchases and comparison shop before you buy. Doing so will not only get you the best deal for your money; it also might sway your decision against making the purchase at all.

1

- If you do use a credit card to pay for a major purchase, be smart about how you repay. If available, take advantage of offers of "zero-percent interest" on credit card purchases for a certain number of months. Be mindful, however, of when and how interest charges begin and what that does to your monthly payment amount. Always pay as much as you can before interest charges kick in so that you are paying interest on a lower balance than the purchase price.

▶ **Getting too deeply into debt.** Sure, this seems obvious. Don't spend what you don't have. That's simple, right? Unfortunately, our ability to borrow (via credit cards and other means) is all too easy these days. And borrowing helps us get what we want, when we want it. With this reality comes the fact that millions of adults of all ages find themselves struggling to pay their loans, credit cards, and other bills. Learn to be a good money manager and to recognize the warning signs of a serious debt problem. Some of these warning signs include the following:

- Borrowing money to make payments on loans you already have

- Getting payday loans. A payday loan (also called a paycheck advance) is a small, short-term loan that is intended to cover a borrower's expenses until his or her next payday.

- Deliberately paying your bills late

- Putting off doctor visits or other important life activities because you don't have enough money

▶ **Tarnishing your financial reputation.** The simplest way around this is to pay your bills on time, every month. While one or two late payments on your loans or other regular financial obligations (rent, for example) will probably not hurt you in the long run, a pattern of late bill payment can adversely affect your credit scores and credit report. Here's how that can happen:

- **Credit bureaus** are companies that prepare credit reports used by lenders, employers, insurance companies, and others to assess your financial reliability, generally based on your track record of paying bills and debts. They produce credit scores that evaluate a person's credit record based on a point system. If your credit scores are low and your credit report is damaged by your inability to pay your bills on time, you will likely be charged a higher interest rate on your credit card(s) or on a loan that you really want and need. You could also be turned down for employment or renting an apartment. Even your auto insurance may be negatively impacted.

▶ **You own a fistful of credit cards.** The general rule of thumb is that two to four credit cards are a sufficient amount for most adults. These include any cards from department stores, oil companies, and any other retailers. Why shouldn't you carry more than this suggested amount?

- Temptation, plain and simple. The more cards you have, the more tempted you may be to use them to fuel costly impulse buying.

- Each card you own, even if you don't use it, represents money that you *could* borrow up to the card's spending limit. For each new card you acquire, you are seen as someone who could potentially get into greater debt. And that could mean qualifying for a smaller or costlier loan.

▶ **Not tracking your expenses.** It's easy to overspend in some areas, most likely for the things you want (not necessarily need), and to shortchange other areas, including that savings account that you were so good about opening. Devising a tracking/budget system that works for you is your best bet for setting and sticking to your financial limits.

▶ **Watch out for those fees.** Financial institutions love to charge noncustomers anywhere from one dollar to four dollars for using their automated teller machines (ATMs). They are also quick to charge for bounced checks, that is, writing checks for more than you have in your account. These fees can range from 15 to 30 dollars for *each* check. You can take the following steps to mitigate these unwanted fees:

- Whenever possible, use your financial institution's ATMs (including branches) or ATMs that are a part of an ATM network to which your bank belongs.

- To avoid bounced check fees, keep your checkbook balanced and up to date, including recording all debit card transactions. This task becomes easier with the use of online and phone banking, both of which are free services. In addition, be sure to record those ATM withdrawal slips within your check register or cross-reference them online. If not closely monitored, those unrecorded $20 ATM transactions can result in your account being overdrawn (Federal Deposit Insurance Corporation, 2005).

Chapter 9 discusses financial management in greater detail.

CHAPTER SUMMARY

This chapter introduced you to the changing workplace and the new demands that rapid advancements make on individuals in the workplace. The relationship between success in school and success as an employee was emphasized. This chapter addressed goal setting and issues such as personal organization and time management, financial management, and maximizing the benefit you derive from your education. These basic self-management tools will lay the foundation for developing and refining your skills using the information and activities in the remainder of *100% Student Success*.

Throughout this textbook, consider how what you learn supports you in developing basic self-management skills. More detailed information in these areas will help you to select from and personalize a variety of methods that will support your development as a student and provide the basis for becoming a successful professional.

POINTS TO KEEP IN MIND

In this chapter, numerous main points were discussed.

- Advances in technology continue to have an impact on the need for new jobs and individual skill requirements.
- Higher education offers the opportunity to gain skills and grow intellectually, in addition to broadening your view of the world.
- Taking responsibility for your education experience begins with self-reflection and assessment of your goals, attitudes, and motivation.
- Setting goals should incorporate both short-term steps and long-term plans.

▶ Written goals that are specific and measurable are more likely to be accomplished than unwritten and unspecific goals.

▶ Individuals who see opportunity in and learn from difficulties will be valued in the classroom and later as professionals.

▶ Persevering and completing difficult tasks will pay off.

▶ Understanding your need to improve and identifying specific areas for improvement are the first steps in developing your organizational abilities.

▶ Time management requires focusing on what needs to be accomplished and determining the amount of time available for each task.

▶ Time management tools include both paper and electronic planning systems.

▶ Communication tools for the classroom include the syllabus, grades, and classroom and school policies and procedures.

▶ It is important to learn the many monetary pitfalls that young adults may face when starting out on their own.

CHECK YOUR UNDERSTANDING

Visit www.cengagebrain.com to see how well you have mastered the material in Chapter 1.

SUGGESTED ITEMS FOR LEARNING PORTFOLIO

▶ Analysis of Paper Planning Systems
▶ Web Research

REFERENCES

Federal Insurance Deposit Corporation (Spring 2005). FDIC Consumer News. Special Guide for Young Adults. Retrieved January 18, 2013, from http://www.fdic.gov/consumers/consumer/news/cnspr05/spring_05_bw.pdf

Mind Tools. (2010). *Personal goal setting*. Retrieved January 18, 2013, from http://www.mindtools.com/page6.html

Human Behavior

LEARNING OBJECTIVES

By the end of this chapter, you will achieve the following objectives:

▶ Explain the importance of understanding human behavior in school and the workplace.

▶ Describe three major influences on human behavior and the possible effects of each.

▶ Compare self-concept and self-esteem.

▶ Describe how self-image influences behavior.

▶ Describe steps for developing a realistic self-image.

▶ Describe steps for developing a healthy self-esteem.

▶ Describe needs and motivation according to Maslow and McClelland.

▶ Describe the relationship of personality, motivation, self-image, and self-esteem to achievement and success in school.

2

BE IN THE KNOW

Embracing Human Behavior

Humans behave differently from each other for a wide variety of reasons. As you will learn, influences on human behavior help to shape who we are.

Now that you are in school and are pursuing a degree in your field of study, you will find that your classroom and other campus experiences will open you up to a whole new world of people and your encounters with them. Gone are the days of just being with your high school friends, people with whom you have likely grown up and have come to count on for support and the sharing of opinions and beliefs about a wide range of topics.

Here is your opportunity to interact with students and professors from different cultures, backgrounds, and beliefs. They will exhibit different behaviors than you simply because of those factors, among others.

One of the exciting things about this is the chance to learn in a "united nations" type of atmosphere. Having exposure to other peoples' opinions, beliefs (religious or otherwise), the environment in which they grew up, and their customs, for example, will hopefully broaden how you view the world around you.

Take advantage of this opportunity presented to you. You may never have such a wide open peek into human behavior again.

SELF-ASSESSMENT QUESTIONS

- What are your beliefs about human behavior?
- How does behavior influence interpersonal relationships?
- How well do you interact with others?
- How might you be able to improve your relationships with others?

? CRITICAL THINKING QUESTION

- How has the emergence of social media and your use of it influenced your ability to sustain relationships?

THE IMPORTANCE OF UNDERSTANDING HUMAN BEHAVIOR: AN OVERVIEW

Academic success involves more than simply achieving good grades. Success in any environment comes from the ability to interact effectively with others by understanding your own behavior, the behavior of others, and your relationships. Success depends on your ability to manage your behavioral responses and understand their effect on your success in school. Chapter 2 emphasizes the influence of these factors on success in school.

INFLUENCES ON HUMAN BEHAVIOR

To understand why individuals think or feel certain ways requires exploring what makes people tick. Honeycutt and Milliken (2012) suggest the following three factors that influence people's behavior:

▶ **Heredity.** Heredity is what makes individuals unique. Heredity determines an individual's physical appearance and can also influence a person's likes, dislikes, abilities, and personality.

▶ **The developmental process.** Humans develop in physical, emotional, intellectual, and spiritual areas. People's physical and mental health can be greatly influenced by heredity, the environment in which they grow up, personality traits, and how they view themselves. Development in each dimension can be affected by environmental and life conditions. For example, individuals from an abusive home situation may display certain personality characteristics. It is also important to recognize, however, that although childhood greatly influences who we are as adults, as adults we can choose to learn and grow. Recognizing childhood influences on behavior will help in this growth process.

▶ **Environment.** Environment can be divided into the physical and social environments. The physical environment includes location, climate, level of urbanization, type of living structure, and other tangible resources. For example, the experiences of an individual who has grown up on a tropical island will be quite different from those of the person from a large northern city. The social environment refers to relationships and the types of human influences that have an impact on an individual as he or she matures. The amount and quality of involvement that an individual has had with people will determine his or her ability to sustain relationships.

It is also important to recognize that individuals develop abilities at different rates and to develop patience and understanding for those who may be slower in the growth process. For example, some individuals may be challenged by growing socially, whereas others may find intellectual growth more demanding. Recognizing these individual differences will help you communicate more effectively with a greater number of people.

SELF-ASSESSMENT QUESTIONS

- How has your development affected who you are as an adult?
- In what areas do you need to develop your skills?
- How will understanding individual differences help you to communicate effectively?

CRITICAL THINKING QUESTION

▶ Which do you find more challenging, growing socially or growing intellectually?

success steps for understanding human behavior

- Take a person's heredity and environment into account.
- Think about childhood and other developmental influences.
- Recognize individual differences, strengths, and weaknesses.
- Consider personality factors.

apply it

Web Research

Find printable activities on the companion web site for this book, accessed through www.cengagebrain.com.

GOAL: To learn more about influences on human behavior

STEP 1: Conduct a web search for articles on what influences human behavior. Consider search terms such as "human behavior," "influences on human behavior," and "social influences on human behavior." Also, consider substituting "social" with terms such as "genetic" or "developmental" to obtain specific results.

STEP 2: Find one web site that you consider to be of high credibility and that contains an article that is useful in furthering your knowledge of influences on human behavior.

STEP 3: Read the article and write a brief analysis of your findings. Consider questions such as:

  a. Do you agree with what is being presented? If so, why? If not, why?

  b. What made you think this information had high credibility?

  c. What did you learn about influences on your own behavior?

STEP 4: Consider placing this analysis in your Learning Portfolio.

2

PERSONALITY DEVELOPMENT AND HUMAN BEHAVIOR

Another factor that influences human behavior is personality. Although the term "personality" often is used to describe an individual's demeanor (e.g., "She has a pleasant personality."), personality also refers to the sum of a person's traits accumulated over time. Several theorists have contributed ideas regarding the development of personality.

Abraham Maslow proposed a hierarchy of needs ranging from the most basic survival needs (such as food) to self-actualization needs (such as recognizing and fulfilling one's potential). According to the hierarchy, shown in Figure 2-1, all humans have needs that are satisfied by elements in the environment. Maslow's hierarchy is represented by a triangle. The base of the triangle represents the most basic human survival needs. Each level of the triangle represents an additional need that is met only when the need below it is satisfied. For example, think of the homeless person for whom survival is the primary concern. The homeless person is probably not concerned with self-actualization or other needs higher on Maslow's hierarchy. Another example might be the individual who is facing an abusive situation and is more concerned with safety than love

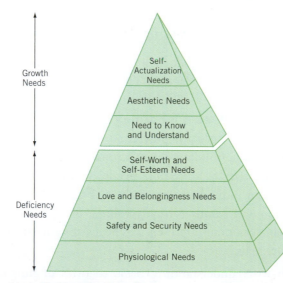

Figure 2-1   Maslow's hierarchy of needs.

Source: Text material adapted from D. Martin and K. Loomis, *Building Teachers: A Constructivist Approach to Introducing Education* (Belmont, CA: Wadsworth, 2007), pp. 72–75.

2

and affection. Needs change as life events occur, and individuals may find themselves at different points in the hierarchy at different times. In addition, needs play a significant role in motivation, which will be discussed shortly.

David McClelland defined his theory of personality in terms of various factors that motivate people (Osland & Turner, 2013). He suggests that three needs motivate individuals: the need for affiliation, the need for power, and the need for achievement. These terms are defined as follows:

▶ **Affiliation.** The individual who is motivated by affiliation seeks strong relationships. As the name suggests, an individual who is motivated by affiliation needs seeks to be a member of and accepted by a group.

▶ **Power.** Individuals who are motivated by power generally have a need to be in control and to influence others. Being motivated by the need for power can be expressed positively as leadership or negatively, as in cases of manipulation or abuse.

▶ **Achievement.** Individuals with a need for achievement find their motivation in accomplishing their goals and engaging in self-improvement strategies. These individuals tend to take responsibility for their actions and thrive on appropriately difficult challenges. Individuals who are motivated by achievement needs value feedback on their performance and apply it.

McClelland concluded that each individual is motivated by varying degrees of each of these factors. The strength of each motivating need varies depending upon the person. For example, you might be motivated by a high need for achievement, a moderate need for affiliation, and a low need for power. A classmate might be highly motivated by power, moderately motivated by achievement, and minimally motivated by affiliation needs. Cultural influences can help determine an individual's motivation. For instance, in cultures where affiliation with family is highly valued, those relationships will take priority and maintaining them will be a strong motivating factor for these individuals.

To summarize, understanding basic theories of human behavior offers individuals the opportunity to appreciate the reasons for people's behaviors. Understanding and consciously considering these influences can help you to understand what motivates your behavior, as well as provide a greater understanding of others.

SELF-ASSESSMENT QUESTIONS

- What level are you currently at in Maslow's hierarchy of needs?
- What goals might you set that would help fulfill the current needs you have?
- Consider an interaction that you had recently. How can you better understand that interaction based on Maslow's theory?

❓ CRITICAL THINKING QUESTION

▶ How would you rank your need for affiliation, power, and achievement (high, medium, low) as described by McClelland?

PERSONALITY DEVELOPMENT, HUMAN BEHAVIOR, AND SCHOOL

Personality traits influence behavior and a significant number of characteristics related to school performance. Examples of characteristics that will be discussed here include motivation, self-image, self-esteem, and locus of control. Consider how the following characteristics might affect school performance and your interpersonal relationships.

MOTIVATION

In addition to contributing to overall long-term personality development, Maslow's hierarchy can also help to determine factors that might influence shorter-term motivation levels. Review Figure 2-1 representing Maslow's hierarchy. Recall that needs are satisfied in order, beginning at the bottom of the pyramid with needs related to physical well-being and safety. If an individual lacks physical/physiological security and a safe environment, that individual is not likely to be concerned with higher levels of the pyramid until the basic needs are met.

Ideally, a student will have resources related to these basic areas in place before starting school. Achieving and succeeding in school is a higher level need and is best supported with strong relationships (belonging, affiliation) and feelings of esteem. Understanding this relationship of needs and success can help an individual recognize a lack of motivation and allow relevant issues to be addressed.

McClelland's identified motivators of affiliation, power, and achievement can help individuals understand what drives them forward and how their priorities affect their success in school and their relationships. For example, an individual who realizes that he or she is motivated by gaining power may need to learn to prioritize other factors to have effective relationships in school. An individual who prioritizes affiliation needs over achievement may need to learn to adjust his or her motivating influences to focus more on achievement in school.

SELF-IMAGE AND SELF-ESTEEM: AN OVERVIEW

Self-image and self-esteem are both important factors in your school success. Both play a role in how you view yourself, which in turn affects your school performance and relationships. You

SELF-ASSESSMENT QUESTIONS

- What motivates you?
- How have your parents or culture influenced your motives for accomplishing certain goals in your life?
- How do your needs affect your motivation at school and work?
- What is motivating you to attend and complete college?
- What problems can you think of that might deter you from your goal?
- How might you be able to motivate yourself during problem times?

? CRITICAL THINKING QUESTION

- How might you recognize a lack of motivation in yourself? What steps might you take to regain your motivation?

Keith Brofsky/Photodisc/Getty Images.

The manner in which adults interact with children has a significant impact on their self-image.

2

can use motivation factors to influence your self-image and self-esteem.

SELF-IMAGE

Self-image is the way in which we view ourselves, including our abilities, talents, physical appearance, and personality traits. Your self-image can be realistic in terms of your actual attributes, meaning you have a realistic sense of your strengths and weaknesses. Self-image can also be inflated, in which you see your attributes as better than they really are. Conversely, self-image can be low, resulting in an evaluation of your own abilities and traits that is lower than it should be.

CASE IN POINT: WOE IS ME

Read the scenario below. Then, in groups or as a class, discuss the questions at the end.

Tim Johnson has been attending the local college for one semester. Tim is an A student. He never has had to struggle with grades, and he is pleased that this trend has continued with his college studies. However, Tim is unhappy. He likes his program, but Tim has the following complaints:

- Tim feels alienated from his classmates. They never invite him to any social events and leave him out of conversations on class breaks.

- Tim believes that his instructors pay more attention to other students than to him.

- Although career services helped him find a part-time job, Tim doesn't like the job and feels career services could have found him something better.

- How might Tim's own behavior and attitude be contributing to any of these situations?

- Could Tim's view of himself be affecting his view of these situations? If so, how?

- What are some constructive ways in which Tim can address these issues?

- Did you learn anything about yourself through evaluating Tim's situation? If so, what?

Influences of Self-Image

How you see yourself influences many (if not all) aspects of your life. Consider the following examples of areas that can be influenced by your self-image:

▶ **Performance.** The way in which you perceive your abilities influences the way you set goals and ultimately determines your success. For example, individuals with a poor self-image are likely to set lower goals based on how they view their abilities, thus compromising the potential to move ahead. Individuals with an inflated self-image may set goals that are too lofty, resulting in failure and a lack of achievement. Likewise, individuals who have not effectively addressed their needs will be frustrated until basic needs are met. An objective assessment of skills, abilities, and motivations leads to an accurate self-image that allows realistic performance and improvement goals to be set.

▶ **Relationships with others.** Your self-image can vary considerably from the picture that others have of you. Expectations of relationships can vary depending on the way in which the individuals involved perceive themselves and each other. For example, if your supervisor or instructor perceives you as less capable than you see yourself, you may feel bored or unchallenged due to his or her low expectations.

▶ **General adjustment.** If self-image issues are having a negative influence on your performance, relationships, or other areas of your life, your general level of adjustment and satisfaction can be affected. If these issues are significant to you, evaluating and understanding the role that your self-image may be playing may be helpful to you.

Creating a Realistically Positive Self-Image

Having a realistic self-image means that you know your strengths and weaknesses. You credit yourself for your skills and talents and set goals to develop areas needing improvement. An important concept to remember is that everyone has strengths as well as weaknesses and that perfection is not the goal. The following suggestions are based on recommendations from Mountain State Centers for Independent

SELF-ASSESSMENT QUESTIONS

• What is your self-image? How do you perceive yourself?
• What about your self-image do you want to change?

❓ CRITICAL THINKING QUESTION

▶ How might you evaluate and understand the role that your self-image is playing in your life?

2

2

Living (n.d.) as well as ideas from this chapter and are intended to help you recognize strong attributes as well as put weaknesses in perspective.

▶ **Understand your motivations.** Use the information from the previous section to understand what motivates you and how you might address your needs and adjust your priorities to see yourself in a more positive light. Addressing issues that are most pressing can reduce anxiety and build a strong foundation of resources and support systems. Fulfilling needs at the base of Maslow's pyramid lays the groundwork for realizing more complex goals.

▶ **Assess skills realistically.** It is realistic to expect that you have strengths in some areas and weaknesses in others. Assess your skills and abilities and realistically determine an objective way to measure them against an accepted standard. Give yourself credit for your strengths and set goals for improvement in areas you wish to develop.

▶ **Avoid exaggeration and the need for perfection.** Expecting perfection is unrealistic, and if you expect perfection in what you do, you may be exaggerating the negative. For example, if you need to improve certain areas of math performance, it doesn't mean that you can't do any math at all or that you are a failure in school. Conversely, an individual who believes he or she excels in all areas has an equally exaggerated self-image and is set for failure and alienating others. Be realistic in your expectations, work to the best of your ability, and honestly assess your performance. Set realistic goals to improve where you can.

▶ **Pay attention to your thoughts.** Monitor your thoughts and the messages that you send to yourself. This is called "self-talk," and self-talk that exaggerates either strengths or weaknesses can distort your self-image. Judge your performance by objective standards, set positive goals, and emphasize realistic goals.

▶ **Accept responsibility appropriately.** You are in control of your choices and feelings. Assess and understand what is in your control and what is not. Use your skills to control what you can, and avoid frustration by understanding that you are not accountable for or able to fix situations over which you have no control or responsibility.

2

success steps for creating a positive self-image

- Assess your skills objectively and realistically.
- Avoid exaggeration and the need for perfection.
- Pay attention to your thoughts. Monitor how you think about yourself.
- Focus on the positive.
- Accept responsibility appropriately.

SELF-ESTEEM

Self-esteem is defined as the way an individual feels about him- or herself. Self-esteem is closely related to self-image, as individuals may like or dislike what they see in themselves. Similarly, the way in which self-image influences performance and relationships can also influence self-esteem. A poor or unrealistic self-image that negatively affects performance and relationships often results in poor self-esteem. A negative cycle is set when low self-esteem causes an individual to doubt his or her abilities, reinforcing a poor self-image.

The Influences of Self-Esteem

Consider how you function on a day when you are feeling bad about yourself. Hopefully, this is a temporary state, but the effects of feeling this way can lower your confidence levels, reduce your energy and ability to take on and complete various tasks, negatively influence how you respond to others, and increase anxiety levels. Consider how these states can influence success in school, particularly if they persist over time.

Developing Healthy Self-Esteem

As it is possible to develop a positive self-image, it is also possible to build healthy self-esteem. Some of the methods for developing self-esteem reflect the techniques that were discussed for a positive self-image. Having a realistic self-image can contribute to healthy self-esteem by allowing you to recognize your strengths as well as improve areas of weakness or accept them. The following suggestions are based

Accepting constructive criticism from trusted colleagues as well as listening to your "inner voice" can be useful in personal relationships.

© Andresr/Shutterstock.com.

2

on recommendations from the University of Texas at Austin Counseling and Mental Health Center (2007):

▶ **Use your realistic self-image as a guide.** Develop your self-image. Focus on recognizing both your strengths and weaknesses. Give yourself credit for your achievements and skills and set goals for what you wish to change. Decide what you are willing to accept.

▶ **Listen to your thoughts.** Pay attention to how you are thinking about yourself, others, and your environment. The messages that you are sending yourself may be based on old experiences or unsubstantiated information and may be detrimental to your self-esteem.

▶ **Use your objective assessment.** Refer back to your objective assessment of your skills, strengths, and weaknesses. Remind yourself of your strong points and the goals toward which you are working. Remember that perfection is unnecessary and impossible.

▶ **Take care of the basics.** Remember that basic needs must be met first. Our previous example of losing a job is extreme, although not unusual in the 21st century. A less extreme example is the person who neglects his or her health and misses class or has poor performance as a result. When you attend to your basic needs, you will feel better physically and mentally and have energy available to develop skills and attributes that contribute to healthy self-esteem.

---

success steps for developing healthy self-esteem

- Use your realistic self-image as a guide.
- Listen to your thoughts. (How do you think about yourself?)
- Use your objective assessment.
- Take care of the basics.
- Use your resources.

2

EFFECTS OF SUCCESS AND FAILURE ON ACHIEVEMENT

Self-image and self-esteem are closely related to success and failure. In addition, the effects of your successes and failures can have a great impact on your performance and the development of your abilities. An individual who has experienced repeated failures may be more likely to develop low self-confidence and self-esteem. Figure 2-2 illustrates the cyclic nature of self-image, self-esteem, and performance. When you have a realistic perception of your strengths and weaknesses, you select tasks to perform that use your strengths and provide an appropriate challenge to develop weaker areas. If you see yourself as capable of something that is actually beyond your abilities, the discrepancy between self-image and actual aptitude can result in disappointing performance and difficulties with colleagues.

Individuals who have high self-esteem have typically experienced more successes than failures and are able to perpetuate successes.

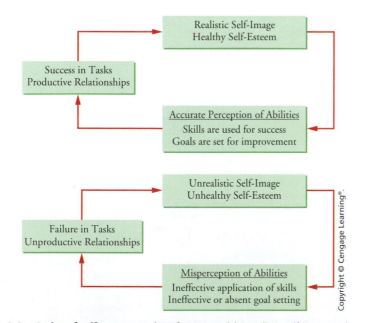

Copyright © Cengage Learning®.

Figure 2-2   Cycles of self-esteem and performance. (a) A realistic self-image and healthy self-esteem have a positive influence on the use of skills and goal setting, resulting in success in tasks and relationships. (b) An unrealistic self-image and unhealthy self-esteem negatively influence skill use and goal setting, resulting in failure in tasks and relationships.

2

From their experiences, they have learned that mistakes and disappointments do happen, but their self-worth is not affected. These individuals are usually able to view failure as a learning experience. Individuals with a less healthy self-image and self-esteem more frequently experience failure at tasks, adding to a poor self-image and unhealthy self-esteem.

Individuals who have multiple failures can develop what is called *failure expectation*. The cycle of failure affects expectations and can be damaging to an individual by creating self-doubt that minimizes chances for future success. Figure 2-3 illustrates failure expectation.

In a similar fashion, success influences how an individual thinks about himself or herself. Recognize that both small and large successes contribute to building self-confidence, which can greatly impact future successes. It is important to recognize *all* successes, such as making a relevant contribution to a class discussion.

Successes are specific to each individual. Avoid comparing yourself to others. For example, for some students, achieving a C in certain subjects is as much of a success as it would be for others to achieve an A. The success might be improving a grade or mastering a difficult concept. If a higher grade can be achieved or is desirable, the objective self-assessment can be used to analyze how improvement can be made for future classes.

Figure 2-3   The Failure-Expectation Cycle illustrates how self-doubt and expectations contribute to failure.

Source: From Milliken, Understanding Human Behavior, 6e. © 1998 Cengage Learning.

apply it

Research and Presentation

Find printable activities on the companion web site for this book, accessed through www.cengagebrain.com.

GOAL: To develop an understanding of how culture and environment can affect self-image and self-esteem

STEP 1: Form groups of no more than four or five students.

STEP 2: Each group selects a culture to research, such as Latin American, Asian, or European.

STEP 3: Each group conducts research on the effects that an individual's culture can have on self-image and self-esteem. Consider the elements discussed in the previous sections.

STEP 4: Use a variety of methods of research, such as interviews with individuals from those cultures, books, and articles.

STEP 5: Each group writes a brief report and presents its findings to the class. Visual aids such as PowerPoint, posters, handouts, or overhead transparencies should be used.

STEP 6: Consider putting this Research and Presentation activity in your Learning Portfolio.

MOTIVATION AND ACHIEVEMENT

An examination of the motivation to achieve reveals a relationship to self-image and self-esteem.

- **Motivation is related to meeting needs effectively.** Meeting your needs and achieving success in order of priorities also provides a sense of accomplishment. Ensure that your basic, foundational needs are met to support your success.
- **Motivation requires an appropriate level of challenge.** Recall that having a realistic self-image allows you to identify strengths and weaknesses and set goals accordingly. Knowing your attributes allows you to be successful, leading to healthy self-esteem. Too much challenge can be intimidating, whereas too little challenge can result in boredom; both

Working diligently on school projects and assignments and assessing the reasons for your successes and failures will add to your long-term success.

2

extremes can decrease motivation. An accurate self-image and healthy self-esteem contribute to motivation by guiding you in the selection of appropriately challenging tasks and goals.

▶ **People are more motivated when they believe they can affect outcomes.** McClelland's research suggested that individuals are more motivated when they believe that their efforts will influence a result or outcome (Accel-Team.com, n.d.). If your level of challenge is appropriate, you are more likely to believe this to be true.

▶ **Motivation and achievement are related to personal accomplishment.** Another of McClelland's findings indicated that achievers are more concerned with their personal accomplishment than with external rewards. Recognizing both your large and small successes and setting and meeting achievable goals contribute to your feelings of personal accomplishment.

▶ **Motivation and achievement are enhanced by feedback and reflection.** Part of motivation is understanding your performance and how to improve it. By thinking about (reflecting on) your performance and getting feedback from trusted individuals, you can increase your motivation levels, as well as develop your self-image and self-esteem.

As a student it is important to understand the motivating factors that led you not only to attend college, but also to succeed. People are motivated internally, so identifying motivating factors and tasks is critical to success. An instructor can tell a student to work hard or study more, but the student must be motivated to do so based on his or her own needs. The instructor's encouragement may support the student's internal motivation, but it is the student's personal incentive that will lead to success.

success steps for enhancing motivation for achievement

- Recognize your needs and their relationship to achievement.
- Set goals that are appropriately challenging yet achievable.

2

- Focus on your personal accomplishments rather than on external rewards.
- Reflect on your goals and performance.
- Obtain feedback from trusted sources.

CHAPTER SUMMARY

This chapter focused on elements of human behavior that contribute to success in school and the workplace. The chapter began by emphasizing the importance of understanding behavior in terms of working effectively with other people. A summary of the influences on human behavior, such as heredity, the developmental process, and environment, was provided. Following this general overview, factors that influence individual behavior and success in school were reviewed. Self-image, self-esteem, success and failure, and motivation were discussed in detail.

It is important to consider how other topics in the *100% Student Success* textbook support your behavior and success. For example, goal setting was discussed in Chapter 1. How can you relate goal setting to developing your self-image? How does goal setting relate to motivation? Also, consider how self-image and self-esteem factor into other topics to be presented in subsequent chapters. Examples include how self-concept and self-esteem influence your decision-making ability and how motivation contributes to living a healthy lifestyle. Understanding these types of relationships between concepts presented in the text will help you to make the best use of the information.

POINTS TO KEEP IN MIND

In this chapter, numerous main points were discussed in detail:

- Three factors that influence people's behavior are heredity, developmental process, and environment.
- Adults can change their behavior if they so choose.

2

▶ Abraham Maslow's hierarchy of needs emphasizes that all humans have basic needs, and these needs are affected by the presence or absence of things such as nurturing, acceptance, love, and a sense of belonging and self-worth.

▶ A person's self-esteem, self-worth, and self-concept can greatly affect his or her ability to have satisfying relationships.

▶ Self-image is defined as how an individual sees him- or herself.

▶ Self-esteem is defined as how an individual feels about him- or herself.

▶ Poor self-esteem affects one's confidence, which can also have a negative impact on the ability to communicate well and effectively interact with others.

▶ Examples of steps to increase one's self-esteem are practicing self-nurturing and asking for help from others.

▶ Individuals with multiple failures can develop failure expectation.

▶ Self-doubt can create such havoc that future success on other tasks can be affected.

▶ Success comes in many forms, including accomplishing tasks and demonstrating kindness and courtesy.

▶ Learning from failures is important for future successes.

▶ People are motivated internally by a combination of the need for affiliation, the need for power, and the need for achievement.

▶ Setting well-stated and clear goals helps individuals remain motivated.

CHECK YOUR UNDERSTANDING

Visit www.cengagebrain.com to see how well you have mastered the material in Chapter 2.

SUGGESTED ITEMS FOR LEARNING PORTFOLIO

▶ Research and Presentation
▶ Web Research

REFERENCES

Accel-Team.com. (n.d.). Employee motivation, the organizational environ-ment, and productivity. David McClelland: Achievement motivation. Retrieved January 22, 2013, from http://www.accel-team.com/human _relations/hrels_06_mcclelland.html

Honeycutt, A., & Milliken, M. E. (2012). *Understanding human behavior: a guide for health care providers* (8th ed.). Clifton Park, NY: Delmar Cengage Learning.

Mountain State Centers for Independent Living. (n.d.). *Positive self-image and self-esteem.* Retrieved January 22, 2013, from http://www.mtstcil .org/skills/image-3.html

Osland, J. S., & Turner, M. E. (2013). *Organizational behavior: An expe-riential approach* (9th ed.). Englewood Cliffs, NJ: Pearson Academic Computing.

University of Texas–Austin, Counseling and Mental Health Center. (2007). *Self-esteem.* Retrieved January 22, 2013, from http://cmhc.utexas.edu /selfesteem.html

2

Common Concerns of the Adult College Student

LEARNING OBJECTIVES

By the end of this chapter, you will achieve the following objectives:

▶ Define issues, barriers, and deterrents common to students in various situations.

▶ Identify methods of addressing barriers and deterrents and locate resources for addressing them.

▶ Describe professionalism and professional conduct and demonstrate it through actions and behavior.

3

"ADULT" AND "TRADITIONAL AGE" STUDENTS

Adult college students can be defined as those over the age of 25 who have life experience outside the classroom. Additional descriptions of the adult learner include other characteristics such as an individual who once served or is currently serving in the military, someone who is returning to academics after a break of four or more years of other activity, such as employment, or someone who takes on more than one adult role, such as parent, spouse, employee, and student (The Penn State Commission for Adult Learners, 2012). Traditional-age students are those who are younger and have had minimal life experience. An example of the adult student might be a 40-year-old mother of two with a nursing background who is returning to school for an additional degree. An example of a traditional student is a new high school graduate, entering college for the first time. As the 21st century sees many individuals returning to school for retraining and to pursue career changes, it is not unusual to have a blend of both types of students in the classroom.

There are certainly variations on these definitions of "traditional" and "nontraditional" students. There are older students who have never been to college, and there are younger students with considerable experience and insight. Use the information in this chapter to identify your individual needs and resources, regardless of how you fit the definitions of adult student and traditional student.

THE GREAT BALANCING ACT

It is generally recognized that adult students have multiple responsibilities, including family, financial obligations, employment commitments, and the daily concerns of home management. When school is added into this complex picture, the situation becomes even more challenging for the adult learner. The learner who enters the college environment with these priorities may have different concerns from the student who does not have the same responsibilities.

Students commonly have at least one of these responsibilities. For example, many college students who are considered traditional age have employment commitments and/or families. Students who do not have these types of responsibilities may face other issues, such as adjusting to the college environment, which require management of time, priorities, and finances. Although adult students are typically viewed as having more commitments than traditional-age students, all college students have responsibilities that require awareness of self and resources.

Regardless of whether you are a traditional or adult student, the great balancing act is successfully achieved by making sure that all priorities are effectively met—and this is sometimes easier said than done. Meeting priorities effectively means making careful assessments, knowing your resources, and engaging in creative problem solving. Often, balancing outside responsibilities and school will require making choices based on your priorities at a given time. It also means communicating with instructors and taking responsibility for your decisions.

PRIORITIES IN LIFE

If you have children, you know how illness can interfere with the daily routine. If you don't have children of your own, consider parents, friends, or colleagues who do have children. An ill child presents a significant challenge when the caregiver must be at work or school. Caring for elderly family members or attending to household emergencies can also require immediate attention.

School, gainful employment, family, and home are all *priorities* in your life. At times, certain priorities (such as an ill family member) become more *pressing*. In other words, the more pressing priority requires your focus at a given time and is the priority that receives your immediate attention. Temporarily giving your attention to a more pressing issue does not mean that other aspects of your life are less of a priority—they still are—but they are not the topic of current focus.

SETTING PRIORITIES RESPONSIBLY

Most instructors are accepting of the fact that students are juggling a variety of commitments; they recognize that life sometimes makes demands other than those related to school. The student's responsibility is to prioritize coursework along with other life responsibilities. Although most students set priorities respectfully and appropriately, some do not. Problems arise when students make excuses and when other aspects of life continually take priority over school assignments. It is important to recognize that instructors and institutions must comply with certain regulations and that this puts constraints on how flexible they can be with students. For example, schools often have attendance requirements to meet regulations associated with receiving federal funding for various programs. Instructors are obligated to uphold these requirements. Students who consistently neglect school responsibilities put instructors and the school in a precarious situation, which sometimes results in policies that are restrictive and seem disrespectful of students' other commitments. It is important to set your priorities responsibly and to communicate your reasons and intentions to your instructor. In addition, instructors must maintain a "stream of fairness" and apply policies equally without showing partiality. Keep in mind the important concept of setting priorities responsibly as you read the remaining sections of Chapter 3.

success steps for setting priorities

- Know your priorities and understand how to determine when some are more pressing than others.

- Understand that instructors and institutions must comply with regulations that often limit their flexibility on certain issues.

- Make thoughtful decisions regarding prioritizing and communicate professionally with instructors about your needs.

3

HELPFUL AND RESPONSIBLE ATTITUDES

An attitude that reflects an understanding of the instructor's position, balanced with an assertive approach, contributes to effectively balancing priorities. The following suggestions are provided for you to consider as methods for maintaining a positive and helpful attitude and maintaining motivation.

▶ **Keep your long-term goal in mind.** Your ultimate goal is to achieve your educational objective by graduating and entering the profession that you have chosen to pursue. Remember that the stresses of being a student and carrying out your other life responsibilities are temporary. Remind yourself of the rewards that await you. Each challenge that you overcome is a step toward meeting your long-term goal.

▶ **Negotiate and compromise.** Instructors typically respond positively to being approached in a nondemanding manner that reflects a desire to honor school as well as other life commitments. Present your case, let the instructor know you are trying to manage your "balancing act," understand the instructor's commitments and responsibilities, and seek a middle ground that respects both of you. Use compromise to negotiate a workable solution.

▶ **Imagine you're in the workplace.** If you faced the same dilemma in the workplace, you would need to address the situation with your supervisor and devise a mutually workable solution to your dilemma. Interact in a manner that would be appropriate in the workplace, and incorporate elements of professionalism, tact, and assertiveness in your communication with your instructor.

3

SELF-ASSESSMENT QUESTIONS

- How well do you balance your priorities?
- How effective are your negotiation and compromise skills? How can you develop these communication necessities?

? CRITICAL THINKING QUESTION

- How do you keep your long-term goal of graduation and career in front of you despite temporary obstacles in your way?

success steps for maintaining a helpful and responsible attitude

- Keep your long-term goal in mind.
- Negotiate and compromise.
- Imagine you're in the workplace.
- Weigh your options.

▶ **Weigh your options.** If you believe that you truly have a dilemma that cannot be resolved by negotiation and compromise, you may need to consider other alternatives. You may elect to choose your most pressing priority and accept consequences for doing so. You may seek outside support from the appropriate resource at your school. The ultimate decision is up to you and will be based on your situation and the resources available to you.

BARRIERS AND DETERRENTS FACING ADULT STUDENTS

© iStockphoto.com/Catherine Yeulet.

Negotiating and compromising in a professional manner can help you collaborate with instructors to balance your commitment and responsibilities.

Recall from Chapter 2 the concepts of self-image and self-esteem. Typically, the nontraditional student returning to the classroom has a self-image reflecting his or her current situation, which does not include the role of student. The new self-image that includes "student" is likely to be discrepant with the individual's current self-image. This inconsistency may contribute to a need for returning students to be aware of their new role and seek to fulfill the needs associated with it. For example, basic needs such as supplying care for children must be addressed. Support from family and friends contributes to belonging and esteem needs.

Quigley (1998) elaborates on Patricia K. Cross's (1992) barriers and deterrents to adult learners. The barriers that these educational researchers discuss include elements that pertain to a student's responsibilities, perceptions of school, and processes within the school.

Cross (1992) and Kerka (1986) point out that *barriers* are in reality *deterrents*. In other words, challenges to completing your education are not barriers that prevent you from reaching your goals. Instead, they are influences that may discourage you, but not alter your course. To emphasize this point, we will use the term *deterrent* in our discussion. Individual circumstances and perceptions also significantly influence how one responds to challenges.

SITUATIONAL DETERRENTS

Situational deterrents are those circumstances in your environment that have an effect on your ability to give your full attention to school. Examples include family-related issues such as lack of day care, transportation problems, financial issues, and home or family management concerns.

Situational deterrents are most effectively met by being aware of the resources upon which you can draw (Quigley, 1998). It is your responsibility to pursue and make arrangements for using resources that are available to you. Your school may offer a listing of resources for you to explore.

DISPOSITIONAL DETERRENTS

Dispositional deterrents are internal factors that affect your perception of or attitude toward school. Quigley (1998) identifies dispositional deterrents as having the greatest impact on learners. Consider these carefully and strive to develop an understanding of how they might influence you. Dispositional deterrents include your perceptions of school based on previous experience, your expectations, and how you perceive your abilities and level of confidence.

INSTITUTIONAL DETERRENTS

Institutional deterrents are those elements of school policy and procedure that present difficulties for adult learners. Examples include scheduling, processes that require significant time investment, or other procedures that are cumbersome and not easily completed.

It is important to keep in mind that institutional deterrents often arise from requirements over which schools have little control. Federal regulations and accreditation standards frequently require certain procedures and deadlines to be in place, and schools must abide by these in order to be in compliance. Failing to comply can hold serious consequences for a school, such as loss of accreditation or federal funding.

TYPES OF DETERRENTS TO ADULT LEARNERS

Deterrent	Definition	Examples	Solutions
Situational Deterrents	Circumstances in your environment that have an effect on your school attendance or ability to give your full attention to school	▶ Family-related issues such as lack of day care ▶ Transportation problems, financial issues, home and family management concerns ▶ Adjusting to the college environment	▶ Student services ▶ Contacts and acquaintances ▶ Other community resources ▶ Financial aid office
Dispositional Deterrents	Internal factors that affect your perception of or attitude toward school	Your perceptions of school based on ▶ previous experience ▶ your expectations ▶ how you perceive your abilities and level of confidence	▶ Talk to your instructors. ▶ Seek support from trusted sources. ▶ Assess your perceptions. ▶ Evaluate your responses. ▶ Recognize your strengths. ▶ View needs for change as professional growth.
Institutional Barriers	Those elements of school policy and procedure that present difficulties for adult learners	Examples include ▶ scheduling ▶ processes that require significant time investment ▶ other procedures that are not designed in a way to make them easily completed	▶ Seek help from student government representatives, student focus groups, and quality circles

Adult learners typically face various types of deterrents. Careful consideration of possible solutions to deterrents can help you stay focused and on track with your educational goals.

CASE IN POINT: LEARNING TO JUGGLE

Read the scenario below. Then, in groups or as a class, discuss the questions at the end.

Lindsay Dillon is a single parent who works as a receptionist for a physician at a family practice. She recently enrolled in an evening medical assisting program at a local technical college, which she attends after her daytime job. She has two children, both in elementary school. Lindsay's mother lives in the same town and works three days a week. She is willing to help with child care on her days off but is unable to offer assistance on the days that she does work. Lindsay is the first in her peer group to attend college. In addition, she was last in school 15 years ago, when she attempted a nursing program but dropped out to have her family. Lindsay wonders how she is going to balance caring for her children, being employed full time, and keeping her friends while still succeeding in school.

▶ Think about your personal situation and your academic training. How do Lindsay's challenges relate to those that you face?

▶ How can Lindsay find a way to balance all of her responsibilities? What are some resources that might be available to her?

▶ What challenges do you think Lindsay might face from her friends?

▶ How might Lindsay's self-image and self-esteem be influenced by her return to school after 15 years? What feelings might Lindsay have?

METHODS FOR OVERCOMING DETERRENTS

It is important to remember that although deterrents can be stressful and at times discouraging, there are methods for overcoming them. When outside concerns take temporary priority, it is important to recognize them as transient. Keep in mind that they are short-term issues within your larger goal of building your career. Remember to evaluate the most pressing priority, weigh your options, and choose the best approach for the circumstances.

> ### success steps for overcoming situational deterrents
>
> • Remember deterrents are short-term issues.
> • Evaluate your most pressing priority.
> • Weigh your options.

CHOOSING THE BEST APPROACH FOR THE CIRCUMSTANCES: RESOURCES AND METHODS FOR OVERCOMING SITUATIONAL DETERRENTS

There are organizations and offices on and off campus that may be able to offer resources for addressing situational deterrents. Consider the following possible options.

Campus and Community Resources

Student services. Many schools have a student services department that provides support for advising, career development, and other areas related to students' professional growth. Some departments maintain lists of resources that students frequently need, including child care resources, area housing options, and other resources relevant to students' needs. Advising on a variety of topics, including adjusting to the college environment, may be available through student services. Students are responsible for contacting, evaluating, and making arrangements with the department.

Contacts and acquaintances. Word of mouth between friends and family can also be helpful. For example, friends who have children may have referrals for day care, and those with older children can be a valuable source of helpful suggestions based on experience.

Other community resources. The community in which you live can also provide an abundance of resources. For example, churches and synagogues frequently have resources for day care and other support services. Brainstorm a list of possible resources that you have available to you based on your circumstances.

Financial aid office. The financial aid office at your school has information regarding student loans, grants, work-study programs, and scholarships. It may also have information regarding off-campus financial resources if it does not have resources that meet your needs. Consider contacting financial aid personnel at your school if you have financial concerns, even if you believe you don't qualify for funds. Financial aid counselors are trained in identifying the best resources available for your needs and may have creative ideas that can be helpful to you.

The digital and traditional library. Remember the library as a support source. There are numerous publications that summarize resources for a variety of financial and other topics. Ask the reference

Use all available campus and community resources to help you overcome situational deterrents.

ZUMA Press, Inc./Alamy.

3

librarian (which you can do online as well) for assistance in locating resources that are relevant to your needs.

Online groups. Local agencies and professional groups frequently have online resources for professional networking, at-home moms, and other groups whose members share similar concerns or have similar needs. For example, in the Denver area, the Denver Regional Council of Governments (DRCOG) offers a carpool matching service. Explore groups such as these that may be offered as a public service in your locale.

Strategies for Addressing Situational Deterrents

There are definitive actions that you can take to lessen the burden of situational deterrents. Other students also face the same dilemmas, and you may be able to create effective solutions by working with peers. Consider the following strategies.

Carpooling. Find classmates who live in your area and arrange to help each other out in the event of a transportation emergency. You might want to consider carpooling on a regular basis if it fits in with your other schedule demands. Some students have found that carpooling with others from a similar locale a distance from campus allows an opportunity for a "study group" during lengthy commutes. If you need to get to work immediately after class, carpooling may not be an effective option. If it does fit your schedule, carpooling can save you money and provide an opportunity to get to know your classmates.

Mass transit is one community resource that can provide a convenient and economical alternative for students.

Public transportation. It may be to your benefit to learn what public transportation is available in your area. Many mass transit systems offer discounted fare options for students who present valid school identification. Public transportation eliminates the stress of traffic and long commutes, is typically less costly than purchasing gasoline, and gives you time to read or study while someone else does the driving.

Child care co-ops. An alternative to day care providers or other child care services is a child care cooperative developed and managed by students with children. Creating a co-op requires thoughtful coordination, as you need to find a compatible mix of people who can be reliable and available at various times to be the care provider. Your student services office may be able to assist you in organizing a child care co-op.

Community child care options. In addition to home and commercial child care options, there are organizations in the community

3

that may be a resource or can offer one. For example, *MOPS (Mothers of Preschoolers)* and *Mothers and More* are organizations that advocate for families and may have suggestions for meeting child care needs.

Creative work opportunities. Financial issues are common concerns of college students. For adult learners with family responsibilities, this matter can become even more pressing. Research creative job opportunities that can provide flexible hours and good income. For example, many companies rely on Internet research or data entry. These are jobs that can typically be done at home at hours that are convenient to you, provided that deadlines are met.

Community financial resources. The financial aid office at your school is the most appropriate place to start if you are seeking financial assistance. Community sources, such as your bank, are also options. Banks may be able to suggest low-interest student loans or refer you to appropriate resources. Ask the customer service department or personal bankers at your bank for more information.

Consider online learning options. Online learning can add flexibility to your education by allowing you to complete requirements according to your schedule. Research online options at your school and consider taking advantage of online learning if it is available. If online courses are not available at your school, it is sometimes possible to take an online course from another institution and transfer the credits in. Check with your academic department to see whether this is a viable option.

Use other technologies. E-mail, social networking, online chat, and other technical tools have greatly facilitated communication and the exchange of information. Use technology to your advantage. For example, being able to text or chat online with an instructor may eliminate the need for you to make a trip in for office hours. Today, many instructors use online tools for posting course materials, grades, and announcements. Using these resources when they are available can save time and provide access to important course information. Various student support groups may be available through social networking sites. As with any resource, carefully evaluate the information and advice you get from these sources.

METHODS FOR OVERCOMING DISPOSITIONAL DETERRENTS

Dispositional deterrents are internal and are part of who you are rather than being a part of your external environment. Experiencing difficulty adjusting to the college environment (for any reason) is an example of a dispositional barrier. Addressing concerns related to these types of issues requires self-reflection and self-awareness and may be closely related to the motivational, self-image, and self-esteem issues discussed in Chapter 2. You may find it helpful to review those concepts and apply them here. The following suggestions are actions you can take to gain insight into your internal process and address concerns related to dispositional deterrents.

Talk to your instructors. Quigley (1998) emphasizes the importance of communicating with your instructor regarding personal concerns. Research has shown that students who talk with their instructors regularly are more successful at persisting in school. Communicating with instructors gives them the opportunity to understand your concerns and work with you to reach a mutually agreeable solution to issues.

Seek support from trusted sources. Make a list of people in your life whom you respect and trust. Examples include clergy, relatives and friends with whom you are close, former or current instructors, and other personal and professional contacts. Reviewing problems aloud and getting feedback may help you gain insight into solving problems. Discussing your personal concerns and getting honest opinions from people you trust may help you overcome dispositional deterrents.

Assess your perceptions. Kerka (1986) emphasizes the importance of the individual's perception of his or her situation. Research suggests that deterrents have less impact on students who perceive the deterrents as obstacles that can be overcome. Evaluate your perceptions of the deterrents that you face and engage in a logical problem-solving process to arrive at solutions. Consider a brainstorming session with a trusted individual as part of the problem-solving process.

Getting feedback and advice from a trusted source can provide insight into your strengths, as well as areas to develop for your academic and professional success.

Evaluate your responses. Your responses to events in the environment are also important (Kerka, 1986). Reacting to situations in a manner that prevents you from approaching a problem in a logical and thoughtful manner is generally detrimental to overcoming deterrents that you face. For example, reacting emotionally in anger or withdrawing from a problem situation greatly reduces the opportunities for effective problem solving.

Recognize your strengths. Everyone has strengths that can be applied to their professional growth. Use feedback from others to develop an understanding of your strengths and explore ways to use them advantageously in your field. Recognizing your strengths

3

- How do you perceive deterrents in your environment?
- How do you respond to deterrents in your environment?
- How does your self-image influence your response to deterrents?

? CRITICAL THINKING QUESTION

▸ What method(s) might you use to overcome your dispositional deterrents?

success steps for overcoming dispositional deterrents

- Talk to your instructors.
- Seek support from trusted sources.
- Assess your perceptions.
- Evaluate your responses.
- Recognize your strengths.
- View the need for changes as professional growth.
- Be aware of your needs, self-image, and self-esteem.

and using them to market your skills and talents appropriately is an important part of professionalism and finding your professional niche. Ask your trusted source for feedback on your strengths.

View the need for changes as an opportunity for professional growth. Just as everyone has strengths, they also have areas of challenge and areas in which they can improve. Rather than a "weakness," consider areas of challenge a "strength gap" and set goals for professional development. Your trusted source can also provide you with insight into areas you might need to develop and help you brainstorm ideas for setting and achieving goals.

Be aware of your needs, self-image, and self-esteem. Ensure that your needs are being met in a way that supports your role and success as a student. Use your successes to build a positive self-image and enhance your self-esteem.

apply it

Monitoring Perceptions and Responses

Find printable activities on the companion web site for this book, accessed through www.cengagebrain.com.

GOAL: To increase your awareness of your responses to deterrents and maximize productive responses

STEP 1: Divide a piece of paper into three columns. In the left-hand column, write a list of the deterrents that you personally face. In the middle column, identify and describe how you react to that deterrent. For example, if your method of transportation is unreliable (the deterrent) and you react by getting angry and missing class, describe that in the middle column. In the right-hand column, record alternative reactions and solutions to the deterrent. Take the actions that you need to take to implement alternative solutions (for example, familiarizing yourself with public transportation). (Note: You can create this document electronically if you prefer.)

STEP 2: Reflect on the deterrents, responses, and alternatives that you have listed. Make it a point to be conscious of these and keep them in your awareness.

STEP 3: When you face one of your deterrents, recall your list. If you are a visual person, consider carrying the list with you as a reference. Take a few seconds to monitor your response and consider whether it is the most productive response you can make. For example, if you get angry and decide to miss class, stop and consider if this is the most helpful reaction. Consider the alternative responses and actions that you recorded.

STEP 4: Replace any nonproductive emotional response with your constructive alternative response. Note your emotional response when you take the more productive action.

STEP 5: Record your progress in a journal. Over time, you should see a change in your initial response to deterrents that you encounter. Put the journal entries in your Learning Portfolio.

METHODS FOR OVERCOMING INSTITUTIONAL DETERRENTS

Institutional deterrents may be the most difficult deterrents for students to address because some of the policies may be in place for compliance reasons and cannot be changed. However, it may be possible to streamline some procedures.

If you find policies and procedures that seem unnecessarily restrictive, first find out if they are in place for a reason, such as compliance with federal regulations or accreditation standards. If they are not, approach the situation in a professional and thoughtful manner. Demonstrate professionalism by knowing your facts and presenting them logically and through appropriate channels. The following types of student groups have traditionally addressed institutional issues:

- ▶ **Student government.** Some campuses have a formal student government, typically composed of elected officers and representatives whose job is to organize events, represent concerns of the student body, and serve as a liaison between students and administration. Student government representatives can be contacted regarding concerns about policies and procedures that seem unnecessarily restrictive to adult students.

- ▶ **Student focus groups.** If a formal student government is not available, student focus groups can be formed to research issues and develop input from the student perspective. Your school may have a procedure for initiating this process. Check with your student services department, department chair, or other administrator to ensure that you are working within acceptable boundaries. Following established and accepted protocol will increase your chances for success.

- ▶ **Quality circles.** Quality circles are groups that meet on a regular basis to review and monitor the school environment and to advocate for processes that contribute to quality education. Quality circles typically consist of students, faculty, and possibly administrators. Membership usually rotates so that new and different perspectives are represented.

Image 100 Ltd./Getty Images.

Effective verbal and nonverbal communication skills, as well as facilitation skills, are incorporated into classroom activities such as giving presentations.

success steps for addressing institutional deterrents

- • Determine whether a policy or procedure is required for compliance with regulations and standards.
- • Research the issue thoroughly.
- • Know your facts.
- • Present your case through appropriate channels.
- • Be professional and logical.

apply it

Success Resources

Find printable activities on the companion web site for this book, accessed through www.cengagebrain.com.

GOAL: To increase your awareness of available resources to address deterrents

STEP 1: Create three columns in an electronic document or on a sheet of paper. (For ample space, use the landscape orientation for your page.) Label the columns "Situational Deterrents," "Dispositional Deterrents," and "Institutional Deterrents." Then divide each of the three columns in half. Label each pair of subcolumns "Concerns" and "Resources."

STEP 2: List the deterrents that you experience in the "Concerns" column and list potential sources for support in the "Resources" column. Note the outcomes of contacts with resources and record important contact information for future reference.

apply it

Resource Brainstorming

Find printable activities on the companion web site for this book, accessed through www.cengagebrain.com.

GOAL: To share and develop resources for addressing deterrents often encountered by college students

STEP 1: Create a group of peers who share a desire to create a resource bank for common student needs, such as day care.

STEP 2: Decide on the format for your group. You may wish to meet in person and elect a recorder for the group. One of the benefits of meeting in person, at least for the first meeting, is the positive energy generated in a face-to-face brainstorming group. Another convenient method is to create an e-mail or social networking group so that each participant receives a copy of the resource and the group can be asynchronous (you don't have to be in the same place at the same time to be effective). You may choose a combination of formats. It is important to select a format that works for the group members.

continued

3

continued

STEP 3: Share ideas and information regarding resources that group members might find helpful. Social networking allows members to post needs related to long-term planning ("I need a new babysitter beginning next school term") or for more immediate concerns ("I need a babysitter for next week"). General information can also be posted ("My neighbor just started a day care, if anyone is interested").

PROFESSIONALISM AND PREPARING FOR THE WORKPLACE

SELF-ASSESSMENT QUESTIONS

- How do you define professionalism?
- What can you do in school to develop the professional skills you will need in the workplace?

? CRITICAL THINKING QUESTION

▶ What do you consider to be the single most important element of professionalism? Why?

Developing professional attitudes and behaviors is as important as (some would say more important than) gaining technical experience. Professionalism consists of behaviors that are acceptable in the workplace as well as how you present yourself and are perceived by coworkers and customers or clients.

ELEMENTS OF PROFESSIONALISM

Professionalism is a combination of many factors. In total, these elements provide the impression that you give to those around you. Consider how the following elements blend to convey a sense of professionalism.

Professional Presentation

Professional presentation includes appearance and dress. It also refers to the overall image as observed in a composite of behaviors such as attitude, interpersonal skills, ethics, and numerous other personal characteristics. Professional presentation can be broken down into the following components.

Personal Traits

Many personal traits contribute to one's professional presentation. Personal traits are subject to some degree of subjective interpretation and indeed much of how we are viewed by others is based on subjective responses. The following traits are generally accepted as professional:

▶ **Attitude.** A professional attitude is one that is positive yet realistic and conveys a "can-do" orientation to tasks. A professional attitude communicates self-confidence with openness to growth and learning, as well as a cooperative spirit and a concern for the welfare of the group and group goals. Self-motivation and taking responsibility for oneself within the group boundaries are also part of a professional attitude.

▶ **Dependability and responsibility.** Dependability means arriving on time for class or work, being prepared, and completing projects on time. If circumstances prevent this, the professional gives ample notification and suggests alternative solutions for completing the task.

▶ **Self-management.** Self-management is the ability to be aware of one's behavior and manage it in such a way that professional standards are consistently met. Professionalism entails being aware of schedules and deadlines, being able to manage time and prioritize tasks, and monitoring one's performance for quality.

Ethics

Professionalism reflects an awareness of and concern for high standards of behavior and doing what is right based on universal principles. Most professions have a code of ethics that members of the profession are expected to uphold in their daily activities. Examples of universal ethics principles include honesty, fairness, and beneficence (acting for the good of another person).

Effective Communication

Effective communication means providing adequate information, ensuring that you receive adequate information to complete an assignment or task, and being able to exchange information in a variety of settings. The following examples of communication are important to the professional.

▶ **Group skills.** In most professional settings, the ability to work cooperatively to meet a group goal is essential. Group skills include being able to compromise, negotiate, contribute, and collaborate to build ideas and solutions.

▶ **Facilitation skills.** Facilitation skills contribute to leading effective meetings, guiding communication to reach group goals, and giving effective presentations.

3

▶ **Verbal communication.** Communicating effectively involves being assertive, being polite and tactful, using acceptable language, and conveying messages accurately and on time.

▶ **Nonverbal communication.** Many people believe that nonverbal communication communicates more than verbal communication. Nonverbal communication includes your facial expressions, posture, and eye contact. Nonverbal communication can convey impressions such as whether you are paying attention or showing respect. If your verbal and nonverbal messages are inconsistent, the listener will typically respond to your nonverbal message versus the verbal one.

▶ **Effective listening.** Listening is one of the more essential components of communication. Listen carefully to what others tell you and pay attention to what they are communicating nonverbally. Effective listening also involves being able to clarify to ensure understanding, receiving messages with an open and objective attitude, and demonstrating sensitivity to the emotional content of messages.

▶ **Effective written communication.** Whether in a letter, e-mail, or other online tool such as a social networking profile or blog, written communication is often the first impression you make in the business world. Professional written communication demonstrates accurate grammar and spelling as well as language appropriate to the professional setting. It also includes keeping required records and documentation using accepted formats and protocols. If you know that your spelling or other element of your written communication is weak, consider using tools such as an electronic spell checker or having someone that you trust review your work. Be aware that spell checkers are not always accurate. For example, if a word is spelled correctly but used in the wrong context, the spell checker will not recognize the error.

It is also important to select the most appropriate communication method to achieve your goal. For example, if you need an immediate response, a phone call, text message, or instant message may be more effective than an e-mail, which may not be read right away. If you have corrective feedback to give, a face-to-face meeting is generally preferable. Consider what you are trying to accomplish with your communication and proceed accordingly.

▶ **Diversity in communication.** Communication practices frequently vary cross-culturally and depending on the way in which an individual has been raised. Levels of assertiveness, the manner of interacting with authority figures, and the meanings of words and nonverbal gestures are examples of communication elements that can vary. As much as possible, it is important to understand the individuals with whom you are communicating and remain sensitive to their responses during your interactions with them.

Diversity Awareness

Diversity awareness is the demonstration of respect for individuals with disabilities and from different cultural groups, lifestyles, age groups, socioeconomic groups, and genders. It includes being aware of words and actions that may be offensive to others and refraining from using offensive elements in communication and other activities. Diversity awareness has expanded to include such aspects of diversity as various learning styles and learning differences as well as ways of thinking. The "smallness" of the world in the 21st century requires an open mind and willingness to learn from and about a variety of sources.

Professional Development

Professional development includes meeting the requirements of your profession, as well as taking the responsibility to maintain current knowledge in your field. Staying current in the following areas is also part of professionalism.

▶ **Credentialing and licensing.** You are responsible for acquiring any certification and license that is required in your field. It is your responsibility to know credentialing and continuing education requirements and any changes affecting them.

▶ **Professional conduct.** Many professions are regulated legally and have standards of practice. You are responsible for understanding these parameters and for conducting yourself accordingly. You are obligated to practice within the boundaries of your expertise and skills and refer to another professional if you are not qualified to perform a certain task. Being aware of liability issues and preventing unsafe conditions is also a professional expectation.

▶ **General business knowledge.** Professional behavior includes using technology appropriately and keeping up to date with the technical and business developments in your field. You must understand the significance of financial and marketing issues as well as administrative and management concerns and roles in daily business operations.

▶ **Lifelong learning.** Professionalism involves the ability and responsibility to remain current in your field and to be aware of recent developments and new knowledge. Effective professionals recognize the need for continued education beyond school and set professional goals for their continuing development. They are able to locate and use resources effectively in order to stay current in their field.

▶ **Technical knowledge.** All professional fields are becoming more "tech savvy" and rely on technology to accomplish organizational goals. Knowing how to leverage technology to complete your job effectively and efficiently will contribute to your success as an employee. Stay current with developments in the technology field and be proficient in the technical tools utilized in your organization.

apply it

Web Research

Find printable activities on the companion web site for this book, accessed through www.cengagebrain.com.

GOAL: To research professionalism and methods for professional development online

STEP 1: Conduct an Internet search using the terms "professionalism" and "professional development." (You are likely to get results from professions other than your own, but the information is usually applicable to all professionals.)

STEP 2: Bookmark or print articles that would be a good resource for understanding professionalism.

STEP 3: Share and exchange resources with classmates who are doing this activity.

apply it

Professional Development Journal

Find printable activities on the companion web site for this book, accessed through www.cengagebrain.com.

GOAL: To build a strategy and set goals for professional development

STEP 1: Select a format that you will use regularly. Some people prefer an electronic journal, whereas others prefer the traditional bound type. Choose the type that you will use.

STEP 2: Start by reflecting on and recording your strengths. Write about your strengths, how they can benefit you, how you can use them, and how they can contribute to your professional growth. Add observations and thoughts that are important to you.

STEP 3: Next, reflect on your "strength gaps" (challenge areas). How would you like to develop these? How can your strengths support you? Set short-term goals for developing these areas and note resources and methods for goal achievement.

STEP 4: Write in your journal at least once or twice weekly, more often when you reach a milestone or make an observation that you want to make sure you remember. Record developing strengths and new elements of yourself that you wish to develop. Review your journal regularly to see your progress.

STEP 5: Based on the entries in your journal, set goals as part of a professional development plan.

In addition to the technical knowledge you are developing in school, also be aware of opportunities to consider and practice professional skills. These are skills that transcend subject matter and are relevant in all classes and areas of study. The skills are also known as *transferable skills* and include as examples effective problem solving, teamwork, and the ability to use technology effectively. Think about these skills on a daily basis and increase your awareness of opportunities to practice them.

CHAPTER SUMMARY

This chapter addressed deterrents that often pose difficulties for students who are getting an education while fulfilling numerous other life responsibilities. Situational, dispositional, and institutional deterrents were discussed, and methods for addressing each of these were suggested.

The remaining chapters in *100% Student Success* provide recommendations for self-management and professional development that can support you in addressing challenges that you face during your education. Strategies suggested throughout the text can provide a foundation for sound self-management techniques that can help you keep organized and minimize disruption from challenges that arise. As you read through the text, personalize the information provided to meet your individual needs.

POINTS TO KEEP IN MIND

In this chapter, several main points were discussed in detail:

▶ Adult learners must balance a variety of life priorities such as family, school, life management tasks, and employment.

▶ Although all life priorities are important, some priorities become more pressing at times.

▶ Most instructors understand the adult student's need to balance priorities and appreciate open communication and the sincere effort on the student's part to prioritize coursework appropriately.

▶ Assess the deterrents that you face and use appropriate resources to address them.

▶ Develop your professional presentation, skills, and behaviors.

CHECK YOUR UNDERSTANDING

Visit www.cengagebrain.com to see how well you have mastered the material in Chapter 3.

SUGGESTED ITEMS FOR LEARNING PORTFOLIO

▶ Success Resources

▶ Resource Brainstorming

▶ Web Research

▶ Professional Development Journal

REFERENCES

Cross, K. P. (1992). *Adults as learners: increasing participation and facilitating learning.* San Francisco: Jossey-Bass.

Kerka, S. (1986). *Deterrents to participation in adult education.* ERIC Digest No. 59. Retrieved January 24, 2013, from http://www.ericdigests.org/pre-924/overview.htm

Penn State Commission for Adult Learners (2012). The Penn State Commission for Adult Learners. Retrieved January 24, 2013, from http://www.outreach.psu.edu/commission

Quigley, B. A. (1998). The first three weeks: A critical time for motivation [Electronic version]. *Focus on Basics, 2,* A. Retrieved January 24, 2013, from The National Center for the Study of Adult Learning and Literacy web site: http://ncsall.net/index.html@id=420.html

U.S. Department of Education (2013). Projections of Education Statistics to 2021. Retrieved March 22, 2013, from http://nces.ed.gov/programs/projections/projections2021/sec5c.asp

part 2

Shaping and Communicating Your Ideas

Part II of *100% Student Success* focuses on the fundamental skills and strategies that you will need to acquire in order to be an effective learner and communicator in both the classroom and the workplace.

As a holistic being, you are a product of your physical, psychological, social, and spiritual self. Contributing to all of these are your interpersonal and learning styles, your self-image, and your self-esteem. **Chapter 4: Learning Strategies** explores how you can use your attributes to develop skills that will contribute to your success.

Chapter 5: Communication Skills for Student Success introduces elements of communication that are important to success in school and in the workplace. Communication is a skill that employers highly value in employees. Effective communication prevents errors, adds to cost-effectiveness, and builds successful interpersonal relationships.

Chapter 6: Critical Thinking and Problem Solving summarizes critical and creative thinking and provides suggestions for using both processes effectively. Using these skills successfully and appropriately in school can greatly add to your success.

4

Learning Strategies

LEARNING OBJECTIVES

By the end of this chapter, you will achieve the following objectives:

▶ Explain the concepts of "natural learning" according to Caine and Caine.

▶ Describe the relationship of natural learning to self-image, self-esteem, and achievement.

▶ Define active learning and teamwork.

▶ Explain the impact of the functions of the brain on the learning experience.

▶ Discuss the various learning styles.

▶ Explain the importance of determining your preferred learning style.

▶ Describe an effective study environment.

▶ Explain how to improve reading skills.

▶ Describe methods used for effective note taking.

▶ Discuss methods for studying and learning math effectively.

▶ Discuss methods for studying and taking tests effectively.

▶ Discuss methods to minimize test anxiety.

▶ Explain the differences between preparing for an objective exam versus an essay exam.

▶ Explain the basic principles of using selected memory enhancement techniques.

▶ Describe skills needed to succeed in online courses in the 21st century.

BE IN THE KNOW

Teamwork

You may have heard the expression "There is no *I* in team." While this statement is both literally and figuratively true, there are several "I" statements of which you should be aware as they pertain to being a successful team member in both the classroom and the workplace.

Consider the following points. Read them and put yourself in a team situation. Do you agree with these statements as they apply to you? What actions might you take to make yourself a better team member?

- *I* need to be accountable to my team members to complete the work I have been assigned.
- *I* am as valued as a team member as anyone else on the team.
- *I* value the contributions of all team members.
- *I* fully participate in discussions and decisions that affect the outcome of the project.
- *I* am a team leader and other team members look to me to fill that role.
- *I* weigh all suggestions equally before coming to a conclusion.
- *I* care about the success of the project as much for my team members as I do for myself.
- *I* meet or exceed deadlines and provide quality work that positively affects that outcome of the project.
- *I* voice my opinions and concerns to the team in order to make the project as successful as possible.
- *I* recognize that different team members bring different skills to the team.

What other "I" statements can you think of as they relate to being a successful team member? GO TEAM!

FUNCTIONS OF THE BRAIN IN LEARNING

Over the years, research has been conducted to understand how the brain functions and how individuals learn. For years it has been known that elements such as stress, anxiety, and lack of sleep can affect

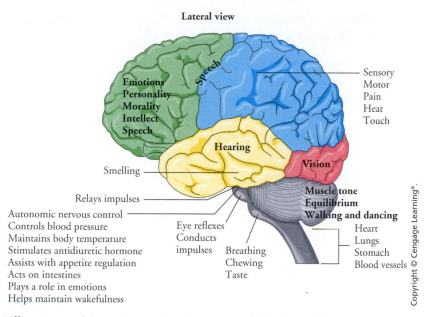

Lateral view

Emotions
Personality
Morality
Intellect
Speech

Speech

Sensory
Motor
Pain
Heat
Touch

Hearing

Vision

Smelling

Muscle tone
Equilibrium
Walking and dancing

Relays impulses

Autonomic nervous control
Controls blood pressure
Maintains body temperature
Stimulates antidiuretic hormone
Assists with appetite regulation
Acts on intestines
Plays a role in emotions
Helps maintain wakefulness

Eye reflexes
Conducts
impulses   Breathing
Chewing
Taste

Heart
Lungs
Stomach
Blood vessels

Copyright © Cengage Learning®.

Different parts of the brain control various aspects of behavior and learning.

the ability to learn. To further understand the effects that the human brain can have on learning, Caine and Caine (n.d.) proposed principles of "natural learning" (known as "brain-based learning" in their previous publications). These principles help to explain how the brain functions and the impact that these functions can have on learning experiences. Some of these principles are listed here:

▶ Due to the connection of body and mind, effective learning involves use of all senses as well as physical involvement.

▶ Physiological reactions of the body, including responses to stress, fatigue, poor nutrition, and illness, affect the brain's functions and learning capacity. Individual development rates also affect learning.

▶ Social interaction is an integral part of learning. Learning occurs through relationships with others, participating with others, and when socialization needs are met.

▶ Recall other needs that were discussed in Chapter 2. When needs are effectively met, learning occurs more easily.

▶ Humans are innately motivated to seek information, explore knowledge, and make sense of input from the environment.

Motivation increases with the meaning and level of interest in the information.

▶ Information is better learned when it is well organized. If information doesn't make sense, the brain naturally tries to organize the information into some sort of pattern. Well-organized information allows you to focus on the material rather than attempting to try and make sense of information that is unclear or seemingly unrelated.

▶ Emotions play a critical role in learning. Learning is largely dependent on how you feel about yourself (recall our discussion regarding self-esteem), your attitude toward the material, your preconceived ideas, and how you are responding to the environment on a given day. Emotions also affect the ability to memorize and recall information. How you respond to information throughout the learning process will influence how well you learn it. Information that is appropriately challenging is more motivating than information that is threatening or that evokes negative responses.

▶ Learning occurs in a context. Putting facts in a story, demonstrating them in a presentation or project, or being involved in some other type of activity enhances learning. Specifics are better retained when they are presented as parts of a whole.

▶ Reflection supports learning. Thinking about, reviewing, and applying what you have learned facilitates learning by allowing processing to occur on both conscious and unconscious levels.

▶ The brain remembers information in at least two ways. The spatial memory system occurs without a conscious effort to remember information. For example, remembering that a streetlight is at the end of the block by the school is something that is automatically placed in the memory. It didn't have to be intentionally memorized. Experiencing or seeing something new motivates this system into action. Another system in the brain stores information such as facts and skills and is dependent on rote memory and repetition. Learning facts and skills should occur through use of both memory systems. Remembering occurs more readily when learning involves a variety of activities such as demonstrations, projects, field trips, visual imagery, stories, drama, and so forth. Make use of both memory systems by taking advantage of various activities offered in your classes that involve all your senses in the learning process.

▶ Learning follows the same developmental pattern in humans, yet each brain is unique and responds to information in its own way. Being aware of your own preferences and style can facilitate your learning.

LEARNING STYLES AND TYPE PREFERENCES

Understanding your preferred learning style can contribute to optimal learning. Each person has a preferred way of learning information. For example, some students learn and retain information most effectively when it is portrayed in illustrations (visual learning style), whereas other students learn most effectively by listening to a lecture (auditory learning style). Others may learn best by engaging in activity and trying it out (kinesthetic learners), and some may learn best by building, writing, or manipulating objects or tools in some other way (tactile learners).

You may find that learning new material is easiest for you when you use your preferred learning style. Being able to create methods based on your learning style to support your studying will benefit you throughout school as well as in the workplace. Letting instructors and employers know your preferred learning style will support them in helping you to develop your skills.

It is important to remember, however, that it is of value to you to be able to learn using all styles, and it is to your advantage to develop your skills in all learning areas. Success in your academic studies and as a professional requires not only an understanding of your preferred learning style but also calls for the ability to incorporate other learning style models into your skill set. For example, even though an individual might naturally be more comfortable using illustrations, it is advantageous to be able to learn techniques by listening to a verbal explanation.

SELF-ASSESSMENT QUESTIONS

- What did you learn regarding the impact your brain has on your learning?
- Based on what you have learned, what might you change to enhance your learning?

? CRITICAL THINKING QUESTION

▶ How has stress, fatigue, poor nutrition, or illness affected your learning capacity?

4

SELF-ASSESSMENT QUESTIONS

- What is your preferred learning style?
- How can you improve in utilizing the other learning styles to accomplish your academic goals?

? CRITICAL THINKING QUESTION

▶ How might you create methods based on your learning style to support your studying?

Learning styles are commonly categorized into auditory, visual, tactile (touch), and kinesthetic (movement and doing) modes. Figure 4-1 illustrates these four learning styles and gives examples of activities that support each. Remember that it is important to learn using all of these modes; however, you may be most successful in learning new information using the mode that comes to you most naturally.

There are other models that describe how individuals learn, including Kolb's Learning Style Model, the Herrmann Brain Dominance

LEARNING STYLES AND SUPPORTING ACTIVITIES

Learning Style	Sensory Modality	Activity Examples
If your style is . . .	You learn best using . . .	Activities that are likely to support your learning are . . .
Auditory	▶ The sense of hearing	▶ Lectures
	▶ Verbal information	▶ Discussion
		▶ Recordings
		▶ Reciting aloud
		▶ Reading (although it uses visual sense) may be effective because of its verbal nature
Visual	▶ The visual sense	▶ Illustrations
	▶ Diagrammed information	▶ Pictures
		▶ Visualizing
		▶ Charts
		▶ Diagrams
		▶ Written instructions
Tactile	▶ Touching	▶ Writing
	▶ "Hands on" activity	▶ Diagramming information yourself
		▶ Putting something together
Kinesthetic	▶ Participation	▶ "Jumping right in"
	▶ Trying before learning	▶ Experiential learning
		▶ Field trips
		▶ Active involvement
		▶ Laboratory exercises

Figure 4-1   Learning Style and Activity Chart. By identifying your preferred learning style, you can select activities from which you will learn most effectively. Even though you probably have one preferred style, it is to your benefit to learn from all types of activities.

apply it

Learning Models

Find printable activities on the companion web site for this book, accessed through www.cengagebrain.com.

GOAL: To develop a better understanding regarding your own personal learning style preference

STEP 1: Conduct an Internet search using "learning styles" as your search term.

STEP 2: Compile a print or electronic file of articles pertaining to various learning models. Consider how each applies to your individual learning style. Complete learning inventories and use other tools that you find in your research.

STEP 3: An alternate activity is for each individual in the class to research one learning model. Provide copies of the articles or e-mail links of your findings to fellow group members so that each concludes the activity with a variety of resources.

STEP 4: Consider placing your resources in your Learning Portfolio.

Instrument (HBDI), and the Felder-Silverman Learning Style Model. The Myers-Briggs Type Indicator (MBTI) is also a popular tool. Although not a learning model per se, the MBTI can provide an individual with insight into how to interact with his or her environment in a way that supports learning.

You are encouraged to explore other learning models to support your awareness of your learning style.

ACTIVE LEARNING

As pointed out in the last section, there are various ways that people learn. The traditional and primary method of teaching in the academic environment is lecture. Advancements have been made in understanding the need to incorporate active learning into the classroom as a way to engage students in the learning process. Active learning involves practicing a specific skill, reflecting on its effectiveness, and practicing again to incorporate changes and improvements, as opposed to passively listening to a lecture. Active learning not only makes learning more enjoyable but can also appeal to all types of learning styles by incorporating elements such as problem solving, formulating and answering questions, discussing, debating, and brainstorming (Felder & Brent, 2003). Activities can include working in teams to solve problems and complete projects or working independently on developing materials such as learning portfolios or journals.

TEAMWORK IN THE CLASSROOM

4

Rubberball/Mike Kemp/
Getty Images.

Working in teams supports the exchange of diverse ideas and supports the development of interpersonal and cooperative skills needed in the workplace.

Depending on individual preference, the ability to work in teams may not be a comfortable skill but is one that must be developed for both academic and employment success. What is teamwork? *The American Heritage Dictionary* (2011) defines *teamwork* as "cooperative effort by the members of a group or team to achieve a common goal."* Learning how to work with others requires individuals to look beyond individual goals and work toward achieving the common goal in a way that benefits all team members. Successful completion of group projects requires the group to become a cohesive team. Successful formation of a cohesive team requires agreement on a common goal, effective use of individual skills within the group, and effective communication in order to include all team members and resolve conflict (NDT Resource Center, 2001–2012).

SELF-ASSESSMENT QUESTIONS

- How might an individual's self-image affect teamwork?
- How might an individual's self-esteem affect teamwork?
- How can different learning styles of team members be used to benefit teamwork?

CRITICAL THINKING QUESTION

▶ What steps might you take to become an effective team member in order to contribute to the success of group activities?

success steps for effective teamwork

- Decide on a group or team goal.
- Use individual talents and experiences in a collaborative effort to achieve a balanced blend of talent to meet the group goal.
- Balance individual and team needs and communicate clearly about both.
- Address and resolve conflict as soon as possible.
- Involve all participants in decisions.
- Emphasize commitment to the successful achievement of the team goal.

*Copyright © 2011 by Houghton Mifflin Harcourt Publishing Company. Reproduced by permission from *The American Heritage Dictionary of the English Language,* Fifth Edition.

It is the responsibility of each student to contribute to the success of group activities by learning how to be an effective team member. Understanding how you best relate to others and how you process information from your surroundings will contribute to understanding how you can best contribute to the group. For example, if you know that you tend to process information from the environment before speaking up or acting on it, you and group members can be aware of your participation style and use your style to process and synthesize various points of view for the group.

At times, students don't work together effectively to achieve success. Understanding the signs that may indicate a lack of team cooperation provides the opportunity to address issues and improve team function. David Pucel and Rosemary Fruehling, in their book *Working in Teams,* list the following characteristics that indicate an ineffective team (Pucel & Fruehling, 1997):

▶ Failure to understand the group goal

▶ Domination of more reserved group members by more aggressive members

▶ Fear of expressing thoughts openly and honestly

▶ Fear of disagreement or conflict

▶ Lack of respect for others' perspectives and opinions

▶ Lack of interest and attention

▶ Decisions reached by a few while other members disagree

▶ Discussions that are out of control or dominated by the leader

▶ Unwillingness to discuss team progress or consider group processes

▶ Unwillingness of members to share personal feelings about the working of the team

▶ Unwillingness of members to complete team tasks

If students do not form cohesive teams when working on group projects, grades can often be affected. The classroom offers an environment that allows students to develop their teamwork abilities.

4

SELF-ASSESSMENT QUESTIONS

• In what classroom activities are you most comfortable?
• If group activities are challenging for you, what can you do to improve your comfort level and group skills?

? CRITICAL THINKING QUESTION

▶ Why do you think it is more effective to take down notes in your own words, rather than what is stated verbatim from your instructor?

CASE IN POINT: COMPATIBILITY

4

Read the scenario below. Then, in groups or as a class, discuss the questions at the end.

Lynn, Dale, Drew, and Bryce have always been a cohesive and successful leadership team at the business of Schmidt and Schmidt. As team leaders of the various departments at Schmidt and Schmidt, these four individuals have accomplished a variety of team projects. In addition to successfully managing cohesive work groups, the managers work effectively as a team to complete project goals and fulfill responsibilities. Upper management at Schmidt and Schmidt has recognized this leadership team for its strong efforts and effective team management and asked Lynn, Dale, Drew, and Bryce to provide a presentation detailing their strategies for their success. The points they presented included the following:

- Understanding and respecting team members' individual learning styles
- Understanding and respecting team members' interpersonal styles and preferences
- Communicating consistently and accurately within and among work teams
- Recognizing and honoring both team and individual accomplishments as projects are completed

Eventually, the need for a fifth team leader became apparent, and the four members of the leadership team were asked to participate in the hiring process:

- How can understanding and respecting various learning preferences help the team select an effective new member?
- How can understanding interpersonal styles and preferences contribute to selection of a team member who interacts with the group in a positive manner?
- Why is recognition of both team and individual accomplishments important? How does recognition contribute to productivity and organizational goals?
- When considering a recent college graduate, how might the four team leaders be able to assess the candidate's abilities in the skills desired prior to hiring?
- As a college student, what can you do while you are in school to understand and develop the learning and interpersonal skills that will be important on work teams?

SUCCESSFUL SKILLS FOR LEARNING

Academic success is achieved through a variety of traditional learning activities, such as reading and note taking. Students who excel academically have developed efficient note-taking, reading, and test-taking skills in addition to participating effectively in classroom activities. The following suggestions for effective note taking, creating a positive study environment, and developing reading skills are based on recommendations from the Middlebury College, Office of Learning Resources (n.d.).

NOTE TAKING

The ability to take effective notes during lectures is essential to the success of college students. Thorough and accurate notes provide you with the information you need to study effectively. You can use your notes according to your learning style by translating notes into a diagram (visual learner), reciting them into a tape recorder and listening to the playback (auditory learner), or applying the notes to an activity (kinesthetic learner). Regardless of how you use the notes, note taking is the vehicle commonly used for obtaining information in class. Consequently, effective note taking is a skill that is important to learn and develop. Skills of listening and interpreting information accurately and quickly are important. A common misconception is that the instructor's word must be written down verbatim; however, it is acceptable and more efficient to write down main themes and ideas. The following are additional suggestions for making note taking more effective and easier:

▶ Position yourself for optimal hearing and seeing. If it is easier to hear and see by sitting near the front and center, then do so. Avoid areas such as doorways or windows, where distractions are more likely to occur. Avoid sitting next to friends who might also be a distraction. Taking meaningful notes that will be easily understood at a later study time requires full concentration.

▶ You may choose to use a word-processing program to record notes on a laptop computer or tablet. Use double or triple spacing and print your notes in black ink.

▶ If you use a notebook, make sure to purchase one that lies flat and is easily kept in order. Some students choose to have a separate notebook for each course; others choose to go with something like a three-ring binder with dividers. Choose a style that is convenient for you and that you will use. Organization of notes may be accomplished more easily with wide-lined paper and with an organization system such as a binder or notebook with pockets that allows you to add documents.

▶ When taking notes, write down main ideas with some details. Avoid writing down what the person is saying word for word.

▶ Leave blank spaces for later additions.

▶ Be an active listener. Write down your questions as they come up, and follow up to get the answers.

▶ Review your notes and reword as needed. If time permits, it may be helpful for some individuals (especially tactile learners) to rewrite notes as a learning tool.

▶ Add drawings and diagrams to illustrate concepts. This method is helpful for students who are visual learners.

There are numerous note-taking systems, such as the Cornell Method. Reading systems often have a note-taking component. One

success steps for taking effective notes

- Select a method of note taking (electronic or traditional) that is best suited to your needs and preferences. For example, use a laptop computer, a single notebook divided into sections, or a spiral-bound notebook for each subject.

- Record main ideas and enough details to allow you to fill in the remaining information later. Avoid trying to write down verbatim what the instructor says.

- Leave space to go back to and fill in additional details while you are studying.

- Write down questions as you think of them.

- Review and rewrite your notes.

- Add diagrams and drawings to illustrate concepts.

- Use recommended note-taking methods, such as the Cornell Method.

of these is SQR4, which stands for Survey, Question, Read, Record, Recite, Review. It is a systematic method that recommends overviewing the material, noting questions about it, reading it in thorough detail, recording notes, and reviewing the data. You are encouraged to explore various note-taking systems and select one that supports your learning. For some examples of note-taking strategies, visit www.cengagebrain.com.

THE STUDY ENVIRONMENT

Effective study habits will minimize distractions and maximize your benefit from studying. Study habits vary individually, and you will need to consider what is most effective for you based on your preferences and style. Consider the following suggestions:

- **Have a consistent study area.** Create a permanent place for your study area. Let other household members know that this is your area and ask that they respect the area by leaving it undisturbed. Your permanent study area should be one that promotes concentration and minimizes the likelihood of interruptions.

- **Apply organizational techniques.** Reflect on the organizational skills that were introduced in Chapter 1. In addition, organize your physical space by grouping supplies and materials. Doing so will not only make them easier to find, but you will know when you need to replenish supplies, and you will avoid last-minute panic. Keep necessary tools for studying in this area so that time is not wasted locating pens, paper, and other supplies. Avoid taking these study supplies for other tasks.

- **Make a healthy physical environment.** Minimize fatigue and eye strain by ensuring that you have adequate lighting and seating that promotes good posture and ergonomically sound positioning. Ensure that the study environment is quiet and at a comfortable temperature. Position your computer at a level that avoids neck strain.

- **Avoid distractions.** Commit to studying when you are in your area. Avoid the temptation to check social media or answer the telephone. Reserve special family time so that your children and spouse or partner don't feel neglected and are more apt to honor your study time.

- **Consider alternative locations.** In some situations, such as when numerous roommates are present in a household,

James Woodson/Digital Vision/
Getty Images.

Study in an environment that is organized and free of distractions so you can focus. Effective study habits contribute to academic success.

setting up a home study environment may not be possible. If this is the case, another location may be your best choice. The school and public libraries are examples of other options.

▶ **Know your personal cycles.** Determine your most productive study time. For example, some people are most alert and productive during the early morning, whereas others have more energy at night. Pay attention to your biological cycles and use your time management skills to develop a schedule appropriate for you. Consider when you think best and when you are the most alert. Determine the time of day when other activities are least likely to compete for your time.

▶ **Define clear goals.** Know what you want to accomplish in each study session. Use the time management skills you learned in Chapter 1 to prioritize each task.

▶ **Take breaks.** Minimize fatigue and maximize concentration by taking breaks. A good rule of thumb is to work for 1½ hours and then rest for 20 to 30 minutes. Achieve a balance between breaks and studying. Use study time wisely to achieve complete tasks and meet your goals for each study session.

success steps for developing an effective study environment

- Have a consistent study area.
- Apply organizational techniques to your study habits and space.
- Create a healthy physical environment that includes ample lighting, ergonomically sound furniture arrangements, and a comfortable room temperature.
- Avoid distractions by turning off the phone, avoiding social media, and asking family members and roommates to avoid interrupting you.
- Consider an alternative study location, such as the library, if home cannot be made distraction free.
- Have clearly defined goals for each study session.
- Take a 20- to 30-minute break for every hour and a half spent studying.

READING SKILLS

College courses typically require significant reading, and developing reading skills can significantly impact your academic success. Reading can be difficult for a number of reasons, including a lack of exposure to reading, poor eyesight, or reading techniques that are not as efficient as they could be. Reading skills can frequently be improved using various techniques. To improve reading skills, consider the following guidelines:

- **Read for concepts.** Avoid reading every word. Instead, learn to find the words that are meaningful and build ideas. It may be helpful to take short notes and record any question that you have on important concepts.

- **Get an overview.** Skim through the reading assignment to determine the main idea and locate significant parts that will require more careful reading. After skimming, go back and reread the areas that need more attention and that enhance your understanding of the content.

- **Quiz yourself.** Ask yourself questions on the material that you have read. Go back and review the material on which you had difficulty answering questions. If studying with others is effective for you, find a partner and quiz each other.

- **Mark important points.** Highlight important content that you will need to know. Use another color to highlight information that requires further attention and study.

- **Use a variety of activities.** In addition to reading, use the material and concepts that you are learning. Test yourself, review, organize related concepts and facts into categories, master the technical terms and formulas, and think of ways to apply the concepts to practical situations.

- **Direct your attention.** Some parts of the reading assignment may not require as much attention as others. Direct your focus and attention to areas that require greater concentration.

- **Use recommended reading systems.** Consider researching and utilizing a reading system, such as SQR4, which (as mentioned previously) includes a note-taking component.

- **Use campus resources.** Investigate and use campus resources that are available to you. Learning resource centers, learning

4

4

success steps for getting the most from your reading

- Read for concepts rather than reading every word.

- Skim the material first for an overview and to get the general idea.

- Quiz yourself over the material that you have read.

- Highlight information to help you learn. Use one color for important points and another color for information that you need to review.

- Use various activities to reinforce your learning. Summarize, make diagrams, and apply the information to practical situations.

- Direct your attention to areas in which you need the most study and review.

- Use effective reading methods, such as SQR4, to organize the material.

- Take advantage of campus resources, such as reading labs and resource centers.

- Vary your reading speed according to the information. Skim familiar information quickly and read more complex, unfamiliar material at a slower rate.

labs, and student advisors are examples of resources commonly available to students.

▶ **Use various reading speeds.** Use different reading speeds, depending on the goal of your reading. Getting the general idea of a piece may require rapid skimming, as might material with which you are familiar. Conversely, unfamiliar material or material that is more difficult typically requires more focused reading at a slower rate. Modify your reading pace according to your needs and the material.

STUDYING MATH

Mathematics often requires study skills that differ from those needed for more verbal subjects. Active learning and doing are especially important in mastering math concepts. The following suggestions for facilitating studying and test taking in math are summarized from tips provided by the Saint Louis University, Department of Mathematics and Computer Science (1993).

▶ **Actively participate.** Active learning is an important component of succeeding in math classes. Mathematical concepts are most effectively understood when they are used to solve problems. Assignments are intended to provide practice in using math concepts, so completion of homework is essential to your success. If you have questions about a step in a problem, write it down and follow up with the instructor. Try other problems using the same concepts to see whether doing a different problem increases your understanding, as sometimes a slightly different perspective will help. Take responsibility for your learning by asking questions in class to clarify confusing concepts and asking questions of the instructor during office hours.

▶ **Remember that math concepts are cumulative.** Math concepts build on one another. What you learn this week is the foundation for what will be taught next week. For this reason, attending class consistently, doing all assignments, and ensuring that you understand every concept are critical components of success. Making it a point to see the relationships among concepts can be helpful. Some concepts will connect with others. Give yourself time to understand the relationships among concepts. If you aren't quite sure you understand during class time, do the homework, reread the material, and see whether the next day's class makes it clearer.

▶ **Make use of all types of assignments.** You are likely to encounter various types of problems, which require diverse skills. For example, you may need to memorize formulas and complete repetitive exercises to reinforce your learning. Other problems may require you to apply what you have learned to practical situations. Understand the purpose of each type of assignment and consider how it fits into the "big picture."

▶ **Recognize differences between high school and college math.** College math courses tend to cover more material in less time and tests tend to cover more material. Homework may be assigned for your practice and benefit and may not be collected or graded by the instructor. This difference places

4

4

> ### success steps for solving math problems
>
> - Understand what the problem is asking you to solve. Read through and think about the entire problem.
> - Draw on what you know to select techniques to solve the problem.
> - Organize the techniques that you identify into a plan to solve the problem.
> - Execute your plan.
> - Review your answer and check your work. Consider how you might use the same techniques to solve other problems.

SELF-ASSESSMENT QUESTIONS

- Do you think you have ever had test anxiety? If so, when? Why do you think you were anxious? What did you do to try and relieve your anxiety?
- How good are you at taking exams? How might you be able to improve?

? CRITICAL THINKING QUESTION

▶ What test-taking strategies to do employ that have given you a measure of success? What additional strategies might you use in order to gain even greater success?

even greater emphasis on the importance of keeping up with the class, asking questions to clarify confusing information, and taking responsibility for your performance.

▶ **Seek additional help if needed.** If you need additional help, seek resources such as a tutor or the learning resource center on your campus. Seek help as soon as you see that you need it to avoid falling behind. Do not procrastinate or skip class to avoid stress related to class, as this will only compound the difficulty.

TEST TAKING

The ability to take tests successfully is a required skill for students in college as well as in many careers for professional licensure or certification. Understanding how to prepare effectively for tests and how to take tests effectively can increase your success and relieve any test anxieties.

Preparation for an exam should not begin the night before the exam but should be a process that has been incorporated into your study habits on a daily basis. Devote a part of your daily study schedule to reviewing material in preparation for upcoming exams. Repetition and building on information as you receive it over time are effective long-term study techniques. Completing assignments and reading the material daily also contribute to the ongoing preparation for an exam. Consider every assignment and project as preparation for exams. It is especially important to record any questions that arise during this process and follow through with the instructor to get your questions answered.

How you prepare for an exam is partly dependent on whether the exam will be an objective or essay-type exam. Determine the range of information that will be included on the test and types of questions that will be asked. Ask your instructor for this information if it has not been provided.

The two main types of questions asked on exams are objective questions (multiple choice, true/false, and matching) and essay questions, which require a written response of a specified length. Objective questions typically require a response that demonstrates knowledge and comprehension of facts. Essay questions usually require you to be more analytical and to synthesize an answer by relating several concepts.

Consider the following strategies for *preparing for an objective exam:*

▶ The technique of formulating questions and answers from course material is an effective method. If you benefit from studying with classmates, this is an effective technique for study groups.

▶ Focus on facts and objective information such as definitions, theorems, and formulas. Using flash cards with a term or question on one side and the definition or answer on the reverse side is an effective method for learning factual material. For example, if you are learning various theorems, you might write the theorem on one side of the flash card and its use on the other. This technique can be used individually or in a study group.

▶ Ensure that you have included all information from textbooks and class handouts. If your instructor has indicated that information from other media (such as videos, CDs, or web sites) will be covered, be sure to review these as well. Find out how to gain access to the media if access is not readily available.

▶ If your objective exam includes calculations such as those common in classes such as math, chemistry, or other applied courses, it is important to drill yourself on the types of problems on which you will be tested. Practice is the key to mastering applied subjects requiring problem solving.

Preparing for essay exams requires different approaches, as you will need to analyze concepts and synthesize them into a cogent response to the question. It is also important to recall the study strategies for objective tests in order to have accurate information from which to draw in answering the essay questions. You need correct information as the basis for the responses that you will develop in an essay test.

Consider the following strategies for *preparing for an essay-type exam:*

▶ As you read course material, pay attention to the relationships among concepts and ideas. Consider the conclusions you can draw from the relationships that you discover.

▶ Develop a system for showing the relationships among concepts. For example, a concept map (also called a "mind map") can effectively illustrate the relationships among ideas. Likewise, concepts written on index cards can be arranged in a variety of ways to illustrate relationships and to formulate a premise for supporting an idea or thesis.

▶ Practice expressing yourself by writing the relationships and conclusions that you find. Use concepts from your English classes to organize your response to include a major thesis and supporting themes. Include an effective introduction and conclusion. If your response is one that appropriately includes your opinion or assessment of a situation, support your opinion with accurate and logical facts and reasoning.

For any type of exam, certain strategies can help you make the most of the time you have to complete the questions. Much of successful test taking is budgeting your time, having a general idea of what is on the test, and reading thoroughly. Refer to the "Success Steps" for detailed tips on successful test taking.

success steps for successful test taking

• Know the amount of time you have to complete the test. Divide the total amount of time that you have by the number of questions on the test to get a general idea of approximately how much time you can spend on each question. Of course, some questions will take longer than others, but this method will help you gauge your time effectively.

• Read through the entire test. Reading through the test will provide you with an overview and general picture of what the test entails. This will also help you to effectively allocate your time to each of the questions.

- Read directions carefully. Misunderstanding test directions can cause you to lose points by using the wrong approach to the questions. Ensure that you understand the directions and request clarification as needed. Read and understand wording and what the question is asking for. For example, pay attention to whether the question is asking for a definition, an example, or an explanation.

- Answer the questions that you know first. Doing so gets them "out of the way" so that you can spend more time on items that require more concentration and time. Answering the questions you know may offer insight into more difficult questions.

- Pay attention to clues that will help you answer more difficult questions. Sometimes, answering one question will provide clues to the answers to other questions.

- Answer all questions. It is usually to your advantage to answer all questions in some way. Even if you are unsure of the entire answer, use the information you do know to provide an answer. Doing so will increase your chances for at least partial credit.

Individuals who experience test anxiety can use the following additional techniques for minimizing anxiety before an exam:

1. Follow the guidelines for preparing for and taking exams. Effective preparation and an organized approach to test taking can significantly reduce anxiety.

2. Take care of yourself. Get a full night's rest before the exam. Fatigue can increase anxiety and reduce effective thinking skills.

3. Review reasonably the night before the exam. Avoid cramming. If you have kept up with your assignments and ongoing review, you won't need to cram at the last minute. Review, quiz yourself, and get sufficient rest. Ensure that you get sufficient sleep and avoid using any type of sleeping aid that could leave you drowsy in the morning.

4. If you believe that you need additional review, allow time in your morning schedule to arrive at school early and review your material. Or, if you prefer, review at home.

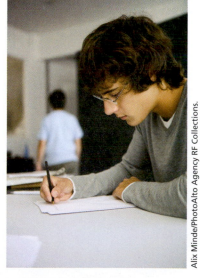

Alix Minde/PhotoAlto Agency RF Collections.

Preparing carefully, studying, and getting adequate sleep and nutrition will support improved test performance.

4

apply it

Study Techniques

Find printable activities on the companion web site for this book, accessed through www.cengagebrain.com.

GOAL: To apply study techniques to your learning experience

STEP 1: Make an honest assessment of your study and test-taking skills. Pinpoint specific areas in which you would like to develop your skills. For example, you may discover that you need to improve your note-taking skills in your literature class. Note area(s) for improvement as specifically as possible.

STEP 2: Research methods for making changes in the areas you identify. For example, if you need to improve your note-taking skills, conduct an Internet search using "note taking" as your search term. Consider the methods mentioned in this chapter (the Cornell Method for note taking and the SQR4 method for reading comprehension).

STEP 3: Set specific goals and create a plan for applying what you learn to your assignments and class work.

STEP 4: Assess your progress and adjust your goals as needed to continue your improvement.

Budget your time so that you are not rushed and can arrive at the test feeling composed and relaxed.

5. Eat a healthy meal before a test. Doing so will maximize your energy and concentration.

MEMORY TECHNIQUES

Knowledge for the exam is important, but remembering the material from classes in preparation for a career is even more critical. Future professional success requires you to recall information learned in the academic environment as well as to apply it to practical situations. Here are several methods that can be used in aiding your memory:

▶ **Imagery.** To use imagery to recall important information, associate an image with the information you are trying to memorize. For example, if you are learning a chemistry formula, you might visualize the corresponding steps in a lab experiment. If you are memorizing the steps in repairing an engine, visualize yourself actually working on the engine. This technique can be adapted to a wide variety of fields and activities.

▶ **Association.** Associating information with things that you already know puts information in a context and links it to something that is already familiar. For example, if you are learning a new computer program, associating its functionality with another similar program can jog your memory as well as allow you to highlight the differences between the two.

▶ **Mnemonics.** Mnemonics are verbal reminders that make use of rhymes, familiar tunes, and acronyms to help you remember information. A well-known mnemonic is "Roy G. Biv," which stands for the order of the colors of the rainbow: red, orange, yellow, green, blue, indigo, and violet. You may find mnemonics that are commonly used in your field, or you might find it effective to create your own mnemonics.

The tools and techniques proposed here are only a few suggestions for memory enhancement. Consider conducting further research to find the memory tool that works best for you. Memory techniques can be found in a variety of resources, including books, articles, journals, and on the Internet.

TECHNOLOGY IN THE CLASSROOM

The college classroom continues to evolve as technology advances. Technology has influenced not only the ways in which students conduct research, but in the ways courses are presented. Your classes may now be face to face (also known as "on-ground"), hybrid or blended (a combination of on-ground and online), or totally online. Internet research has become a standard practice for the completion of in-class and homework activities.

SELF-ASSESSMENT QUESTIONS

- How do you memorize information? Do you use different methods depending on what you are trying to memorize?
- Do you think the method(s) you use work best, or would trying some other methods be helpful?

CRITICAL THINKING QUESTION

▶ Do you find that if you memorize information specifically for an exam that you forget it almost immediately after the exam is over?

© iStockphoto.com/Photodjo.

Computers and technology are a major learning tool in the classroom and have made the hybrid class possible.

4

apply it

Memory Techniques

Find printable activities on the companion web site for this book, accessed through www.cengagebrain.com.

GOAL: To gain further understanding of and appreciation for memory techniques

STEP 1: Conduct a search on the Web to locate various memory techniques. Use "memorization techniques" or "improving memory" as the search terms.

STEP 2: Create a reference tool such as a paper, table, or other visual aid to summarize the memory techniques that you find. Record your ideas for using each and your thoughts regarding the effectiveness of each technique.

STEP 3: Consider placing this worksheet in your Learning Portfolio.

Technology options, known as *platforms,* are used to create and facilitate a course online. Here are some examples of online platforms that colleges use:

◗ Blackboard

◗ E-college

◗ WebCT

SELF-ASSESSMENT QUESTIONS

- How might you benefit from taking a hybrid course?
- What concerns might you have in taking a hybrid course?
- What skills do you have that would make you successful taking an online or hybrid course? What skills do you need to develop?

? CRITICAL THINKING QUESTION

◗ What do you consider to be advantages of taking an online course? Disadvantages?

Both students and faculty need to learn how to make this type of classroom effective. Students who are considering or are currently taking a course with an online component should be aware that the online component requires as much effort and time as on-ground learning. Online course components require participation in online discussion, responses to questions, submission of online assignments, and active learning projects. Successfully completing an online course or an online component of a hybrid course requires attention to course announcements and communications, timely submission of online assignments and contributions to online (threaded) discussions, and effective technical skills that include an understanding of the platform's features and operation. The ability to be self-disciplined, manage time, and organize both online and on-ground components is essential to your success in a hybrid or online course.

success steps for completing online course components

- Be aware of course announcements and communications— check the web site often!
- Submit assignments and complete activities in a timely manner.
- Contribute to online discussions in a timely manner.
- Become knowledgeable about the online platform's features and operation.
- Be self-disciplined.
- Use effective time management skills.

4

CHAPTER SUMMARY

This chapter provided information directed at supporting your learning and improving your study skills and habits. Understanding various learning models and the importance of understanding your preferred learning style were emphasized. You were also encouraged to develop learning styles that may be less comfortable to you but that can enhance your learning. Study skills, test-taking methods, and memorization techniques were also introduced. To gain optimally from this information, you are encouraged to understand and develop your learning styles and create study habits and routines that support them. Study techniques that match your learning style best support your learning.

POINTS TO KEEP IN MIND

In this chapter, the following main points were discussed in detail:

- The ability to manage stress and develop good nutritional, exercise, and relaxation habits is essential for optimal learning.
- Information is learned more effectively when it is well organized.
- Learning occurs when the environment is stable, familiar, and emotionally supportive, as well as challenging.

4

▶ Learning styles include auditory, visual, tactile, and kinesthetic.

▶ Learning models include Kolb's Learning Style Model, Herrmann Brain Dominance Instrument, and the Felder-Silverman model. The Myers-Briggs Type Indicator, although not a learning model per se, can provide information on how you interact with your environment to facilitate learning.

▶ Active learning requires student involvement in activities such as solving problems, answering questions, formulating questions, discussing, debating, and brainstorming.

▶ Teamwork is a requirement of both academic and professional environments.

▶ Students who excel academically have typically developed skills in efficiently taking notes, completing reading assignments, studying, and taking exams.

▶ How one prepares for an exam is partly dependent upon if the exam is to be the objective or essay type.

▶ Hybrid courses combine both online and classroom learning.

CHECK YOUR UNDERSTANDING

Visit www.cengagebrain.com to see how well you have mastered the material in Chapter 4.

SUGGESTED ITEMS FOR LEARNING PORTFOLIO

▶ Learning Models
▶ Memory Techniques

REFERENCES

American Heritage Dictionary of the English Language (5th ed.). (2011). Available at http://ahdictionary.com

Caine, R. N., & Caine, G. (n.d.). *Overview of the systems principles of natural learning.* Retrieved January 25, 2013, from http://www.cainelearning.com/files/Summary.pdf

Felder, R. M., & Brent, R. (2003). Learning by doing [Electronic version]. *Chemical Engineering Education, 37*(4), 282–283. Retrieved January 25, 2013, from http://www4.ncsu.edu/unity/lockers/users/f/felder/public/Columns/Active.pdf

Middlebury College, Office of Learning Resources. (n.d.) *Reading, note taking, and study skills.* Retrieved January 25 2013, from http://www.middlebury.edu/academics/resources/ctlr/olr/study

NDT Resource Center, Iowa State University. (2001–2012). Teamwork in the classroom [Electronic version]. Retrieved January 25, 2013, from http://www.ndt-ed.org/TeachingResources/ClassroomTips/Teamwork.htm

Pucel, D. J., & Fruehling, R. T. (1997). *Working in Teams: Interaction and Communication.* St. Paul, MN: Paradigm Publishing Inc.

Saint Louis University, Department of Mathematics and Computer Science. (1993). Success in mathematics [Electronic version]. Retrieved January 25, 2013, from http://mathcs.slu.edu/undergrad-math/success-in-mathematics

4

CHAPTER OUTLINE

Communication Skills for Student Success

LEARNING OBJECTIVES

By the end of this chapter, you will achieve the following objectives:

▶ Explain the importance of good listening skills.

▶ List reasons why listening can be difficult.

▶ Explain the benefits and characteristics of assertive communication.

▶ Discuss considerations that should be made when sending an e-mail.

▶ Describe how professionalism is demonstrated in written communication.

▶ Explain the purpose of using open-ended questions versus closed questions.

▶ Recognize the importance of body language.

▶ Explain the importance of effective communication.

▶ Demonstrate the ability to create a visual presentation.

▶ Demonstrate the ability to conduct professional correspondence.

▶ Distinguish between social networking and social media.

5

BE IN THE KNOW

Think Twice, Post Once (Maybe)

In the world of woodworking there is a phrase: "Measure twice, cut once." In other words, measure the length of wood you need to cut two times before you cut it, because you cannot lengthen a piece of wood that was cut too short.

This type of advice, probably given by a woodworker with personal experience of a cutting mishap, should also be taken when it comes to social networking. Think about it. How many YouTube videos have you viewed where people are seen participating in out-of-control (legal or not) activities? Or you've gone onto your Facebook page only to find that one of your "friends" posted a picture or two hundred of you at that campus party, drink in hand . . .?

Social networking, and its vehicle, social media, is a phenomenon that is here to stay. And it's not just for entertainment any more. Increasingly, mainstream businesses are adapting social networking as a way to recruit, hire, and retain employees. This is because it is cost-effective and timely, and recruiters can find out much more about a candidate's character through an Internet search than they ever can reading a two-page resume.

Hopefully, your personal social networking experiences to date have not caused you any harm—real or perceived. As you work to get your degree and move into the world of business, bear in mind the woodworker's advice—calculate the risk before you take it.

SELF-ASSESSMENT QUESTIONS

- How effective are your communication skills?
- How could you improve your communication?

? CRITICAL THINKING QUESTION

▶ Do you think communication skills are the same in both the classroom and workplace, or different? Why or why not?

IMPORTANCE OF COMMUNICATION: AN OVERVIEW

Whether at school or in the workplace, it is important to develop excellent communication skills. The significance of effective written and spoken communication skills cannot be understated. In any profession, individuals are valued for their ability to communicate effectively. The focus of this chapter is to review the skills needed for effective communication in both academic and professional settings.

Developing these skills while in school will make a difference to your success as a professional.

EFFECTIVE VERBAL COMMUNICATION

Effective verbal communication is a fundamental skill. Technical aptitude is more useful when it can be expressed clearly. Your success can depend on your ability to apply and communicate your knowledge. Learning how to speak effectively in the classroom and as a professional begins with understanding the basics of effective communication. Communication can be divided into two parts:

Effective communication requires careful and focused attention, clear expression of thoughts and feelings, and mutual respect.

- The Sender: the individual expressing his or her needs, feelings, thoughts, and opinions
- The Receiver: the individual listening and understanding what is being communicated

Effective communication occurs when the receiver of the information interprets and understands the sender's message in the same way the sender intends it.

LISTENING

Listening is one of the most challenging aspects of communication. Ineffective listening can be caused by

- preoccupation and lack of attention
- thinking rather than listening
- closed-minded thinking
- prejudging the speaker or judging what is being said

It is important to make the distinction between hearing and listening. Effective listening begins with taking time to understand what the speaker is thinking and feeling from his or her perspective. To listen adequately involves actively participating in the communication process by focusing on what the speaker is saying; attending to spoken elements as well as unspoken elements, such as emotion and body language; and concentrating on the present moment. Active participation cannot be accomplished if you are preoccupied, thinking about other topics, or anticipating what the "right" response will be to what the speaker is saying.

SELF-ASSESSMENT QUESTIONS

- Are you a good listener?
- How might you be able to improve your listening skills?
- What makes listening difficult for you?

? CRITICAL THINKING QUESTION

- What are some ways that you can take the speaker's perspective when listening to what he has to say?

5

> ## success steps for effective listening
>
> - Take the time to understand what the speaker is saying.
> - Take the speaker's perspective.
> - Attend to spoken as well as unspoken elements.

BODY LANGUAGE

Individuals often communicate feelings or thoughts with their body language.

Arms folded across the chest, lack of eye contact, and fidgeting are revealing elements of body language. Arms folded may signal that the listener is defensive or resistive to hearing what is being communicated. Lack of eye contact can indicate that the individual feels uncomfortable. Evaluating how others perceive your body language is important. Understanding how others may be interpreting your gestures and movements may help you gain insight into the effectiveness of your communication. It is also important to remember that Western interpretations of body language may differ from interpretations in other cultures. For example, in many Asian cultures, making eye contact is interpreted as a lack of respect for authority. Avoid jumping to conclusions and consider that if an individual has been raised with certain cultural expectations, these characteristics are deeply ingrained and are to be respected. If certain behavioral nuances interfere with communication, consider cultural diversity. Work collaboratively to achieve an understanding.

Although body language is important to consider during communication, caution should be taken to avoid overinterpretation or misinterpretation. For example, crossed arms is frequently interpreted as the listener being "closed" to what is being communicated. It may also simply be that crossing the arms is a comfortable position for the listener. Taking all aspects of communication into consideration is important, so be aware of the other components of communication as well. Use a combination of cues from listening, hearing, and interpreting body language to accurately understand what the receiver is communicating verbally and nonverbally. Consider the context of the communication and the situation in which it is occurring.

SELF-ASSESSMENT QUESTION

- Think of a conversation you recently had. Did the individual you were speaking with exhibit any body language? If so, what do you think the body language was telling you?

? CRITICAL THINKING QUESTION

- How conscious are you of the body language you exhibit when speaking with various audiences?

> **success steps for interpreting body language**
>
> - Be aware of how your body language is being interpreted. You may be conveying an unintended message.
> - Consider that certain gestures and other body language can be interpreted differently by individuals from diverse cultures.
> - Be careful not to overinterpret the meaning of body language.

QUESTIONING TECHNIQUES

Asking appropriate questions is another important element of effective communication. Learning how to use questions effectively to discover information is a helpful tool in improving communication. There are two general types of questions: open-ended questions and closed-ended questions.

Open-ended questions require more than a yes or no answer from the receiver. The purpose of asking open-ended questions is to gain more detailed information. An example of an open-ended question would be, "When should open-ended questions be used instead of closed-ended questions?"

Closed-ended questions are typically used to confirm information and often require one or two words to answer. For instance, "Did you go to the office on Monday or Tuesday?" or "Did you say that the test is on Wednesday?"

> **success steps for using effective questioning techniques**
>
> - Use open-ended questions to gain detailed information.
> - Use closed-ended questions to confirm information.
> - Use the appropriate type of question to facilitate communication.

ASSERTIVENESS

Assertiveness is the ability to express your beliefs, needs, feelings, and opinions in a manner that clearly makes your point but that is not intimidating and that demonstrates respect for the feelings and opinions of the receiver of your message.

To better understand assertive communication, it is helpful to compare it with other styles that are usually less effective. Consider the following communication styles:

▶ **Aggressive.** Aggressive communication typically conveys anger and impatience and is generally abrasive. Aggressive communication is typically characterized by a raised voice, strong gesturing, glaring eyes, and harsh words. Aggressive communication tends to alienate the receiver of the message and hinders communication.

▶ **Passive.** A passive communication style is characterized by a soft voice, lack of eye contact, and a tendency to avoid stating needs, feelings, and opinions. Passive communication can avoid immediate conflict but can leave the passive sender feeling "walked on" and as if his or her feelings and wishes are not honored.

▶ **Passive-aggressive.** Passive-aggressive communication occurs when feelings of anger or discontent are expressed passively. An example is the individual who, following a meeting with a coworker, smiles and acts as though nothing is wrong. However, he is actually angry and walks out of the office, slamming the door to express his feelings.

▶ **Assertive.** The individual using an assertive communication style expresses his or her opinions and feelings directly using carefully chosen words. Tone of voice is firm, yet calm and nonabrasive, and is modulated at a conversational level. The sender of the assertive message actively listens to the response of the receiver and respectfully acknowledges the sender's position. Eye contact is direct, but not glaring or threatening.

Developing Assertive Communication Skills

There may be situations in which an aggressive or passive communication style is appropriate and effective. However, generally, and especially in the workplace, an assertive communication style is preferred and usually most effective. It is important to remember that using an assertive style does not necessarily get you what you want, but it may maximize your chances or promote a favorable compromise. Consider the following suggestions for communicating assertively:

▶ **Know what you want.** Clearly identify what you want from a specific communication. Doing so will help you express your-self more clearly and support you in knowing where you can compromise.

▶ **Understand your feelings.** Knowing your feelings will help you to express them clearly, which can serve to clarify a situation. For example, saying, "I am confused about the messages I am receiving" conveys that you are open to hearing clarification and correcting any misunderstandings. Expressing feelings has the added benefit of humanizing the communication.

▶ **Use "I" statements.** The statement "I am confused about the messages I am receiving" puts the responsibility on the sender of the "I" message. An "I" message avoids blame, which can be implied in messages that begin with "you." Consider the difference between "I am confused about the messages I am receiving" and "You are sending confusing messages." An "I" message indicates that the sender is taking responsibility, whereas a "you" message tends to sound accusatory and may put the receiver on the defensive, hindering the communi-cation process. Use "I" statements to express your feelings, needs, opinions, and wishes.

▶ **Communicate from a "win–win" position.** Be prepared by knowing the points on which you are willing to compromise and be willing to negotiate when appropriate. Use "I" state-ments to express points on which you are unable or unwilling to compromise.

APPRECIATING DIVERSITY

Interacting effectively with others requires an appreciation of each person as an individual. Culture and environment can have a sig-nificant impact on communication patterns. Words can have differ-ent meanings depending on an individual's culture. Identifying the

SELF-ASSESSMENT QUESTIONS

- Is your communication style usually passive, passive-aggressive, aggressive, or assertive? What examples can you give to support your observation?
- What changes might you make to improve your communication style? How would making a change enhance your communications?

? CRITICAL THINKING QUESTION

▶ Do you consciously go into conversations knowing the points on which you are willing to compromise?

© Digital Vision/Thinkstock.

Learning to communicate effectively in the classroom provides good practice opportunities for developing the professional interpersonal skills required for employment.

SELF-ASSESSMENT QUESTIONS

- In your communication with others, how do you demonstrate appreciation for diversity in your audience?
- How can you increase your sensitivity to diverse communication practices?

? CRITICAL THINKING QUESTION

- Do you take your own personal cultural background and diversity into consideration when speaking with others?

cultural background of individuals can minimize or avoid confusion or misunderstandings during communication. Home environment can also influence an individual's use of words. Grammar and concepts such as assertiveness can also vary depending on an individual's upbringing. When communicating with others, it is helpful to be considerate and not be too quick to judge an individual's word choice or communication abilities.

VERBAL COMMUNICATION IN THE CLASSROOM

Sending and receiving messages through listening, evaluating body language, and questioning are all parts of the communication process and are critical for successful interaction in the classroom. Learning to communicate effectively in the classroom provides good practice opportunities for developing professional interpersonal skills required for employment. Classroom communication involves both the written and spoken word. It is important to develop your skills in both areas.

There are many opportunities for verbal communication in the classroom, including group activities, discussions, questions, and presentations. To optimize the use of these forums, it is important to follow some simple rules.

▶ **Participate in group activities.** Group activities are successful for individual members and the group only if all members participate. Participation includes not only completing activities but communicating clearly with team members as well. To facilitate group communication, it is helpful for group members to establish guidelines and standards for effective communication. Guidelines should also define group etiquette and expectations for respectful and professional communication between group members. Establishing acceptable methods for communication also supports effective communication. For example, the group may choose electronic forums such as e-mail and threaded discussions for communicating with group members and may limit telephone calls to certain hours.

▌ **Ask questions.** Opportunities to ask questions in class offer an excellent chance to confirm your understanding of material and clarify information. Different types of questions can be utilized in the classroom, but always understand your purpose prior to asking. For example, clarifying information may require a closed-ended question, whereas a more detailed explanation of information may be achieved by asking an open-ended question. Although it is said, "No question is stupid," do try to utilize class time appropriately. Some questions are best answered in a one-on-one meeting with the instructor rather than during class. Use your judgment regarding which format is most appropriate for your situation. Speaking up in class also provides an opportunity to practice making inquiries and speaking up in a group of colleagues, which will be expected in the workplace.

▌ **Develop listening skills.** Listening is an important element of asking and receiving information in class. Listening in class may involve skills other than those used in conversation. For example, in class you may listen for specific information. During the listening process, you may also be actively thinking about how information relates to your existing knowledge and writing notes accordingly. You should balance actively listening to the instructor with recording significant notes for meaningful study at a later time.

▌ **Participate in class discussion.** Instructors sometimes ask reflection questions and critical thinking questions to encourage students to share their opinions and ideas. In-class discussions work best if all students actively participate. Discussion is an excellent way to expand your thinking and understanding of the material and develop critical analysis and thinking skills. Students who develop critical thinking abilities gain

5

5

a valuable tool that will be appreciated later in their careers. Developing respect for diverse opinions and viewpoints during discussions is also important for successful classroom interaction and is critical to success in the workplace. Demonstrating an appreciation for all opinions, regardless of whether you agree and learning to disagree respectfully are basic professional communication skills.

▶ **Give presentations.** In-class presentations require written and verbal communication skills, both of which improve and become easier with practice. Embrace the opportunities to hone these skills in the classroom. You may find it helpful to practice your presentation in front of the instructor or a small group of peers to gain confidence prior to presenting to the entire class. Other factors in developing presentation skills include allowing enough time to become familiar with the material and to revise it as needed, maintaining the organization of material during preparation and presentation, and practicing speaking during class discussions. Pay attention to how classmates interact and speak, and learn from observing others. Use opportunities to speak outside of class as practice. When you speak, practice supporting your statements with verifiable facts. If possible, interact with the professional world by working or participating in internship opportunities. Developing confidence and skill at giving presentations will be a valued skill during your career (Gordon, n.d.).

success steps for communicating effectively in the classroom

- Actively participate in and contribute to group activities.
- Ask questions in class.
- Develop your listening skills.
- Actively participate in class discussion.
- Give presentations to develop both oral and written communication skills.

CASE IN POINT: YOU DIDN'T REALLY WANT A JOB, DID YOU?

Read the scenario below. Then, in groups or as a class, discuss the questions at the end.

After graduation Elizabeth Lanham began searching for a job. In the first two weeks she sent out 25 resumes. She followed up appropriately, checking to find out when interviews might be taking place and whether she was a candidate for consideration. Weeks went by, and she continued to send resumes, but Elizabeth still did not get any interviews. Over time Elizabeth began to wonder why she had not gotten even one call from all the resumes she had sent. She knew she was well qualified for the entry-level jobs for which she was applying. After six months Elizabeth finally got her first interview. It wasn't until this first interview that Elizabeth finally found out why she had not been receiving any earlier calls for potential jobs. During the interview Elizabeth was informed that her resume and cover letter had spelling and grammatical errors. The interviewer said that Elizabeth was very qualified for the job but that the lack of attention given to her resume and cover letter had indicated a lack of attention to detail that could affect her ability to perform the required job duties. Elizabeth did eventually get a job. By using the interviewer's feedback, Elizabeth made the necessary changes and corrections to her documents so they exhibited the professionalism required for employment.

▶ Is it right for employers to rule out applicants due to errors on the resume and/or cover letter? If so, why? If not, why not?

▶ How important do you think written and spoken communication will be in the job that you will be seeking after graduation?

▶ What can Elizabeth do in future written communication to make sure she shows professionalism?

▶ If you lack skills in either written or spoken communications, how do you plan on improving them?

▶ What sources might be available to you for improving these skills?

5

To summarize, effective verbal communication skills are learned. As a student, take advantage of every opportunity to learn and grow in this area. Employers will expect excellent verbal communication skills, and your overall success depends on these skills.

EFFECTIVE WRITTEN COMMUNICATION

Much like oral communication, communicating effectively in writing requires developing skills and taking the time to write correctly. Well-written communication delivers your message with clarity and effectiveness. Poorly written communication can cause confusion and misunderstandings. As with spoken communication, effective written communication is critical to success not only in school but also in the business environment.

WRITTEN COMMUNICATION IN THE WORKPLACE

Examples of written communication in the workplace include completing inventory forms, writing financial statements, completing work orders, filling out patient charts, sending electronic messages, and making sales or other types of presentations. Most importantly, daily interactions with colleagues and customers often require clear and effective written communication.

As a student, it is important to clearly understand the requirements that future employers will expect from you as a professional and to practice and apply these skills in the classroom. Written communication is effective when attention is given to the following elements:

▶ **Professionalism.** Professionalism is indicated by the appearance of the communication. For example, the appearance of a letter can indicate professionalism or a lack of care. Written communication that has grammatical errors or misspellings presents an unprofessional image. In correspondence, elements such as font selection, paper quality, organization, and neatness convey professionalism. Likewise, the manner in which an e-mail is written can either increase your professional credibility or diminish it.

▶ **Organization.** Organization is critical to professional image. If a term paper is disorganized, the information in the paper may be misunderstood, resulting in a poor grade. A business proposal that is well organized is more likely to achieve a business goal. Effective organization of written communication allows the information to flow, giving the reader a better opportunity to easily comprehend the ideas that are presented.

▶ **Quality.** Grammatical and punctuation errors, misspellings, and disorganization of information are examples of a lack of quality in written work. Errors that reflect a lack of quality reflect poorly on your ability to perform other tasks well. Although this may seem presumptuous, impressions conveyed by written communication (particularly when your communication is your only introduction to another person) make a strong impact. Developing high standards of quality for written communication while you are in school will lay the foundation for continuing to apply care and attention to details in your future professional communications.

WRITTEN COMMUNICATION IN THE CLASSROOM

The classroom provides an excellent environment for developing your writing skills. Opportunities for developing writing skills in the classroom include note taking, tests, term papers, projects, and presentations. Although some of these tasks seem a bit mundane, practicing clarity of written expression in each will contribute to your overall skill development, as well as enhance your learning.

It is important to be clear regarding what the instructor requires. Meet the requirements and go beyond them to cover your topic in a thorough manner that reflects high standards. Keep in mind that the quality of work done for classroom assignments should represent not only what is required in the classroom, but should reflect the type of work you would do on the job. Also, demonstrating writing capabilities in the classroom can be to your benefit if you use the instructor as an employment reference.

Presentations

Various software programs have significantly changed how the written component of classroom presentations is created. Software programs such as Adobe Persuasion, Microsoft PowerPoint, Corel Presentations, Keynote, MediaShout, and Harvard Graphics give individuals the opportunity to produce highly visual presentations. The written component is displayed visually in this type of presentation, making clearly written and precise communication all the more critical. The purpose of using a presentation tool is to enhance the material and visually convey the message. Presentations that have a clear message, are well organized, and are visually appealing will be received more positively.

The following recommendations for creating electronic presentations are based on Hakim (2005):

▶ Know the purpose of the presentation and who your audience will be.

▶ Make sure the colors and font styles chosen for your presentation don't cause the audience to focus on the colors and styles versus the content. Colors and styles should be appealing and easy to read, but not the center of attention.

▶ Have a headline for each slide to focus your audience on each topic presented.

▶ Use background colors that affect your audience positively. Different colors can create different feelings.

▶ Make sure your lettering can be clearly seen. For instance, depending upon the background color, your ink may be more visible if it is white instead of black.

▶ Have your colors complement each other. Colors that do not go well together will be distracting to your audience.

▶ Use a font that is not too busy. Typically, Arial, Verdana, and Times fonts are chosen for their simple and plain appearance.

▶ Pay attention to font size. A general rule of thumb is to make sure your audience in the back of the room can read each line clearly. A font size that is less than 22 points will be very difficult to read. One that is larger than 36 points may be overwhelming.

▶ As much as possible, limit bulleted items to one or two lines. Bulleted items should be written in phrases rather than full sentences.

▶ Make sure slides are not overwhelming with either images or text.

▶ Only use clip art, animations, and other visual aids if they strengthen your message. Remember that sometimes "less is more," so aim for simplicity while effectively conveying your message.

▶ Review each slide for accuracy prior to presenting.

▶ Before the presentation, be familiar with the equipment you will use and have a backup plan, such as handouts, in the event the equipment malfunctions.

▶ When showing the slide presentation, be sure you are facing the audience.

SELF-ASSESSMENT QUESTIONS

- How much experience have you had in giving presentations?
- What strengths and weaknesses do you think your presentation skills have?
- How do you plan on improving your presentation skills?

? CRITICAL THINKING QUESTION

▶ How important do you think it is to understand your target audience when preparing a presentation? How will that knowledge affect your delivery of information?

5

success steps for giving effective electronic presentations

- Have a purpose that applies to your audience.
- Use colors, design, and font styles that are appealing, but not the focus of attention.
- Select a plain font (such as Arial, Times, or Verdana) that is of an appropriate size (22–36 points).
- Limit bullet points to one or two lines.
- Write bullet points in phrases rather than sentences.
- Use clip art and images only to illustrate your point. Too much embellishment detracts from the presentation.
- Review carefully for accuracy before presenting.
- Face the audience, not the slides.

apply it

Find printable activities on the companion web site for this book, accessed through www.cengagebrain.com.

Presentation Tool Analysis

GOAL: To demonstrate the ability to effectively communicate within a team environment, to analyze a presentation tool, and to produce a good presentation

STEP 1: Form a group of no more than four students.

STEP 2: Each group should research one presentation tool. For instance, Group 1 may research everything about Power-Point. Group 2 could research what the presentation tool Adobe Persuasion offers. Group 3 could research Keystone.

STEP 3: After each group has conducted its research, students should write a brief analysis of their findings.

STEP 4: Each group should prepare a presentation of its brief analysis. If possible, have each group use the tool it researched as its presentation tool. If only one tool is available in the classroom, all students should use that tool for their presentations.

STEP 5: Consider putting this Presentation Tool Analysis project in your Learning Portfolio.

TOOLS TO ASSIST WITH WRITING

In addition to the numerous articles on effective writing that can be found on the Internet, there are a variety of available tools that are worthwhile for use in the classroom and later in business. A few tools include these:

- A dictionary
- A thesaurus
- *The Elements of Style* by Strunk and White

▶ *Modern Language Association Handbook* (MLA style)

▶ *Publication Manual of the American Psychological Association* (APA style)

▶ *Turabian's A Manual for Writers of Research Papers, Theses, and Dissertations* (simplified Chicago style)

▶ Software programs such as ScholarWord

▶ Web search engines such as Google Scholar

▶ Campus resources, such as writing labs, tutors, and your instructor

IMPROVING YOUR WRITING SKILLS

Employers often indicate that writing is one of the most desirable skills a job applicant can possess. Kaplan (2004) offers the following suggestions for improving writing skills:

▶ Prepare an outline. Use the outline to indicate what should be included in the finished piece of writing and to organize its content.

▶ Write a draft. A draft is just that. At the draft stage, don't worry about spelling, word choice, or grammar. Simply express your thoughts and ideas.

▶ Correct spelling and review the document for improvement on wording. Planning ahead and managing your time will leave you ample time to review and revise.

▶ Use the tools mentioned previously to assist in improving wording, grammar, and style.

▶ Write the final draft, paying attention to choice of words and important details such as spelling and grammar. Allow ample time to set the final draft aside for a day or so and then review it with a fresh perspective. Make revisions as needed based on your final review. If the content is not of a confidential nature, you might ask a trusted colleague to proofread the document.

▶ Write as often as possible and consider writing to be a skill that can be worked on and developed. Competence and confidence develop with practice.

5

5

TECHNOLOGY AND WRITTEN COMMUNICATION

Advancements in technology have made effective written communication an even greater requirement. The speed at which electronic communication takes place requires thoughtfulness and attention to tone, choice of words, and accuracy.

E-MAIL

With the increased use of e-mail as a communication tool, knowing how to use e-mail effectively is important. As with any type of written communication, attention should be paid to who the audience is and the purpose of the e-mail. A social e-mail will be different from an e-mail sent for business. Dowling (2008) suggests the following tips for writing e-mails:

▶ Prior to sending an e-mail, review it to determine whether it is clear, concise, useful, and necessary.

▶ Remember that you can be held accountable for whatever you write.

▶ Be aware of the length of the e-mail. At times, it might be more effective to write a short note with more detailed information included as an attachment.

▶ E-mail is not always confidential. Send only that which you don't mind having shared. Select other forms of communication, such as a face-to-face meeting, a telephone conversation, or regular mail, for certain types of communication.

▶ As with any correspondence, be professional. E-mail is not to be used for disciplining the reader.

▶ Make sure your e-mail is necessary. If you send too many unnecessary e-mails containing jokes and other trivial communications, receivers of your e-mail may choose to ignore messages from you that may be important. Be aware that in the workplace, sending e-mails of a nonprofessional nature may violate company technology use policy.

▶ Use grammar and punctuation that reflects traditional written communication. Appropriate punctuation makes the message easier to read and reflects on your professionalism.

▶ Observe e-mail etiquette (also called *netiquette*). There are expectations that apply uniquely to e-mail. For example, using all capital letters is considered to be "yelling at" or responding aggressively to your reader. When appropriate, carefully placed capitals can provide emphasis. Using all lowercase does not follow the rules of English grammar and usage.

▶ Use the subject line appropriately to catch the attention of the receiver. The subject line should accurately (but briefly) describe the content of the e-mail.

▶ Always proofread your e-mail before sending it. Make sure it represents you professionally.

Ariel Skelley/Getty Images.

Using electronic communication, such as e-mail, requires attention to accuracy, detail, and rules of etiquette.

5

SELF-ASSESSMENT QUESTION

- When writing professional e-mail, how might you change your writing style from that used for social e-mails?

? CRITICAL THINKING QUESTION

- What is your reaction to the person who sends e-mails that you consider frivolous, distasteful, or annoying?

success steps for sending a professional e-mail

- Remember that you are accountable for what you write in e-mail.
- Keep the e-mail brief, with concise information. If a more detailed explanation is needed, consider sending it as an attachment.
- Send only necessary e-mail. Sending jokes and trivial communications may cause recipients to ignore your e-mail.
- Know your organization's e-mail policy. There may be consequences for sending e-mail that is not job related.
- Remember that e-mail is not confidential and that records are available.
- Use traditional grammar and spelling rules.
- Observe netiquette.
- Use the subject line to communicate what the e-mail is about.
- Maintain professionalism. Do not write an e-mail when you are angry or to discipline someone.
- Proofread your e-mail before sending.

apply it

Find printable activities on the companion web site for this book, accessed through www.cengagebrain.com.

Style Research

Goal: To develop a clearer understanding regarding requirements stated in the MLA and APA handbooks

STEP 1: Research the requirements set forth by the MLA and APA style books (the *Modern Language Association Handbook* and the *Publication Manual of the American Psychological Association*).

STEP 2: Compare and contrast the style suggestions and write a brief explanation of both styles.

STEP 3: Prepare to share your thoughts with the class.

STEP 4: Consider placing this worksheet in your Learning Portfolio.

SOCIAL NETWORKING AND SOCIAL MEDIA

Social networking and social media have revolutionized how we communicate. It is not just a "social" event anymore to use the likes of Facebook and Twitter to convey information. Businesses, law enforcement, sports teams, airlines, and governments, for example, all use social networking and social media to disseminate information in a professional setting.

As a student, it is wise to embrace the use of these communication tools in the classroom. The chances are probably very good that your school is using Facebook, Twitter, blogs, message boards, and other media to provide information, conduct aspects of classroom activities, and to otherwise interact with the student body under the auspices of education, and not just socialization.

How you translate the use of online communities and the information they provide from your social world to your academic world becomes even more meaningful as your enter the workforce. The aptitude that you acquire using social networking and social media in a professional sense while you are in school will help make you more marketable, as employers place high regard on employees who possess these skills (Baker, J. 2013).

CHAPTER SUMMARY

This chapter introduced elements of communication that are important to success in school and in the workplace. Listening, nonverbal gestures, questioning, and assertive communication were emphasized as significant elements of oral communication. Professional presentation, quality, and clarity were emphasized as aspects of effective written communication. Considerations specific to electronic communications and presentations were also reviewed.

Effective communication is a skill that is foundational to many other skills and to success in school and the workplace. Your development of all of the skills addressed in *100% Student Success* can be enhanced by effective communication abilities. You are encouraged to consider how developing your communication skills can support all of your academic and professional endeavors.

POINTS TO KEEP IN MIND

In this chapter, the following main points were discussed in detail:

- ▶ Communication has two participating parties: the sender and the receiver.

- ▶ Lack of attention and closed-minded thinking can reduce the effectiveness of listening.

- ▶ By listening, hearing, and interpreting body language, the receiver may more accurately understand what the sender is communicating verbally and nonverbally.

- ▶ Two general types of questions are open-ended and closed-ended.

- ▶ Respect for individual diversity is essential for effective communication.

- ▶ Learning how to communicate effectively in the classroom offers good practice for the professional communication skills required for employment.

- ▶ In-class group activities are successful only if all team members participate.

- ▶ Listening well facilitates learning from in-class questions.

- ▶ Giving attention to professionalism, organization, and quality of the material makes written communication more effective.

- ▶ The purpose of using presentation tools is to enhance the material and visually convey the message.

- ▶ The use of social and networking and social media in academic life can translate well into the workplace.

CHECK YOUR UNDERSTANDING

 Visit www.cengagebrain.com to see how well you have mastered the material in Chapter 5.

SUGGESTED ITEMS FOR LEARNING PORTFOLIO

▶ Presentation Tool Analysis
▶ Style Research

REFERENCES

Baker, J. (2013). *How students benefit from using social media*. Retrieved April 16, 2013, from http://edudemic.com/2013/02/how-students -benefit-from-using-social-media

Dowling, E. (2008). *10 tips for effective e-mail.* Professional Training Company. Retrieved January 29, 2013, from http://www.protrainco .com/essays/emltip.htm

Gordon, D. E. (n.d.). *Five keys to acquiring better verbal communication skills.* CollegeRecruiter.com. Retrieved January 29, 2013, from http:// www.beyond.com/articles/details-101-article.html

Hakim, C. (2005). *Essentials of effective PowerPoint presentations—PowerPoint presentations that work.* Retrieved January 28, 2013, from http://www .unleash.com/chakim/essentials/index.asp

Kaplan, R. M. (2004). You can improve your written communication skills. Retrieved February 20, 2005, from http://www.job-resources.com /0103tip.htm

CHAPTER OUTLINE

Critical Thinking and Problem Solving

LEARNING OBJECTIVES

By the end of this chapter, you will achieve the following objectives:

▶ Describe the differences between critical and creative thinking and be able to explain when to use each.

▶ Explain the steps of critical thinking and describe common thinking errors.

▶ Describe the steps of problem solving and apply them to a real-life situation.

▶ Describe the steps of decision making and apply them to a real-life situation.

▶ Explain the importance of using statistics appropriately.

▶ Apply basic concepts of using statistics to critical thinking activities.

6

BE IN THE KNOW

Are You a Critical Thinker?

While you are in school you will have many opportunities to read literature and conduct scholarly research for papers and projects. You will also be engaged in discourse with your instructors and fellow students on myriad topics. So what do you do with all of this information that is swimming around in your head?

Successful college students learn to become critical thinkers while in school. In turn, they take this highly desirable skill to the workplace. The ability to think critically is the foundation for assessing and analyzing information and to effectively apply that information in order to make sound decisions and solve problems. Thinking critically does not mean, however, that you are critical of the information being presented. Instead, it means giving a critical eye to the information, questioning its validity and usefulness.

Critical thinking also removes emotion from the equation. Emotional decisions are reactionary in nature and are generally not well thought out. Critical thinking removes that hurdle, thus giving a clear path to using information in the best possible way in order to make well-informed decisions and allow for creative solutions to problems.

Thinking critically allows you to question and even challenge the information in front of you. For example, do you feel the author is somehow biased in his opinion? Are the facts accurate? We all know that anyone can put anything up on the Internet and some people have their own agendas for doing so. A cursory search for information may yield hundreds, if not thousands, of "hits," but there is no guarantee that what pops up first on a search engine is the most complete, accurate, and thorough information on the topic.

With practice, you will learn to become a critical thinker. You will also learn to use your critical voice in creative ways that help you to solve problems and make sound academic and business decisions. Learning to become a critical thinker, and then applying that skill in school and in the workplace, is a sure sign of academic and professional success.

Are *you* a critical thinker?

CRITICAL AND CREATIVE THINKING

Critical and creative thinking go hand in hand but are two different processes. *Critical thinking* is the ability to effectively analyze and use information. *Creative thinking* is the skill of applying acceptable standards and procedures in an innovative and effective manner. This is sometimes referred to as "thinking out of the box."

CRITICAL THINKING

Critical thinking is a process in which you consider information in a methodical and disciplined manner. Developing your critical thinking skills will benefit you in the classroom as well as in your career by strengthening your ability to present ideas and conclusions supported by accurate data. Critical thinking is also known as logical thinking or analytical thinking.

Critical thinking entails systematic thinking and requires conceptualization, the ability to logically analyze information from multiple perspectives, and the ability to synthesize a conclusion from your analysis. For critical thinking to be useful, you must be able to apply your conclusions to daily activities.

Critical Thinking Processes

Precise thinking skills are necessary in order to think critically. Understanding these skills can help you keep them in your awareness and apply them to your thought processes. Asking yourself questions during the critical thinking process will help you identify important elements to consider. The questions suggested below are based on recommendations from the Foundation for Critical Thinking (2011).

- What is my purpose? What am I trying to accomplish?
- What question do I need to answer to achieve my goal or purpose?
- What information do I need to answer the question?
- Is my information from verifiable and reliable sources?
- Am I using sound and logical reasoning to make sense of my information and reach a sound conclusion?
- Are there alternative perspectives that should be considered?

SELF-ASSESSMENT QUESTION

- How do you use critical thinking in your daily life? In school?

6

CRITICAL THINKING QUESTION

- Do you consider yourself analytical? How does your ability to analyze information play into your critical thinking abilities?

Critical thinking is an important component of successfully completing assignments and includes skills such as conceptualization and analysis of ideas.

Bananastock Ltd./Jupiter Images.

▶ What conclusions can I make from my information?

▶ Are my conclusions unbiased and logical based on reliable information?

The following suggestions are actions you can take to develop critical thinking skills.

Remain Objective

Personal opinions and values are important but should not be a part of professional decisions. Critical thinking requires the setting aside of personal opinion and judgments. It requires you to evaluate information on the basis of its merits related to the issue at hand and to use valid facts in the process.

Use Dialectical Thinking

Dialectical thinking is the ability to consider more than one viewpoint or perspective at a time. It is an important part of critical thinking, as it allows you to take into account all aspects of a problem or question. Considering multiple perspectives of an issue helps you to understand the issue in greater depth, which in turn provides the opportunity for more accurate analysis and a more effective presentation of your information. Understanding additional viewpoints also enables you to more effectively defend your position, as you will have anticipated other perspectives and potential arguments.

Consider the Breadth and Depth of Your Thinking

Breadth of thought refers to taking multiple points of view into consideration and is related to dialectical thinking. Consciously consider multiple perspectives that may be related to your subject.

On the other hand, *depth of thought* refers to the level of detail that you consider related to your topic. Determine the amount of detail that you need and present enough information to logically support your point without overwhelming your audience.

Consider Multiple Causality

It is important to recognize that there are usually several causes for any given event. A situation may appear to be a consequence of an action or event, but circumstances are rarely (if ever) products of direct cause and effect. Thinking critically requires consideration of all events and conditions that contribute to a situation.

Consider the Situation and the Context

No two situations are exactly alike. Considering information critically requires taking into account the circumstances, environment, and the individuals who are involved. Each of these individual factors contributes to the uniqueness of each situation, making a customized approach necessary for effective thinking.

On the other hand, past situations that are similar to present circumstances can give you ideas for addressing current issues. Think about past experiences that might lend insight into current thinking. Effective critical thinking requires considering both the differences and similarities of past and current situations.

Use Metacognition

Metacognition is consciously monitoring your thought processes to understand how you are thinking, and is an important process in the development of critical thinking skills. Pay attention to how you think and the elements of critical thinking that you use. Reflection is the process of thinking back over the way you reached your conclusion and can provide insight into the way that you think. Reflection allows us to understand our assumptions, become more aware, and become conscious of alternatives (Stein, 2000; Frank & Davie, 2001).

success steps for assessing your thinking

The following steps are adapted from Paul and Elder (2008).

- Know and clearly explain what your reasoning is supposed to achieve.
- Identify your assumptions, make sure they are valid, and understand how they are influencing your thought process.
- Identify your point of view and contrast it with others' viewpoints. Understand the strong and weak points of both.
- Support points of view with quantifiable data.
- Explain relationships and concepts clearly.
- Make sure that the points you make are consistent and don't contradict one another.
- Make sure that the conclusions that you draw are consistent with the concepts and points that you have stated.

Obstacles to Critical Thinking

Obstacles to critical thinking occur when information that you have available is considered inaccurately, incompletely, or both. Errors of this nature can result in ineffective decisions and information that is presented in an illogical manner. Developing the habit of making the following considerations will contribute to more effective critical thinking.

Assumption versus Fact

Critical thinking requires you to use solid facts and evidence in your analysis of information. An argument or conclusion loses its credibility when personal biases or assumptions are used as facts supporting a decision or argument. Errors in critical thinking and in subsequent decisions are more likely to occur when assumptions are used in place of verifiable facts.

Thinking Superficially

Superficial thinking means considering only the very obvious or superficial facts and aspects of an issue. Thinking in depth requires identifying related information, considering the context of the issue, and understanding the relationships of all factors. Discussing, writing, diagramming, and reading are methods for delving into an issue in greater depth.

Jumping to Conclusions

Another error in thinking and one that can significantly interfere with effective critical thinking is determining a conclusion before all relevant data is received. If all important facts are not available, it is difficult (if not impossible) to draw a logical conclusion. One element that can contribute to the tendency to jump to conclusions is an emotional reaction to information or circumstances. It is normal and expected to have emotional responses to certain issues that you encounter. However, emotional reactions must be tempered with an objective and rational consideration of the facts in order to think effectively and reach reasonable conclusions.

All-or-None Thinking

All-or-none thinking occurs when one believes that because something happens in a certain way one time, all future events will occur in the same manner. Another aspect of all-or-none thinking is the conviction that because one believes in a certain way, that way of thinking is the only way to think and is always true. All-or-none thinking is believing that there is one universal way to think about something and to apply information. Effective critical thinking requires flexibility, recognizing that there is usually more than one way to do or think about something.

Cause and Effect

Multiplicity, or the idea that events usually have more than one cause, was discussed earlier in this chapter. The related error in critical thinking occurs when an event is viewed as a direct result of another event or situation. It is generally more productive to think in terms of correlated events, or circumstances that are related to a result. Considering one event or circumstance to be the cause of a situation or issue usually limits other aspects of critical thinking because it limits your perspective. To be credible, you must be able to explain the relationship between the cause and the outcome. Figure 6-1 shows the process of critical thinking.

6

DIAGRAM OF THE CRITICAL THINKING PROCESS

Define the $\longrightarrow$ Identify $\longrightarrow$ Identify your point $\longrightarrow$ Clarify and state purpose for your of view and your point of view your reasoning. assumptions. compare it to others' and support it with $\longrightarrow$ Draw and state viewpoints. quantifiable data. conclusions.

Ask these questions:	Ask these questions:	Ask these questions:	Ask these questions:
▶ Are you remaining objective?	▶ What are the strong and weak points of each viewpoint?	▶ Are the relationships clear and logical?	▶ Are your conclusions consistent with the concepts you have presented?
▶ Are your assumptions valid and relevant?	▶ Do you need to consider another point of view and possibly incorporate it into your thinking?	▶ Are the concepts clearly articulated?	
▶ How are your assumptions affecting your thinking?		▶ Are there any contradictions?	
	▶ Have you considered multiple causes?		

Figure 6-1   Thinking critically means systematically sorting and analyzing information. Critical thinking is an important skill to develop for school and professional activities. Following the steps outlined here can support you in developing this skill.

Adapted from Paul and Elder (2008).

Steps for Thinking Critically

- Differentiate facts from assumptions.
- Consider issues in depth.
- Consider all important facts and perspectives before reaching a conclusion.
- Avoid all-or-none thinking. Expect some ambiguity.
- Recognize that events usually have multiple causes.

apply it

Find printable activities on the companion web site for this book, accessed through www.cengagebrain.com.

Problem-Solving Techniques

GOAL: To learn and apply strategies to be used in the problem-solving process

STEP 1: Conduct an Internet search using "idea mapping," "concept mapping," and "visual learning methods" as your search terms.

STEP 2: Review the results of your searches and select a method that you believe will be effective for you.

STEP 3: Use the method to approach a problem or to arrive at a creative solution.

STEP 4: Reflect on your outcome and compare the results to other problem-solving techniques you have used. Write a brief reflection to include in your Learning Portfolio.

CASE IN POINT: BEING CRITICAL *AND* CREATIVE

Read the scenario below. Then, in groups or as a class, discuss the questions at the end.

Todd Whitmore is employed by a medium-size organization and works in the Research and Development Department. Todd is prompt, has minimal absences, abides by company policy, and follows directions for his assignments accurately. Considering these elements, one might say Todd is a model employee.

Todd, however, is experiencing frustrations. He has worked with this company for over four years and believes that he is ready to be promoted to a more responsible position within the department. He has applied for several positions within the department and has been declined a promotion each time.

Todd recently approached his supervisor to discuss the issue and his frustrations. His supervisor, although supportive, told Todd that even though Todd was a good employee, he needs to develop his critical thinking skills and logical thought processes in order to achieve a promotion. Todd's supervisor gave Todd examples of scenarios where Todd had contributed to problem-solving processes but had not taken into consideration all relevant factors, resulting in an incomplete solution and an inappropriate decision for the department. The supervisor also revealed that Todd needed to be more creative in order to move ahead as a contributor in the department and the company.

Todd's supervisor was supportive of Todd's efforts and desire to expand his responsibilities and skills within the Research and Development Department. Todd and his supervisor proceeded to set goals and devise strategies to help Todd develop his critical and creative thinking abilities.

6

▶ What are some critical thinking processes that Todd might have been lacking?

▶ How do critical thinking skills contribute to effective problem solving and decision making?

▶ What are some methods that Todd might use to develop his critical thinking skills?

▶ How might Todd's self-image, self-esteem, and interpersonal skills influence his creative contributions to his department?

▶ What are some methods that Todd might use to develop his creative thinking?

CREATIVE THINKING

Creative thinking is the ability to sort out problems, identify pressing issues, and arrive at effective solutions. Scott Isaksen and Donald Treffinger (1985, p. 13) define the purpose of creativity as follows:

▶ To encourage the identification of possibilities

▶ To think in new and varied ways

▶ To consider different points of view

▶ To think of new approaches and strategies

▶ To generate and encourage the use of new ideas

Photographer's Choice/Bob Handelman/Getty Images.

Creative thinking requires reflection to identify problems, generate ideas, and analyze possible solutions.

apply it

Find printable activities on the companion web site for this book, accessed through www.cengagebrain.com.

Critical Thinking Journal

GOAL: To increase your awareness of your thought processes and to develop your critical thinking skills

STEP 1: Understand the elements of critical thinking. You may discover variations on these themes as you complete this activity.

STEP 2: Consciously use these elements in two ways: (1) Analyze information or a problem in your usual manner and reflect on the process to determine which elements you used, and (2) think of each element and apply it to a problem or information that you are analyzing. You may wish to try the first approach followed by the second for the same problem and compare the processes.

STEP 3: Review your critical thinking process. Evaluate what you have learned and think about how you might apply your findings in the future.

STEP 4: Record your thinking process and your observations about your thinking process. Compile your observations into a critical thinking journal. Review your progress regularly.

6

Whereas critical thinking involves the systematic analysis of information and arriving at logical conclusions based on fact and circumstances, creative thinking is the ability to apply those conclusions in unique ways to meet goals. Creative thinking may also be a part of critical thinking, in that the critical thinking process may require innovative approaches to finding and interpreting information. You will also find that critical thinking has a place in the creative thinking process. There is certainly overlap between the two types of thinking, although you are likely to use each for specific purposes.

Creative thinking can benefit your problem-solving efforts in personal and professional circumstances. The ability to effectively solve problems and manage others in the problem-solving process is a skill that is highly valued by employers and is valued in the 21st-century world where rapid change occurs as a result of advancing technology and a growing knowledge base.

An important element to keep in mind about creative thinking is that it is not a license to do whatever you want. Effective creative thinking requires the consideration of professional, legal, and ethical boundaries and the development of innovative solutions within acceptable limits.

PROBLEM SOLVING

Isaksen and Treffinger (1985) suggest clearly defined steps to take in the creative problem-solving process. By consciously completing each step, you may be more focused and able to arrive at creative solutions more effectively. Isaksen and Treffinger's creative problem-solving steps are summarized as follows.

MESS FINDING

Mess finding refers to the process of determining an area that might benefit from creative problem solving. Your "mess" might be obvious to you, or you may need to prioritize areas to which you would like to direct your problem-solving efforts.

DATA FINDING

In the *data finding* stage you collect information that will help you begin the problem-solving process. Data can consist of your knowledge, information from other sources, opinions of people whose input you value, and any other facts and figures that are useful to you. You should also record any questions, concerns, or feelings that you have about your "mess." The purpose of this step is to sort out and assess where you stand in the problem-solving process.

PROBLEM FINDING

During this step, you review the information that you have collected and determine whether you have accurately pinpointed the problem. Once all of the data has been reviewed, you may find that there are several issues within your "mess" to consider. For example, there may be smaller concerns leading up to the larger problem that will have to be addressed in order of importance. The *problem finding* step is where you clarify and prioritize the most pressing issues.

IDEA FINDING

Idea finding is similar to the brainstorming process that occurs within a group. During this step, you identify as many ideas and approaches to your problem as possible. As you identify ideas, take the same approach as in a brainstorming session. Do not censor or negate any idea. Record all thoughts that come to mind, even if they seem outlandish or impossible. They may be springboards to other ideas. Keep in mind that the more ideas you can generate, the more likely your chance of finding a workable solution. Consider completing this step in several sessions, as you are likely to develop additional ideas over time. Isaksen and Treffinger (1985, p. 18) suggest letting ideas "simmer" to allow new perspectives to come to mind and new ideas to develop. Jot down ideas as they come up so that you don't forget them.

When you are confident that you have accumulated a sufficient number of ideas, begin to sort them by combining similar ideas, determining feasibility, and discarding those that are not practical.

SOLUTION FINDING

In the *solution finding* step, you determine the merit of your ideas based on standards and criteria that you have set. Assess the advantages and disadvantages of each idea based on your criteria and decide which ideas have the most potential as a solution for your problem. During this step of the process, you may find it helpful to make a list comparing pros and cons.

ACCEPTANCE FINDING

Acceptance finding is the stage where you put your solution into action. You will consider the strengths of your ideas and avenues to pursue them, as well as anticipate barriers and obstacles that you might encounter. At this stage, some individuals and organizations conduct a SWOT analysis. SWOT stands for

▶ **s**trengths (the strong points of your solution),

▶ **w**eaknesses (components of your solution or skills that you need to develop),

▶ **o**pportunities (possibilities to promote your solution or idea), and

▶ **t**hreats (elements in the environment that may impede your success).

Identifying each of these components reveals the strategies necessary to maximize your chances of success.

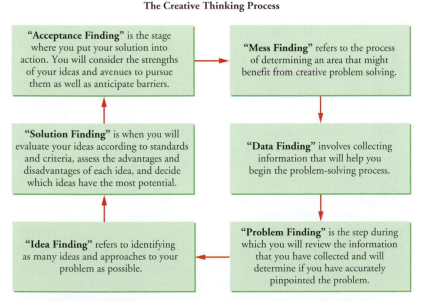

The Creative Thinking Process

"Acceptance Finding" is the stage where you put your solution into action. You will consider the strengths of your ideas and avenues to pursue them as well as anticipate barriers.

"Mess Finding" refers to the process of determining an area that might benefit from creative problem solving.

"Solution Finding" is when you will evaluate your ideas according to standards and criteria, assess the advantages and disadvantages of each idea, and decide which ideas have the most potential.

"Data Finding" involves collecting information that will help you begin the problem-solving process.

"Idea Finding" refers to identifying as many ideas and approaches to your problem as possible.

"Problem Finding" is the step during which you will review the information that you have collected and will determine if you have accurately pinpointed the problem.

Like critical thinking, creative thinking is a process of steps and consciously considering your options.

Adapted from Isaksen & Treffinger (1985).

6

success steps for developing creative thinking skills

- Carry a smart phone, tablet, or small notebook with you and jot down ideas as you think of them.
- Give ideas time to "brew," as this helps them to develop.
- Consider *all* ideas, even if they seem outlandish at first.
- Use creative learning tools, such as idea mapping, to analyze your ideas.
- Consciously reflect on your thought processes.

apply it

Find printable activities on the companion web site for this book, accessed through www.cengagebrain.com.

Creative Problem Solving

GOAL: To apply the steps of creative problem solving as defined by Isaksen and Treffinger

STEP 1: Identify a topic or issue for which you would like to brainstorm creative options.

STEP 2: Electronically or using several sheets of paper, write each one of Isaksen and Treffinger's creative problem-solving steps (mess finding, etc.) at the top of each.

STEP 3: As you complete each step of the problem-solving process, record your thoughts and ideas on the appropriate sheet.

STEP 4: Review each step to understand how you arrived at your solution. Be sure to evaluate your solution for effectiveness. If necessary, review the steps of the process to determine how you might improve the process next time.

apply it

Find printable activities on the companion web site for this book, accessed through www.cengagebrain.com.

Creative Thinking on the Web

GOAL: *To explore ideas and resources for developing creative thinking and lateral logic and to apply principles of creative problem solving*

STEP 1: Conduct an Internet search using the search terms "creative thinking," "creative problem solving," and "lateral logic." Look for strategies for creative problem solving that provide steps that you can apply to a real-life issue. Print the articles and strategies that you find most interesting.

STEP 2: Select one of the approaches you find for creative problem solving and familiarize yourself with its principles. You may wish to do further research to learn more about the strategy that you select.

STEP 3: Apply the strategy to a problem that you are currently trying to solve. Follow through on each of the recommended steps and keep a written journal of your progress and findings.

apply it

Find printable activities on the companion web site for this book, accessed through www.cengagebrain.com.

Group Brainstorming and Problem Solving

Goal: *To gain experience in the brainstorming process and to apply brainstorming to the problem-solving process*

STEP 1: Assemble a group of people who are working to develop a solution to a common problem. This might be related to a school assignment or a project outside of school.

continued

continued

STEP 2: Ensure that all group members understand the ground rules of brainstorming, which are summarized here:

- Consider all ideas for all of the stages of creative problem solving. For example, in the problem-finding stage, collect as many ideas as possible regarding what the actual problem is. During idea finding, collect as many ideas as possible for addressing the problem. You may already have identified your "mess" or the issue that you are addressing. If not, you can also implement group brainstorming for mess finding.

- Do not pass judgment on any ideas at this stage of brainstorming.

- Write all ideas on a whiteboard or flip chart. Complete this process for each step of the problem-solving process.

STEP 3: Use brainstorming guidelines to implement the stages of mess finding, problem finding, idea finding, and solution finding.

STEP 4: Following each of the stages of problem solving from Step 3, analyze the ideas that have been generated. Combine similar ideas, sequence suggestions, and organize your information. During this process, you will condense your many ideas into smaller, workable chunks. Distill your many ideas into a workable plan for each step of the problem-solving process.

STEP 5: Implement a SWOT analysis (if appropriate) to implement your plan. This process will be completed over time and its details will depend on your particular project and environment.

DECISION MAKING

The quality of the decisions you make is directly related to the quality of your thinking. Critical thinking processes are essential to decision making. Creative thinking can be a vital element in developing good alternatives for decisions. Major decisions typically require more attention to critical thinking than smaller, everyday decisions. Understanding how critical and creative thinking influence the decision-making process will support you in making more effective decisions.

PERSONAL TRAITS AND DECISION-MAKING SKILLS

Chapter 2 discussed aspects of self-image and self-esteem. Consider how a negative self-image might impact the ability to make decisions. Recall that self-image is the way in which one views the self; self-esteem is the way one feels about the self. If an individual perceives the self in a negative way, that individual may not anticipate that their decisions will lead to success. The result of anticipated failure can lead to indecisiveness or poor decisions, negatively impacting the individual. Poor outcomes can in turn impact self-esteem.

apply it

Find printable activities on the companion web site for this book, accessed through www.cengagebrain.com.

Decision-Making Review

GOAL: *To reflect on decision making and identify constructive elements, as well as those that may negatively influence the process*

STEP 1: Identify a decision that you need to make. It could be related to school or a decision in your personal life.

STEP 2: Using the elements outlined earlier in this chapter (and listed below), create a hard copy or computer document with the elements listed down the left-hand side.

Elements to Consider in Decision Making

Assumption versus fact (What verifiable facts do I have?)

- Jumping to conclusions (Do I have all the information that is available to make a good decision?)
- All-or-none thinking (Am I considering that there may be other alternatives and some ambiguous areas, or am I thinking in absolutes?)

continued

SELF-ASSESSMENT QUESTIONS

- How do you use critical thinking processes in your decision making?
- How could you develop your critical thinking skills to support better decision making?
- How does your self-image influence your decision making? What works well? What would you like to change?
- How might self-image and self-esteem influence other aspects of thinking?

CRITICAL THINKING QUESTION

▶ Does your creative thinking sometimes override your critical thinking when making major decisions?

6

continued

- Cause and effect (Am I recognizing that events can have multiple causes or a combination of causes? Am I recognizing that my decision might have multiple effects?)

STEP 3: As you go through your decision-making process (which may extend over a period of days or weeks), make notes about the process. Use the document that you have created as your guide and make your notes in the appropriate areas. Create other categories that you believe would clarify your observations.

STEP 4: Review the outcome of your decision and the information that you have recorded during the decision-making process. What was effective? What was less effective? What might you change in your decision-making strategies?

USING PROFESSIONAL RESOURCES

An important strategy to ensure that you are supporting your thinking, problem solving, and decision making effectively is to use professional literature and resources. All fields have a body of information that is accepted as a professional knowledge base. To be credible, you must be aware of and apply this knowledge base in your professional activities. Before using any statistics, it is important to assess whether your source is reliable. Chapter 7 discusses the credibility of resources and provides guidelines for evaluating credibility.

THE USE OF STATISTICS AND QUANTITATIVE DATA

Statistics and quantitative data (numbers and other "hard" data) can be useful in supporting your thinking and decisions. Statistics are generally viewed as credible supporting evidence to arguments and plans. However, statistics can be misleading and must be used appropriately to be effective. Elements such as the context that the statistic is drawn from, the wording, and other factors influence the trustworthiness of a statistic. The following are some elements to think about when using statistics or other data as part of your reasoning.

Reading Research

When you are reading research in your field, it is important to understand how the research terms and processes are used. Although introductory research is beyond the scope of this text, there are some general points to understand.

In their book on research analysis, authors Jeffrey Gliner, George Morgan, and Nancy Leech (2009) summarize the following important concepts to consider when using or reading research that uses statistics:

▶ Statistical analysis is used to show a correlation between events. Statistics do not *prove* cause and effect.

▶ Correct use of statistics and statistical analysis depends on several factors, including the way in which the study or the presentation of information is designed.

▶ It is helpful to acquire a basic understanding of quantitative research analyses, for example, *t*-tests and analysis of variance (ANOVA), so that you can better understand how information is being compared and interpreted.

▶ It is helpful to understand terminology such as *independent variable*, *dependent variable*, and *significance*.

When giving presentations or using statistics in other classroom projects, be sure to define the context of your statistical terms so that your information is clear and logical.

The depth to which you need to understand research techniques and strategies will depend on your field. Your specific program curriculum will address research appropriate to your field and education.

Using Statistics Effectively

There may be times when you wish to consider statistics in your critical thinking and decision making. It is important to understand how you are using statistics in order to present your points in a credible and valid manner.

The Online Writing Lab at Purdue University ("Writing with statistics," 2011) suggests examining terms such as *average* and *percentage*. It is necessary to know the basis of averages and percentages in order to understand what they mean. For example, if a claim is made that 50% of students have grade point averages above 80%, do you mean 50% of a class, an entire school, or all college students in the country? The numbers are quite different, depending on the basis of the percentage. In addition, "above 80%" is a relatively wide range. What is the percentage really stating? What is the relationship of the statistic to the point you are making?

SOURCES OF PROFESSIONAL RESOURCES

The resources that you have available to you will depend on your field. Generally, the most effective resources are available from publications and documents that are published by professional organizations and academic institutions. Chapter 7 discusses sources of professional literature and information in depth.

CHAPTER SUMMARY

This chapter summarized critical and creative thinking and provided suggestions for using both processes effectively. You learned critical thinking processes and their relationship to decision making, and explored obstacles to critical thinking. You learned an approach to creative thinking and steps that can be used to arrive at solutions to problems you encounter. Finally, you received an overview of the use of statistics and professional data in critical thinking. You are encouraged to expand on this information in a manner appropriate to your field of study.

Critical and creative thinking skills can be applied to your academic and professional development in many ways. In addition to using critical and creative thinking techniques in your studies, consider how they can be applied to your development of the areas covered in *100% Student Success*. For example, concepts of problem solving can be applied to troubleshooting difficulties with studying or preparing for exams. Decision-making skills can be applied to financial decisions, and creative solutions can be found for balancing a busy schedule. You are encouraged to keep critical and creative thinking concepts in mind throughout your work with this text.

POINTS TO KEEP IN MIND

In this chapter, several main points were discussed in detail:

▶ Critical and creative thinking are separate, yet related, processes.

▶ Critical thinking is a process in which you consider information in a methodical and disciplined manner.

▶ Critical thinking involves the use of certain skills such as considering multiple perspectives, understanding multiple causality, conceptualizing, and analyzing data logically.

▶ Metacognition is the ability to think about and understand your own thinking process and is an important factor in the critical thinking process.

▶ Errors in thinking, such as jumping to conclusions, using assumptions rather than facts, thinking superficially, engaging in all-or-none thinking, and assuming cause-and-effect relationships, can impede the critical thinking process.

▶ The purposes of creative thinking include increasing awareness of possibilities, encouraging new ways to think, and considering multiple points of view. Creative thinking techniques help us think in new ways and generate new ideas.

▶ Effective problem solving and appropriate creative thinking are skills that are highly valued by employers.

▶ Effective problem-solving skills are imperative in a world where rapid change occurs as a result of advancing technology and a growing knowledge base.

▶ There are clearly defined steps to take in the creative problem-solving process. By consciously completing each step, you may be more focused and successful in your problem-solving efforts.

▶ An important strategy to ensure that you are supporting your thinking, problem solving, and decision making effectively is to use professional literature and resources.

▶ It is important to understand how you are using statistics in order to present your points in a credible and valid manner.

6

CHECK YOUR UNDERSTANDING

Visit www.cengagebrain.com to see how well you have mastered the material in Chapter 6.

SUGGESTED ITEMS FOR LEARNING PORTFOLIO

▶ Reflection and Critical Thinking Questions: Include your written responses to these questions. Use them to review your development over time.

REFERENCES

Foundation for Critical Thinking. (2011). *The critical mind is a questioning mind: Learning how to ask powerful, probing questions* [Electronic version]. Retrieved January 31, 2013, from http://www.criticalthinking.org/articles/critical-mind.cfm

Frank, C., & Davie, L. (2001). Creating online communities for critical thinking, reading, and writing. Paper presented at TCC (Teaching in the Community Colleges) 2001 Online Conference. Kapi'olani Community College, The University of Hawaii. Retrieved January 31, 2013, from http://tcc.kcc.hawaii.edu/previous/TCC%202001/frank.html

Gliner, J. A., Morgan, G. A., & Leech, N. L. (2009). *Research methods in applied settings: An integrated approach to design and analysis* (2nd ed.). Fort Collins, CO: Colorado State University.

Isaksen, S. G., & Treffinger, D. J. (1985). *Creative problem solving: The basic course*. Buffalo, NY: Bearly.

Paul, R., & Elder, L. (2008, February). *The analysis and assessment of thinking (Helping students assess their thinking)*. Foundation for Critical Thinking. Retrieved January 31, 2013, from http://www.criticalthinking.org/pages/the-analysis-amp-assessment-of-thinking/497

Stein, D. (2000). *Teaching critical reflection: Myths and realities No. 7* [Electronic version]. Ohio State University, College of Education, Center on Education and Training for Employment. Retrieved January 31, 2013, from http://www.eric.ed.gov/PDFS/ED445256.pdf

Writing with statistics [Electronic version]. (2011). Purdue University, Online Writing Lab. Retrieved January 31, 2013, from http://owl.english.purdue.edu/handouts/research/r_stats.html

part 3

Harnessing Information

Part III of *100% Student Success* addresses two critical issues in the classroom: being information literate in the digital age, and understanding—and complying with—ethical and legal issues that arise in the academic environment.

Chapter 7: Information Literacy for the 21st Century emphasizes the importance of information literacy and its role in learning and professional development in the 21st century. Becoming information literate will allow you to remain current in your field, promote your credibility, and add to your success in your chosen profession.

Abiding by legal and ethical standards is an expectation of students and professionals alike. In addition, students and professionals are protected by and have certain rights under the law. **Chapter 8: Legal and Ethical Issues in the Academic Environment** summarizes the laws and standards that define your responsibilities as well as specify your rights.

Information Literacy for the 21st Century

LEARNING OBJECTIVES

By the end of this chapter, you will achieve the following objectives:

▶ Define *information literacy* and explain the necessity for developing the skills for academic and career success.

▶ Define *digital literacy* and explain its relationship to information literacy.

▶ Describe common library resources and explain their use in finding school- and career-related information.

▶ Demonstrate the ability to use Internet resources effectively in research.

▶ Demonstrate the ability to assess the credibility of information sources.

▶ Define *copyright* and *plagiarism* and demonstrate the ability to avoid plagiarism and cite resources correctly.

BE IN THE KNOW

Effective Research: Questions to Ask

As you read through this chapter, and subsequently conduct research for papers and projects assigned to you, keep the following questions in mind. Answering these questions will help you to formulate a solid plan for creating your final product.

Questions to Ask to Find Useful Information

- What kind of information do I need? (facts, figures, statistics, opinions, sides of an issue, historical/background, profile, interview, primary, secondary, etc.)
- How much information do I need? (limited scope, in-depth coverage, summary or overview, etc.)
- What parameters should I follow? (time period, geographical location, age or gender, point of view, etc.)
- Who will be receiving this information? (practitioners, professionals, laypeople, scientists, team members, colleagues, clients, patients, etc.)
- What information sources should I use? (encyclopedias, professional journals, people, directories, databases, popular magazines, maps, videos, etc.)
- Where do I find these resources? (library, Internet, individuals, companies, government resources, librarian, etc.)
- How do I search for the information within each resource? (index, electronic search engine, etc.)
- How should I retrieve the information once I find it? (download, photocopy, interlibrary loan, print, etc.)
- How do I manage the information that I retrieve? (electronic files, print file folders, etc.)

Questions to Ask to Effectively Evaluate Information

- Is the information current?
- Is the information credible?
- Is the information accurate?
- Is the information relevant to the need?

- Is the information useful?
- Is the information free from bias?

Questions to Ask to Effectively Organize Information

- How do I organize the information so I can find main ideas, key issues, different viewpoints, etc.?

- How can I think about the information in new ways?

- How do I manage a large amount of information?

- How do I organize the information so it is presented logically and appropriately? (chronologically, priority of elements, problem/solution, deductive order, inductive order, etc.)

Questions to Ask to Effectively Communicate Information

- Who is my audience? Am I communicating on a casual topic or for business? Is the setting formal or relaxed? The type of audience and the setting will determine how you will deliver your information.

- What channel should be used to communicate the research results? (written, verbal, visual, electronic, etc.)

- For the selected channel, what specific format best meets the communication need? (proposal, narrative, research report, slide presentation, image, diagram, etc.)

- How do I properly reference the resources I use and give appropriate credit to the original authors of the information?

7

INTRODUCTION TO INFORMATION LITERACY IN THE DIGITAL AGE

In the age of enormous amounts of quickly changing information, students and professionals alike must be able to find relevant information and put it to use effectively. Students must be able to access information beyond textbooks and classroom instructors in order to prepare for the workplace. Professionals must keep current and continuously expand their body of knowledge to be successful and to advance in their careers. Staying successfully updated requires individuals to be *information literate*.

Information can be accessed in many different ways. Traditional libraries, for example, offer many sources of information, and most libraries now provide access to their resources via the Internet. Apart from libraries, the Internet also opens the door to a wealth of additional resources. Entire textbooks can be devoted to information literacy; however, this chapter focuses only on basic and essential skills for students and provides a foundation for more advanced information skills ultimately needed for workplace success.

WHAT IS INFORMATION LITERACY?

Webber (2010) defines information literacy for the 21st century as "the adoption of appropriate information behavior to identify, through whatever channel or medium, information well fitted to information needs, leading to wise and ethical use of information in society." Today, information comes to us from a myriad of sources: the Internet, emerging Web 3.0 tools, podcasts, and traditional media, to name a few. Webber's definition points to the importance of selecting appropriate information from a suitable source and using the information in a credible manner within legal and ethical boundaries. Excellent students will pursue the development of these skills and practice them in each course they take. They will apply the concepts specifically to their field of study and career goals. Information-literate individuals are also able to critically assess information and to use it effectively to solve personal and workplace problems.

ADVANTAGES OF BEING INFORMATION LITERATE

When learners become information literate, they increase their advantages in school and in the workplace. The following list represents just a few of these potential advantages:

- Learners sharpen their critical and creative thinking skills.
- Learners develop higher-order thinking skills essential for excellence in school and the workplace.
- Students develop a deeper and more applicable understanding of the content they are learning and become better prepared for their jobs.

SELF-ASSESSMENT QUESTION

- How information-literate do you consider yourself? What is your level of skill in using the computer and the Internet for finding and using information?

? CRITICAL THINKING QUESTION

- What other advantages can you think of to being information literate?

7

▶ Individuals are able to communicate in knowledgeable, logical, and defensible ways regarding their work.

▶ The ability to effectively participate in problem solving and decision making is enhanced.

▶ Professionals are able to keep up with advancements in their field of study, making them more competent and valuable as employees.

DEFINING DIGITAL LITERACY

As we move further into the 21st century and into an ever-expanding digital age, we find that how information literacy is defined takes on additional significance. According to Jones and Flannigan (n.d.),

> "*Digital literacy* represents a person's ability to perform tasks effectively in a digital environment. The term *digital* means information represented in numeric form and primarily for use by a computer. The term *literacy* includes the ability to read and interpret media (text, sound, images, etc.), to reproduce data and images through digital manipulation, and to evaluate and apply new knowledge gained from digital environments."

The American Library Association (2013) defines digital literacy as "the ability to use information and communication technologies to find, understand, evaluate, create, and communicate digital information, an ability that requires both cognitive and technical skills."

The Association defines a *digitally literate person as* one who:

▶ "possesses the variety of skills—cognitive and technical— required to find, understand, evaluate, create, and communicate digital information in a wide variety of formats;

▶ is able to use diverse technologies appropriately and effectively to search for and retrieve information, interpret search results, and judge the quality of the information retrieved;

7

- understands the relationships among technology, lifelong learning, personal privacy, and appropriate stewardship of information;
- uses these skills and the appropriate technologies to communicate and collaborate with peers, colleagues, family, and on occasion the general public;
- uses these skills to participate actively in civic society and contribute to a vibrant, informed, and engaged community (American Library Association 2013)."

Today, the information-literate learner must combine the knowledge of how to find, evaluate, and communicate information within the context of a digitized environment.

CONDUCTING RESEARCH: STRATEGIES AND ISSUES

Knowing the tools available and how to use the tools to find information are only two of the information literacy skills. An important third element is knowing how to determine what information is needed and how to develop an effective and efficient plan of action for the search. Once information is found, the person who is information literate knows what to do with this information, including how to communicate it to others.

MAKING A PLAN FOR RESEARCH

Good research starts with a plan of action. Being information literate includes the ability to develop a good research plan and use library and online resources effectively and efficiently, avoid unproductive searching, and understand when and where to get help. As with solving any problem, the first step is to understand specifically the task at hand and the parameters within which the task must be completed.

© iStockphoto.com/RapidEye.

Using the library and understanding the resources that are available to you as a student will contribute greatly to your success in college.

RESEARCH ETHICS AND LEGALITIES

Information-literate individuals understand the legal and ethical ramifications of accessing and using information. Important concepts to understand include plagiarism, copyright, and appropriate methods for citing other people's work.

Plagiarism and Copyright

Plagiarism is copying and presenting someone else's work as your own without giving him or her appropriate credit. Copyright is the legal right of ownership to the work.

The advancement of the Internet and technology in general has made it easier to plagiarize the works of others due to the accessibility of information. Important considerations for using information include avoiding plagiarism and correctly documenting or citing information sources to give credit where credit is due. Plagiarism guidelines apply to all information, regardless of the source. Legal and ethical issues surrounding academic research will be discussed in detail in Chapter 8.

success steps for beginning the research process

- Clearly identify the task. If researching for a specific project, be sure to read your project instructions carefully or ask enough questions to understand exactly what the project requires. What is your task? How long does your project have to be? How current does your information have to be? What kinds of resources should you use? Are there a specific number of resources required? For what audience are you writing?

- Develop the topic in detail. A good start to developing a topic is to frame the task in the form of a question. Next, brainstorm a list of additional questions that could be asked to answer the main question. In the brainstorming phase, do not evaluate or judge the questions; just list them. Then, review the question list and develop the topic more fully. If necessary, read about the topic in an encyclopedia or another broadly focused resource to make sure the background has been reviewed sufficiently.

continued

continued

- Create an outline of major topics and subtopics. This strategy works well even for minor research tasks. In some cases, the initial questions and outline may change as you find more information.

- Generate a list of keywords and phrases and subject headings. Organize keywords appropriately to produce a useful list. Refine your search phrases to broaden or narrow the focus as needed. Add to this list as the search continues.

- Conduct the search using online catalogs and indexes or the library. Follow the appropriate procedures for each tool. Ask the reference librarian for ideas or help as needed.

- Locate the actual resource either online or in the library. Review the bibliography of the resources you find to continue finding additional items. Continue revising your search term list and outline as needed.

EVALUATING ONLINE INFORMATION

Once information is found, it must be evaluated to determine whether it is appropriate, credible, and current. Anyone can put information on the Internet and can do so for a multitude of reasons. No individual or organization edits, controls, or verifies the information on the Internet; therefore, Internet users must view information they find very critically. At a minimum, researchers should ask the following questions about the web site from which they are getting information, in order to determine the value of the information they find:

▶ **Sponsorship.** Who or what organization sponsors the web site and what are their motives for doing so? Are they trying to inform, sell something, or persuade the reader to agree to a specific way of thinking? Is there some other motive? What does the URL (uniform resource locator) tell you? Look at the ending of the URL to determine whether the site is an educational site (.edu), a commercial site (.com), a government site (.gov), and so forth. Is the site from a foreign country? (A foreign country's web site does not mean that the information is not valid, but the information might not apply to the laws or policies of the United States.) Is the site hosted by an ISP such as MSN or an agency or organization? What does the "About Us" or other information say about the sponsorship and purpose of the site? Determining the sponsor of a web site can provide insight into the goals of the web site, revealing information about possible biases and agendas.

▶ **Authorship.** Who authored the content and is this person (or organization) qualified to do so? What are this person's credentials? Is this person associated with an organization that lends more credibility to his or her statements, such as a government agency or academic institution?

▶ **Currency.** Is the information dated, revised regularly, and current? Are original and revision dates on the site? Are the cited resources current?

▶ **Quality of information.** Does the information appear to be of high quality? Does it agree with other sources of information you have read? Is it logical? Do the links to other sites work and are these sites credible? Are statements supported with references to other works, as might be found in a scholarly journal? Can you actually find these references? Are permissions to reproduce someone else's information noted? Can the resources be found in a traditional library?

▶ **Objectivity.** Is the site biased toward a specific viewpoint? If so, does the site state that the information is a viewpoint or does it present the viewpoint as fact? Are all viewpoints addressed or just one perspective? Sponsorship can indicate perspective and help you determine the objectivity of a site.

SELF-ASSESSMENT QUESTIONS

- Do you think you have ever plagiarized in your schoolwork? If so, how?
- What specific steps can you take to avoid this practice?

? CRITICAL THINKING QUESTION

▶ Do you think you spend sufficient time critically evaluating the information you find online?

apply it

Find printable activities on the companion web site for this book, accessed through www.cengagebrain.com.

Web Site Evaluation

GOAL: *To develop a checklist for evaluating web sites*

STEP 1: Develop a checklist you can use for assessing any web site using the criteria discussed in this chapter.

STEP 2: Find one web site that you consider to be of high credibility and one site that you consider to be of low credibility.

STEP 3: As a group, write a brief explanation addressing each criterion, explaining how the site does or does not meet the criteria.

STEP 4: Consider placing this worksheet in your Learning Portfolio.

THE INTERNET: BROADENING THE RESOURCE POOL

7

The Internet has made researching easier by providing access to a wide variety of information. In addition, the Internet facilitates searching for information with search engines, online reference resources, online indexes and directories, and entire virtual libraries.

BASIC TOOLS ON THE INTERNET

Hybrid Images/Cultural/Getty Images.

The Internet provides an almost never-ending source of information for use in scholarly research.

Because there are millions of Internet sites, it is essential to have an efficient way of searching. Two important tools for searching the Internet efficiently are search engines and subject directories. Understanding these tools is essential to using effective search strategies to find information efficiently.

Search Engines and Subject Directories

Search engines are tools that facilitate searching on the Internet. Basically, they are a collection of Internet files (not all the files on the Internet, however) that allow an Internet user to search through the files using keywords and a search engine mechanism. Many different search engines on the Internet can be used to find information. However, because each search engine allows searching through only those Internet files in its particular database, using only one search engine supplies only a small portion of the available sites on the Internet. To find a more complete list of web sites and Internet files, multiple search engines should be used. Google is a well-known example of a search engine with a large database. Google Scholar specifically searches through scholarly literature. Search engines are good for general information.

Subject directories are excellent tools for research-oriented searches or when you want to find sites recommended by experts. A subject directory is a collection of links to a large number of Internet resources. Typically the links are organized by topic area. There are two types of subject directories: Commercial directories are general in nature and are less selective in the links they provide. Academic and professional directories are usually maintained by experts and cater to professionals needing credible information. These directories are excellent research tools for highly specialized information. INFOMINE, The Internet Public Library, and Librarians' Index to the Internet are excellent examples of professional subject directories.

Electronic Searching Techniques

There are some basic techniques that can help focus or expand a search using an electronic search tool. To define your search terms more precisely, use Boolean operators such as AND, OR, and NOT. The operator AND is used to retrieve results where *all* the words separated by AND are included. The operator OR is used to retrieve results where either of the words separated by OR are included. Finally, the operator NOT is used to retrieve results where the word preceded by NOT is excluded. Implied Boolean operators include using a plus sign (+) in front of a word to retrieve results that include the word and a minus (–) in front of a word to retrieve results that

7

exclude the word, similar to the AND and NOT operators. Quotation marks around phrases are used to retrieve results where that specific phrase is included. Most search tools have an "Advanced Search" link that provides a form to help focus or narrow the searches. These advanced search tips and tools explain the search language used by that search tool.

RSS Feeds

RSS stands for "Really Simple Syndication" and allows one to subscribe to updates on selected web sites. RSS feeds allow one to obtain current information as it is published, without having to conduct a search and then sift through thousands of results. RSS feeds provide up-to-date information on rapidly changing topics and offer one way to remain current in a specific field or area of knowledge.

RESOURCES AVAILABLE ON THE INTERNET

Many of the resources available in a physical library are now available on the Internet via virtual libraries, subject directories, and

7

success steps for exploring the use of Boolean operators

- Select a topic you would like to research. The topic should be identified by a phrase. "Professionalism" is an example.

- Experiment with the various Boolean operators, both in words and symbols. For example, use "food guide pyramid"; then try "food guide NOT pyramid" and "food guide OR pyramid" and compare your results.

- Try other searches specific to your field. Experiment with various combinations of search terms and operators to gain an understanding of the types of results you obtain.

- Note your observations regarding the results you obtain using different operators in your searches. Note which results would be most useful in various situations.

individual web sites. There are numerous free and fee-based sites that provide information-literate users with valuable resources at their fingertips.

Online Reference Resources

Reference resources such as dictionaries, thesauruses, encyclopedias, almanacs, handbooks, and directories can be accessed online via the Internet. Hundreds of both general and subject-specific resources are available, covering almost every industry. Though some web sites require registration and sometimes a monthly or annual access fee, many sites are free. A few sites allow free use of basic services while charging a fee for more advanced or expanded services. One of the most important benefits of accessing these resources using the Internet is the ability to use search tools to locate the specific information needed.

Online Periodicals

As mentioned earlier, if your library does not subscribe to a desired periodical, one of the options is to find a full-text version of the article online. The general procedure for searching for online full-text articles is basically the same as in a physical library. An online periodical index is used to find the needed information. In many cases, the actual full-text article can be viewed online either for free or for a fee. Many online libraries and subject directories also link to periodical indexes and the articles themselves.

Web Portals

A web portal (sometimes called a gateway) is a web site that provides links to many different kinds of information, either for a general audience or related to a specific interest group or industry. Web portals are useful in finding industry-related information, products, news, periodicals, organizations, chat rooms, people's addresses or phone numbers, and almost anything else related to the industry that can be found on the Internet. Some web portals are maintained by ISPs (Internet service providers, such as AOL and Yahoo!), whereas others are maintained by state governments, professional

7

organizations, or some other special interest entity. There are hundreds of web portals for almost any industry or interest group on the Internet. Note that some web portals are commercial in nature but can still provide useful resources.

Professional and Trade Organizations

Professional and trade organizations include members with similar interests or occupations. These organizations are excellent sources for current information about an industry, trends and current practices, licensure and certification requirements, and networking with professionals. Most organizations have some kind of online presence and many provide excellent information on their home pages. Students and professionals can keep current in their field by participating in a professional organization's activities and learning about current issues. A good starting place to find appropriate professional organization web sites is the Google Directory listing for professional organizations.

LIBRARY RESOURCES: THE BASICS

Information-literate individuals can figure out the organization of the library facilities they visit. They are also able to identify the various resources available and understand how to use these resources effectively. This knowledge provides an important foundation for using an effective search strategy to find the answers to questions or to solve workplace problems. Understanding the resources allows the researcher to know where to most effectively start the search process. Library resources include a variety of reference tools, sources of current and archived information, and other media sources beyond the printed format.

REFERENCE RESOURCES

There are numerous reference resources available in most libraries. Information-literate individuals should understand the information found in each resource as well as how to use the resources efficiently to answer questions.

Dictionaries and Thesauruses

A dictionary is an alphabetical listing of words. Typically, dictionaries also show how to pronounce the words, give variations on spelling and word forms, and provide the different meanings and uses of the word. Although a general dictionary is sufficient for basic writing tasks, information-literate individuals should be aware that technical and discipline-specific terms are not always found in general dictionaries. The information provided in subject-specific dictionaries is typically more detailed and similar to that found in an encyclopedia. Subject-specific dictionaries often include illustrations and other reference information. Examples of subject-specific dictionaries include medical dictionaries, computer user or technical dictionaries, electronic dictionaries, slang dictionaries, and so forth. There are numerous subject-specific dictionaries available.

A thesaurus is a book of synonyms. It can also include antonyms (opposite words) and phrases or slang terms for words. As with subject-specific dictionaries, specialized thesauruses can include specialized expressions for a particular field such as medicine or computer science.

Encyclopedias, Almanacs, Handbooks, and Atlases

An encyclopedia is a collection of detailed articles on a wide range of subjects. Encyclopedias can be either general (e.g., *World Book Encyclopedia*) or subject specific (e.g., *Encyclopedia of Psychology*), just as with dictionaries and thesauruses. Subject-specific encyclopedias contain more detailed articles related to specific fields and are written by experts in that field.

An almanac provides up-to-date figures, charts, tables, statistics, and other information. Almanac producers usually publish a revised edition each year. Almanacs can be found for almost any subject (i.e., sports, countries, history, religion, etc.) and are excellent sources for current facts and statistics.

A handbook provides very concise data, usually in table or chart form, on specialized subject areas (e.g., electronics, human resources,

7

adverse drug interactions, etc.). A handbook is an excellent reference for current statistics, procedures, instructions, or specific reference information on specific topics.

An atlas is generally thought of as a collection of maps; however, atlases can also be a collection of other visual information, such as those used in the study of anatomy. They can also provide a wealth of supplemental information in text, charts, or tables related to the illustrations. As with other reference tools, atlases can be very subject specific, as in historical atlases, anatomical atlases, or political atlases.

Periodicals

A periodical is a collection of articles and other information published at regular intervals such as daily, weekly, monthly, or bimonthly. The focus of each periodical is very specific to a topic area, location, viewpoint, or treatment of the material. Newspapers, popular magazines, trade journals, and scholarly journals are examples of periodicals. Information-literate individuals understand the different purposes of each type of periodical and the kinds of information each provides.

Newspapers are periodicals that provide very current information, including news, stories, and commentaries. Most newspapers concentrate on a specific geographic area. Although most journalists and editors take care to present accurate information, newspapers can be biased toward a specific viewpoint and can include information that is skewed according to a particular perspective. In the 21st century, newspapers are becoming less widely used, in favor of Web-based sources, RSS feeds, and other electronic formats.

Popular magazines, scholarly journals, and trade journals are periodicals that are often confused. Popular magazines (e.g., *Time*, *Glamour*, *Business Week*) are written for the general public and typically have shorter articles written by journalists. The articles are not usually evaluated by experts in the field, and they typically do not include a reference list (a listing of the sources of information) so that readers can check the facts themselves. Popular magazines are filled with advertising, can be biased toward a specific viewpoint, and can contain inaccuracies.

On the other hand, scholarly journals are periodicals written for very specific audiences and typically include longer articles written by subject matter experts using the jargon or specialized terminology of a certain field. Scholarly journals (e.g., *Journal of the American Medical Association*) commonly use a very structured format for their articles, which typically include an abstract (concise overview), introduction, literature review of background information, methodology, results, conclusion, and bibliography. Articles in scholarly journals are generally critically evaluated by experts from the field to ensure that the facts, statements, and conclusions are as accurate as possible. When experts evaluate the articles in a journal, it is called a *refereed* or *peer-reviewed* journal. Scholarly journals have minimal advertising, strive to be nonbiased, and take many steps to ensure the accuracy of information. Scholarly journals report original research and describe research programs, procedures, theories, and concepts.

Trade journals are periodicals that lie somewhere in between popular magazines and scholarly journals in terms of types of articles, authorship, and steps taken to avoid bias and ensure accuracy. Trade journals (e.g., *Pharmaceutical Processing* magazine or *Occupational Therapy Practice*) are written especially for industry professionals in a very specific field. They provide product information and articles on current trends and practices. Trade journals contain advertising very specific to the journal's audience. Though care is taken to avoid bias and to ensure accuracy, these journals are often not as strict as refereed journals.

Databases and Directories

A database is a collection of data organized so that a user can easily access the information. Many different databases are accessible from libraries and from the Internet. Examples include indexes, catalogs, and other kinds of databases in both print and electronic formats. Databases help researchers find additional sources of information.

A directory is similar to a database except that the data are typically an organized listing of information such as names, addresses, phone numbers, members, associations, and so forth, arranged

apply it

Find printable activities on the companion web site for this book, accessed through www.cengagebrain.com.

Journal Analysis

GOAL: To help develop an understanding of the differences between scholarly journals and popular magazines

STEP 1: Find a refereed journal for an area in your field of study. Go to the journal's web site and read the author guidelines.

STEP 2: In the same journal, find a research article of interest and read the article.

STEP 3: In groups of four or five students, compare the article with the author guidelines. How closely do you think the author met the guidelines? Is there anything you especially liked about the article? Is there anything you found to be confusing, invalid, ambiguous, or otherwise problematic? Write a brief analysis.

STEP 4: Answer the following questions about the articles this journal will accept: Is there more than one kind of article that the journal will accept? Is there a length maximum and/or minimum requirement? By whom will the article be reviewed?

STEP 5: Now use a periodical index to find an article in a popular magazine.

STEP 6: Answer the following questions: How is the format of the magazine article different from that of the journal article? Do the magazine articles appear to follow a similar structured format like those in the journal? Can you find author guidelines for this magazine? What other differences are there between the two types of periodicals?

STEP 7: Consider putting this Journal Analysis project in your Learning Portfolio.

7

alphabetically or by category. Directories are available in both print and electronic formats.

Librarians have access to literally hundreds of databases and directories for all kinds of information. Electronic formats allow convenient searching of the resource, using techniques that narrow the focus of the search to pinpoint the exact data needed. Information-literate individuals have developed skill in using these resources to find information.

Multimedia

Information can be in a form other than print or electronic. Many libraries house or have access to a variety of graphic, audio, video, and film media sources of information that researchers may find useful. Examples include maps, microforms, videotapes, CD-ROMs, DVDs, 16-mm films, audiotapes, and so forth. Each library or library system has access to different media or can often borrow a desired media resource from another library using the interlibrary loan system.

CASE IN POINT: UP TO THE MINUTE

Read the scenario below. Then, in groups or as a class, discuss the questions at the end.

Anita Franklin recently graduated with an Associate degree in network administration. She was quickly hired as an assistant network administrator for a medium-size company and has the responsibility for maintaining about 25 computers networked to a main server, as well as several laptop computers used by mobile employees in the field. Tasks in her job description include answering computer user questions and solving computer problems for the company's employees; keeping software and security tools current on employee machines; and researching and providing input into the purchase of new technology tools, including those for general business tasks, for communication, and for meeting the needs of specialized departments. When new tools are acquired

continued

7

continued

and implemented, Anita also must help teach employees how to use the tools accurately and efficiently.

▶ Think forward to the job position you are seeking as a result of your academic training. How do Anita's challenges relate to what you foresee in your own career?

▶ What information challenges do you think Anita is faced with on a daily basis?

▶ Compared to what Anita learned in school, what information do you think has changed since graduation or will be changing soon?

▶ What knowledge and skills do you think Anita must continue to acquire in order to advance in her job and career? Where might Anita get this information?

▶ How will Anita know she has the most accurate and up-to-date information possible?

WORKING WITH YOUR LIBRARIAN

One of the greatest resources available to students during their academic career is the school librarian. Librarians offer a wealth of expertise on finding and evaluating information in a digital environment that even the information-literate student may never acquire. The information-literate learner recognizes that leveraging this additional expertise will aid in success in both the classroom and the workplace.

apply it

Find printable activities on the companion web site for this book, accessed through www.cengagebrain.com.

Resource Listing

GOAL: To develop an organized list of resources that will be useful for work and career research activities

STEP 1: Define each of the following library resources and briefly explain its purpose: dictionaries (general and subject specific), encyclopedias (general and subject specific), directories, newspapers, popular magazines, scholarly and trade journals, periodical indexes, professional or trade organizations, search engines, online libraries, and web portals.

STEP 2: Then give at least two examples of specific resources under each category that apply to your field of study. Include both physical library and online versions of the resources.

STEP 3: Consider using this list as a starting point for the Resource List in your Learning Portfolio.

CHAPTER SUMMARY

Chapter 7 emphasized the importance of information literacy and its role in learning and professional development in the 21st century. Concepts and guidelines regarding plagiarism were reviewed and you were reminded to apply them to your research. You learned how to evaluate the credibility of electronic resources. Online reference tools were also reviewed, with an emphasis on using search engines, databases, and other electronic resources. Finally, you were introduced to a variety of information sources, including those in libraries and on the Internet.

The ability to use information wisely is critical to your learning and success in school as well as in the workplace. Concepts of information and digital literacy can also be applied to your personal concerns and development, such as financial planning and developing other areas of personal interest.

POINTS TO KEEP IN MIND

In this chapter, a number of main points were discussed in detail:

◗ Information literacy means being competent in locating, using, and evaluating information efficiently and effectively.

▶ Information literacy is essential for school and ultimately workplace success.

▶ Information-literate individuals are able to locate and use many different resources, including general and subject-specific dictionaries, thesauruses, encyclopedias, almanacs, handbooks, atlases, directories, databases, periodicals, and multimedia materials.

▶ Digital literacy is an increasingly important component of information literacy in how information is accessed and used.

▶ Information-literate individuals are aware of and know how to find other sources of information on the Internet such as web portals, professional and trade organizations, and multimedia.

▶ Information-literate individuals understand the basic legalities of copyright and appropriate citation methods, as well as other strategies to avoid plagiarism.

▶ Information-literate individuals understand basic search strategies to answer school and workplace problems.

▶ Information-literate individuals know how to evaluate the credibility of information they find on the Internet and understand the importance of doing so.

CHECK YOUR UNDERSTANDING

Visit www.cengagebrain.com to see how well you have mastered the material in Chapter 7.

SUGGESTED ITEMS FOR LEARNING PORTFOLIO

▶ Resource List

▶ Journal Analysis

▶ Web Site Evaluation Checklist

REFERENCES

American Library Association Digital Literacy Task Force (2013). *Digital literacy, libraries, and public policy.* Retrieved February 5, 2013, from http://www.districtdispatch.org/wp-content/uploads/2013/01/2012 _OITP_digilitreport_1_22_13.pdf

Jones, B. and Flannigan, S. (n.d.). *Connecting the digital dots: literacy of the 21st century.* Retrieved February 6, 2013, from http://www.nmc .org/pdf/Connecting%20the%20Digital%20Dots.pdf

Webber, S. (2010, May 25–27). *Information literacy for the 21st century.* Paper presented at INFORUM 2010: 16th Conference on Professional Information Resources. Retrieved February 4, 2013, from http://www .inforum.cz/pdf/2010/webber-sheila-1.pdf

7

Legal and Ethical Issues in the Academic Environment

LEARNING OBJECTIVES

By the end of this chapter, you will achieve the following objectives:

▶ Define academic dishonesty.

▶ Define harassment, sexual harassment, and discrimination.

▶ List and discuss the various laws that prohibit discrimination.

▶ Provide examples of legal and ethical issues affecting college students.

▶ Explain the purpose of the Americans with Disabilities Act (ADA) and discuss how this act protects students.

▶ Explain the differences among the Rehabilitation Act of 1973, the Individuals with Disabilities Education Act, and the ADA.

▶ Discuss the obligations that institutions have toward students with disabilities.

▶ Describe the steps involved in reporting sexual harassment.

▶ Discuss ways to avoid the pressure to cheat.

▶ Explain the purpose of the Family Educational Rights and Privacy Act (FERPA).

▶ Demonstrate the ability to effectively resolve a conflict.

BE IN THE KNOW

Be Right about Copyright

Plagiarism was briefly discussed in Chapter 7, and you will learn much more about it in this chapter. Closely aligned with plagiarism is the topic of "copyright," which is the legal right of ownership to a work.

Copyright reflects the rights given to creators of some forms of expressions of intellectual property, such as literary and artistic works. Copyrights are protected by copyright laws. Ideas are not copyrighted; only the expression of those ideas in some documented format can be copyrighted. Ideas in the form of procedures, methods, facts, techniques, styles, and mathematical concepts cannot be copyrighted. The following are examples of expressions covered by copyright law:

• novels	• films
• poems	• paintings
• plays	• drawings
• reference works	• photographs
• articles in periodicals	• sculptures
• computer programs	• architecture
• databases	• advertisements
• musical compositions	• maps
• choreography	• technical drawings
• applets	• songs
• web pages	• images

The goal of a copyright is to protect the original creators of the work (and their heirs). Copyright assures that the original creator of the work can do with the work whatever he or she wants. The original creators have the right to authorize someone else to use the work, prohibit others from using their work, or sell their copyright to someone else. This means that they can give up their rights (usually for a negotiated fee) to someone else, who then becomes the copyright owner. This new owner becomes protected by copyright law, as was the original owner.

8

Copyright law regulates more than just "copying" the work. It also controls translating the material into another language, performing the material (as in a play), copying electronic versions of a work (as in music or movie CD or DVD), and broadcasting it (on radio, TV, or over the Internet). In short, copyright covers reproducing a work in any way.

As you write papers or complete projects while in school, be sure that, in addition to understanding and adhering to the rules of plagiarism, you also abide by copyright laws. Ask your professor or your librarian for guidance if you are unsure if you are breaking copyright law.

Copyright © Cengage Learning®.

LEGAL AND ETHICAL ISSUES: OVERVIEW

It is the responsibility of every college student to know the policies and procedures established by the college he or she is attending. Students can usually find policies and regulations they should be aware of online at the school's student portal, in the college catalog, or in the student handbook. Specific information regarding the history of the college, its mission statement, and its accreditations and affiliations is also found in the college catalog, as is more general information, such as descriptions of school programs, admission requirements, and available financial aid programs. Students must take responsibility to read and be aware of what is required of and available to them at the college they will be or are attending. "I didn't know" or "No one told me" is not an acceptable excuse for being unaware of expectations and resources.

Students should also be familiar with a variety of legal matters pertaining to the academic environment so as to be better protected, more likely to avoid problems, and in order to know the steps to take if a problem occurs. Legal standards having an impact on the academic environment include those that affect policy dealing with sexual harassment, disability, and other types of discrimination.

Some issues in the academic environment are considered to be of both a legal and an ethical nature, for example, confidentiality is an issue that can be viewed from both legal and ethical perspectives. Depending

Guy Cali/Corbis.

Understanding legal issues that affect you as a student can help you avoid difficulties as well as help you understand what steps to take should legal questions arise.

8

apply it

Find printable activities on the companion web site for this book, accessed through www.cengagebrain.com.

Ethical Issue Research

GOAL: To develop a deeper appreciation regarding the ethical issues that students face in the college environment.

STEP 1: Select one of the references listed in this chapter or find another article or book that discusses various ethical issues that are faced in the college environment.

STEP 2: Write a brief report on what the article or book teaches you.

STEP 3: Prepare a presentation to the class using presentation tools such as PowerPoint.

SELF-ASSESSMENT QUESTION

- Have you ever engaged in any behaviors that were legally or ethically questionable? If so, how did you resolve them?

CRITICAL THINKING QUESTION

▶ Have you familiarized yourself with your school's policies and requirements?

8

on the situation, it may not be illegal to share information with another person, but such a breach may be considered ethically wrong.

In addition to legal issues, ethical principles must guide behavior in the college environment. Cheating and plagiarizing are actions that have serious ethical (and possibly legal) implications. It is important not only to understand the seriousness of academic dishonesty but also to be aware of its consequences.

This chapter will focus on the legal and ethical issues affecting the college environment, how to avoid potential problems, how to document concerns, how and when to report a complaint, and how to effectively address and hopefully resolve the conflict.

LEGAL ISSUES: HARASSMENT AND DISCRIMINATION

There are a variety of legal issues with which students should be familiar. This chapter will focus on legal issues such as sexual harassment and other types of discrimination that can occur on college campuses. In addition to the laws established to protect individuals encountering these issues, schools usually have written policies and procedures to address these situations. Refer to your college handbook, web site, and catalog for information on the policies and procedures specific to your school.

Discrimination is defined in civil rights laws as unfavorable or unfair treatment of a person or class of persons in comparison to others who are not members of the protected class, based on race, sex, color, religion, national origin, age, physical/mental disability, or sexual orientation.

The Office for Civil Rights (OCR) in the U.S. Department of Education is charged with enforcing the federal civil rights laws that prohibit discrimination. Several laws exist to prohibit discrimination, including these:

▶ Title VI of the Civil Rights Act of 1964, which prohibits discrimination due to race, color, or national origin.

▶ Title IX of the Education Amendments of 1972, which prohibits sex discrimination.

▶ Section 504 of the Rehabilitation Act of 1973, which prohibits discrimination based on an individual's disability.

▶ The Age Discrimination Act of 1975, which prohibits discrimination on the basis of age at any institution receiving federal funding.

▶ Title II of the Americans with Disabilities Act of 1990, which prohibits disability discrimination by public entities, including educational institutions, and provides for accommodations to be made to facilitate the functioning of people with disabilities (U.S. Department of Education, Office for Civil Rights, 2010).

Figure 8-1 summarizes the civil rights laws.

Discrimination can occur in a variety of situations. In 2006, enforcement officers of the OCR received 5,141 discrimination complaints. The OCR (2007) breaks down the complaints as follows:

▶ 52% disability

▶ 17% race/national origin

▶ 13% multiple

▶ 6% sex

▶ 11% other

▶ 1% age

SUMMARY OF MAJOR CIVIL RIGHTS LAWS

Law	Provisions
Title VI of the Civil Rights Act of 1964	Prohibits discrimination due to race, color, and national origin
Title IX of the Education Amendments of 1972	Prohibits sex discrimination
Section 504 of the Rehabilitation Act of 1973	Prohibits discrimination based on an individual's disability
The Age Discrimination Act of 1975	Prohibits discrimination on the basis of age at any institution receiving federal funding
Title II of the Americans with Disabilities Act of 1990	Prohibits disability discrimination by public entities, including educational institutions

Figure 8-1   Understanding civil rights laws will help you understand your rights as well as respect those of others. For more detailed information regarding individual laws, conduct Internet research using the name of the law as your search term.

Adapted from U.S. Department of Education, Office for Civil Rights (2011).

As the statistics indicate, discrimination can occur for a variety of reasons. Any individual can be the target of discrimination. As a student, it is important to be aware of discrimination and know how to effectively address the situation. Discrimination can occur secondarily to several circumstances common in education environments. Discipline practices, academic grading practices, treatment of pregnant students, admissions practices, and treatment of students with disabilities can all result in students being treated differently in various situations, increasing the possibility of discrimination.

It is important to be informed and knowledgeable about your responsibilities and the college's responsibilities related to discrimination.

SEXUAL HARASSMENT

Awareness of sexual harassment issues on college campuses has increased. In order to address sexual harassment issues, colleges have worked toward clearly defining what constitutes sexual harassment and creating policies related to these issues.

Harassment of any kind should not be tolerated. There are a variety of types of harassment that can occur on a college campus. All types result in an environment that is negative, creates hostility, and undermines productivity.

Sexual harassment occurs when unwelcome attention of a sexual nature occurs between individuals. Sexual harassment may involve two students or can involve an instructor and a student. Society generally thinks of sexual harassment as a male harassing a female. Although this may be the more typical type of harassment, harassment can also involve a female harassing a male, a female harassing a female, or a male harassing a male. In addition, sexual harassment can take several forms:

▶ **Verbal.** Making comments that reflect evaluation and ranking of sexual attributes, inquiring about or suggesting sexual activity, or making unwanted or derogatory comments fall into the category of sexual harassment. Threats or demands to engage in sexual activity to achieve a benefit, obtain or keep a job, or achieve academically are also sexual harassment.

▶ **Visual.** Cartoons, posters, and other visual representations of material of a sexual nature fall into the category of sexual harassment.

▶ **Electronic.** Sexual harassment includes derogatory comments of a sexual nature sent via voice mail, e-mail, telephone, text message, or posted online, such as on a social networking site.

▶ **Physical.** Inappropriate physical contact of a sexual nature as well as assault constitute sexual harassment.

▶ **Retaliatory.** Actions in retaliation for having reported harassment fall under the same guidelines as sexual harassment.

If you believe that you have been the target of harassment, it may be helpful to seek the advice and support of a trusted instructor or administrator.

At times sexual harassment can occur unintentionally. For example, an individual may make a lewd comment and later realize the inappropriateness of having done so. Due to the harmful effects that sexual harassment can have on individuals, it is critical to be consciously aware of an event or action that may be construed as harassment. If you make a comment that in retrospect seems inappropriate, follow up with the person to ensure that no offense was taken and to rectify any misunderstandings.

Title IX regulations require that all educational institutions that receive federal financial assistance publish and provide a nondiscrimination policy, have a published grievance procedure for dealing with sexual harassment complaints, and designate an individual to oversee Title IX activities and process grievances. The individual designated to coordinate Title IX activities at your school can provide guidelines

8

- Know the individual on your campus who oversees Title IX requirements and activities.
- Document (a) what happened in as much detail as possible, (b) the location of the incident, (c) the date and time, and (d) any witnesses.
- Report the incident to your school official immediately.
- Follow the steps that are recommended by your school's Title IX official.

SELF-ASSESSMENT QUESTIONS

- Have you ever felt sexually harassed? If so, what was the outcome?
- Can you recall ever sexually harassing somebody unintentionally? Did you take any action to correct your behavior? If not, why? If so, how?

? CRITICAL THINKING QUESTION

▶ Are there any personal steps that you can take to lessen the chance of sexual harassment?

8

Patrick Clark/Photodisc/Getty Images.

Equal opportunity and accessibility of campus facilities to students with disabilities is required by federal laws.

for documenting grievances. In general, documentation should be thorough and clear and include information such as the date, time, and location of the incident, and any witnesses.

During any phase of a discrimination incident or its reporting, the student who has experienced the harassment should feel free to ask for help or advice from trusted school advisors, faculty, or other administrative personnel.

DISCRIMINATION AND DISABILITY

The Americans with Disabilities Act (ADA) defines a person with a disability as someone who

▶ has a physical or mental impairment that substantially limits one or more major life activities including walking, seeing, hearing, speaking, breathing, learning, and working.

▶ has a record of such an impairment.

▶ is regarded as having such an impairment.

Since schools receive federal funding, they are required to comply with the ADA. General requirements for complying with the ADA state that

▶ A student with a disability must disclose the disability to the appropriate school personnel and request accommodations.

▶ Accommodations are not retroactive. In other words, accommodations must be provided from the point of disclosure and documentation, but cannot be applied to previous situations.

CASE IN POINT: UP TO THE CHALLENGE

Read the scenario below. Then, in groups or as a class, discuss the questions at the end.

Finishing college was always Susan McPhee's dream. When she walked across the stage to accept her diploma, all she felt was joy and excitement. She had accomplished her life's dream of having a college education. School had not always been easy, and Susan had to overcome many challenges, but in the end she had prevailed. Susan was the first one in her family to obtain a college degree and, consequently, her feelings of pride were even greater. At her first job after college, Susan has excelled. She is respected by her professional colleagues and is frequently asked to take leadership roles in projects. She is currently exploring the role of entrepreneur and becoming the owner of her own business. What makes Susan's story quite unique is that Susan was born blind and as a young girl had been in an accident in which both of her arms were severed.

▌ Over what unique challenges does Susan have to prevail? (In addition to the obvious physical challenges, consider the social and emotional aspects of her situation.)

▌ What characteristics does Susan need in order to overcome the challenges facing her?

▌ What laws supported Susan in her effort to complete her education? What laws support her now that she is in the workplace? What recourse does Susan have under these laws in the event of discrimination based on her disability?

▌ How does the ability to resolve conflict play into Susan's self-advocacy?

8

For example, if a student realizes he is failing his classes due to learning differences and discloses the same half way through the semester, any accommodations can only apply to the second half of the semester. The student cannot "go back" and retake exams that have already been taken.

▌ The school is required to make accommodations that allow a student to participate in academic and extracurricular programs and activities and complete course requirements. Examples of accommodations include course substitutions, adjustments to academic activities such as note taking (for example, having a note taker for a student who cannot write) and test taking (for example, extra time to complete an exam). Accommodations are specific to the student and will vary according to the needs of the student and the school's situation.*

If a student believes that discrimination has occurred, communication with school officials is critical to resolving the issue. Some colleges establish a student legal department to assist students in areas dealing with civil law questions or problems. Many schools also have a department or office, such as Student Services or Student Affairs, that is specifically designated to support students with disabilities and to address any related issues. Check to determine the appropriate office at your school. If a resolution with school officials is not possible, it may be necessary to contact the Office for Civil Rights for further assistance.

CONFIDENTIAL INFORMATION

Confidentiality can be both an ethical and a legal issue. Confidentiality must be a primary consideration during verbal communication. Damage that can occur from disclosing information of a confidential nature may be permanent, even though the sharing of information may not have been illegal. Trust is an important component of relationships among students, their teachers, and administrators. If there is reason to believe that confidentiality has been breached, you should raise the issue with the individual involved.

The Family Educational Rights and Privacy Act (FERPA) defines specific guidelines for access to and confidentiality regarding your school records (U.S. Department of Education, 2012). Laws regarding confidentiality issues in the academic setting deal specifically with the student record. Legal information contained in student education records is protected by FERPA. According to FERPA, students over the age of 18 have the right to

▶ inspect and review their education records

▶ request that the school correct inaccurate or misleading information that is found in the student record

If the school decides not to change the record, then the student has a right to a formal hearing. If this hearing does not lead to the

*United States Department of Justice, 2009.

school amending the record, the student has the right to place a statement in the record indicating his or her viewpoint on the information that is being contested.

FERPA gives schools the right to

▶ charge a fee for a copy of student records.

▶ refuse to provide copies to parents and students unless distance is an issue.

▶ disclose "directory" information without consent. This information includes the student's name, address, telephone number, date and place of birth, honors and awards, and dates of attendance. Schools must inform students of the request for directory information within a timeframe that is reasonable, so that the student has a chance to request that the information not be disclosed.

Generally, schools are required to obtain written permission in order to release information from a student's record. FERPA does allow for some instances where permission need not be obtained. The courts may allow advisors, faculty, and administrators to share information on students if there is a "legitimate need to know" as specified by FERPA. Schools are also required to inform students on an annual basis of their rights under FERPA.

apply it

Find printable activities on the companion web site for this book, accessed through www.cengagebrain.com.

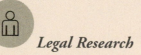

Legal Research

GOAL: To develop a deeper understanding regarding the legal issues that affect college students.

STEP 1: From the various laws discussed in this chapter, select one law to research further.

STEP 2: Read everything about the selected law and then write a report to present to the class. Include in the report what was learned regarding the effects of the law for both the school and the student.

STEP 3: Consider placing this Legal Research activity in your Learning Portfolio.

8

ETHICAL ISSUES: ACADEMIC HONESTY

Acting honorably and with integrity are significant universal values. People generally expect and respect truthful and honest interactions and behavior. It is important for students to demonstrate these qualities in all academic activities. The importance of honesty and integrity in both school and the workplace cannot be overstated. Academic dishonesty occurs when a student cheats or engages in plagiarism.

CHEATING

Cheating involves obtaining and/or providing information by deceitful means. Examples of cheating based on those listed in a college honor code (Foothill College, n.d.) include the following behaviors:

▶ Copying part or all of another student's test answers or assignment.

▶ Handing in another student's previously completed work as your own.

▶ Resubmitting work that you have written, but used previously in another course. (This is acceptable if doing so is part of the assignment from either course and is stated as such.)

▶ Altering grades in hard copy or electronically.

▶ Using unauthorized equipment such as calculators or other aids during an exam.

▶ Seeking information electronically, such as by cell phone or e-mail during an exam.

▶ Obtaining test material by stealing, electronic pirating, or other methods.

The act of cheating and plagiarizing is harmful to both the college and the student body. Cheating is hurtful in many ways to both the honest and the dishonest student. Honest students become frustrated with the fact that cheating is unfair. The student who cheats fails to learn information that he or she will need in subsequent courses and in the workplace. Once caught engaging in unethical behavior, it is probable that the student will have difficulty regaining the trust and

8

respect of instructors and classmates. Dishonest behavior typically has a serious impact on one's reputation and the consequences may follow an individual indefinitely. For example, the student caught cheating may have a difficult time obtaining recommendations from instructors when the student's job search begins.

Cheating at times goes undetected. In some instances the cheating results in an undeserved grade. If a grading curve is being used in the class, grades received by cheating students can skew the curve, ultimately affecting grades earned by honest students. Students who cheat do not benefit from the education that they are paying for and are jeopardizing their future employment successes because they lack the knowledge needed to perform tasks required by employers. Employers expecting qualified graduates are robbed by cheating students, as is the reputation of the college and future graduates.

Consequences of cheating can include:

▶ Receiving an "F" for the work

▶ Receiving a lower course grade or an "F"

▶ Failing a class that is required for graduation

▶ Being suspended or dismissed from school

▶ Damaging your reputation with other classmates, instructors, and family members

As a college student, it is important to appreciate the importance of maintaining your personal integrity and to understand the consequences of your actions and how they affect others. Students who uphold academic integrity will more likely follow the standards and ethics that are required later in their professions. For some students, the pressure to cheat at some point in the college experience may be high. If you experience this temptation, rather than cheat, stop to determine why the pressure to act dishonestly exists. Instead of cheating, try implementing one of

Academic honesty is an important value critical to the development of sound business ethics.

© wavebreakmedia/Shutterstock.com.

8

the following strategies based on those provided by the Student Services Department at College of the Canyons (2001–2013).

▶ **Use time management techniques.** Develop study habits that give you ample time to learn course material.

▶ **Develop your classroom and study skills.** Develop your listening, note-taking, and reading skills. Compare your notes with classmates' and determine what you missed and how you might improve. If in doubt, ask the instructor. Develop a study area that is conducive to studying and that supports your efforts. Clarify information with the instructor as needed. Understand your learning style in order to increase the effectiveness of your studying; use a study method that best supports your style.

▶ **Anticipate.** Consider the type of test you will have and prepare accordingly. For example, you may prepare one way for a multiple choice exam (recall of facts) and use different strategies for an essay exam (drawing conclusions from facts and synthesizing a cogent response). Write your own questions based on what you think the instructor might ask.

▶ **Seek assistance when needed.** If information is difficult or unclear, ask questions of the instructor. Use the learning resource center on campus or obtain a tutor. Get assistance promptly to avoid feeling overwhelmed.

▶ **Individualize your learning.** Recognize your individual learning needs and seek additional activities that will support you in the learning process.

▶ **Come prepared.** Make sure you have all the necessary—and permissible—items for the test. Feeling prepared and settled can reduce anxiety and diminish the feeling that one needs to cheat.

▶ **Sit away from distractions.** Avoid being seated by friends during the exam. Not only will you minimize distractions, you will be less likely to give the impression that you "collaborated" with people that you know.

▶ **Maintain your integrity.** Refuse to be a part of dishonest actions.

8

success steps for avoiding the temptation to cheat

- Use time management techniques.
- Develop your classroom and study skills.
- Anticipate.
- Seek assistance when needed.
- Individualize your learning.
- Come prepared.
- Sit away from distractions.
- Maintain your integrity.

PLAGIARISM

Using someone else's original work without acknowledging the original creator is termed plagiarism. The work can be an idea, actual language, or some other original material. Plagiarism is a growing problem in educational and professional settings, and information-literate individuals take care to avoid this unethical and illegal practice.

Examples of plagiarism are

▶ copying another person's work and submitting it as your own.

▶ presenting work completed by someone else as your own.

▶ taking an idea from someone else and submitting it as your own.

▶ copying text into an original document without indicating the text with quotation marks or correctly acknowledging the original creator of the work.

▶ paraphrasing someone else's work too closely and submitting it as your own.

▶ writing down words spoken by someone else in a face-to-face or telephone discussion and submitting them as your own without acknowledging the original source.

8

▶ copying diagrams, photographs, images, charts, tables, clip art, and similar items as your own without obtaining permission and giving proper credit.

▶ reusing any media that is in electronic form, such as audio files, video files, applets, and software programs, without obtaining permission and giving proper credit to the original creator.

▶ buying, finding, or receiving a paper and turning it in as your own work.

▶ using a web site or information from the Internet without properly acknowledging its source.

The last point—using a web site or Internet information without proper acknowledgment—raises various issues. Many students today, because of the anonymity of the Internet and World Wide Web, fail to recognize that the information on web sites was created by an individual (Howard, 2010). In other words, there is an author, and the work, as that person's property, is subject to the same rules as other material. Material obtained online must be referenced just as any other source.

Regardless of the type of material, if the work of others is presented without giving them proper credit or citing the source of the work properly, this constitutes plagiarism. (For examples of plagiarized work, visit www.cengagebrain.com.)

You do not have to document anything that is your original creation or idea. Examples of things you do not have to document are

▶ your own experiences, observations, insights, thoughts, and conclusions.

▶ your own results from personal observation of an experiment or study.

▶ your own artistic or literary creations such as prose, poems, diagrams, artwork, audio recordings, video recordings, and photographs.

▶ facts that are generally accepted as being true.

▶ common knowledge or observations considered to be common sense.

▶ historical events, myths, and legends.

STRATEGIES TO AVOID PLAGIARISM

To avoid plagiarizing someone else's information, several strategies are outlined as follows:

▶ *Quote.* Using another's exact words is acceptable, but you must copy the exact words, use quotation marks around the quoted words, and cite the source properly. Quotation marks should be used whether the copied words are spoken or written. When adding your own words to quoted text, you must put your words in brackets to distinguish them from the quoted material. Adding your own words is necessary sometimes to put the quote in context or to fill in missing words so the entire message can be understood more easily.

▶ *Paraphrase.* Paraphrasing means rephrasing the words of someone else. It is acceptable as long as the meaning is not changed and the originator is credited properly with a citation. The paraphrase must be accurate, and the source properly cited. Paraphrasing involves more than rearranging the order of words or changing minor elements of a passage. Read the original material and, without looking at it, rewrite the content using your own words. If you have to intersperse exact phrases from the original, place these words within quotation marks. The paraphrase is followed by a statement giving credit to the original author. An example of a paraphrase is:

> According to Smith, when children eat too much sugar, they display abnormal behavior for several minutes and then show significant signs of fatigue and irritation.

▶ *Summarize.* Summarizing requires condensing a significant amount of someone else's work into a shorter statement or paragraph. As is the case with paraphrasing, this is acceptable as long as the meaning is not changed and the originator is given proper credit with a citation. To accomplish this, read the original information and then try to condense the content without looking. If you have used any exact text, place it within quotation marks. Also, place quotation marks around any special words taken from the original text.

▶ *Take effective notes.* To reduce the likelihood of plagiarism, it is a good idea to take careful notes so you can remember exactly which ideas are yours and which are someone else's ideas. One way to keep track is to develop a note-taking strategy that includes a notation or symbol for your idea (such as *MINE*) and a notation or symbol for the ideas of the author of the work (such as *AU*). Put all direct quotes in quotation marks. When you take notes, designate *AU* next to facts, quotes (with quotation marks), paraphrased sentences, and summaries of the author's work. When you write down your own insights and thoughts, use *MINE* (or whatever designation you choose). And be sure to clearly label the source of the information on each page of your notes.

▶ *Save your work.* You can take several measures to maintain the security of your own work. To prevent others from plagiarizing your work, keep copies of your draft work in separate files. For example, rather than revising your original file, save the first draft as draft 1, your second draft as draft 2, and so forth. This will be a reminder that you actually did the work yourself. Save copies of your files in separate places, and make at least one hard copy of your work. Do not allow others to access your computer files.

You can protect your computer and original work by saving documents as protected files that require a password for access. Use the search feature on the "Help" menu to learn the steps for creating a password to protect your documents, using your particular software. There is an option to password-protect the document. Of course, you will have to remember the password so you can open your file. This procedure works in most Microsoft Office applications. Other applications have similar features.

▶ *Use plagiarism detection software.* The advent of the Internet has made plagiarism easier than ever. Cyber-plagiarism, as it is known, has seen a dramatic rise in recent years, especially by students and content writers (bloggers, writers, and other professionals). Schools, colleges, and universities now routinely check for plagiarism using plagiarism detection software, such as Turnitin. In addition, content plagiarized from web sites usually can be identified easily by performing a search using the first line of the material as the search term, which pulls up the document for review. You can avoid a costly mistake by downloading free software that will detect any plagiarism in your work. An information-literate person knows that unintentional plagiarism is still plagiarism.

▶ *Manage your time.* Plan your studying and assignments so that you have time to plan, research, and write your work effectively. Leave time to read and write with careful attention to citing sources and representing other authors' works in an acceptable manner.

▶ *Read and rewrite.* An effective way to avoid plagiarizing is to read the original source, put it away, and complete your writing based on your reading. When your writing is complete, return to the original work and check your facts for accuracy. Cite references appropriately.

▶ *Apply the information.* Discuss the information you are using in the context of your assignment. Expand on ideas. Apply the information in a unique way to the topic at hand. Refer to the original thought or fact, but apply it creatively to your project using your own original ideas.

▶ *Cite your sources appropriately.* Sources should be referenced in the text as well as in the reference list. There are several acceptable styles of source citation and reference, and you should follow the style prescribed by your instructor.

8

success steps for avoiding plagiarism

- Use quotation marks properly.
- Paraphrase.
- Summarize.
- Take effective notes.

continued

continued

- Save your work.
- Use plagiarism detection software.
- Manage your time.
- Read and rewrite.
- Apply the information.
- Cite your sources appropriately.

In addition to upholding your own responsibility for being honest, it is important to participate in helping to make your learning environment one of high integrity. Honest students need to report any possible cheating and plagiarism that may be occurring. Personally confronting a classmate may or may not be an option, but reporting the episode is critical so that the situation can be properly addressed.

apply it

Find printable activities on the companion web site for this book, accessed through www.cengagebrain.com.

Plagiarism Research

GOAL: To develop a better understanding of what plagiarism is and how to avoid it.

STEP 1: Using Internet or library sources, research more about what constitutes plagiarism and how you can avoid it as a student.

STEP 2: Write a short paper regarding your findings. Cite the material used in your research.

CONFLICT RESOLUTION

Conflict resolution is a useful skill for addressing a variety of the topics that have been covered in this chapter. Having to confront an individual who is making lewd comments, demonstrating discriminatory behavior, or asking to plagiarize your work can be quite challenging. Learning how to appropriately confront issues and resolve them effectively is a skill that can be utilized in both the academic and professional settings.

Learning to resolve conflicts calmly, respectfully, and logically with concern for everyone's welfare is an important professional skill.

Conflict is inevitable and will occur throughout life. For some, conflict resolution is a skill that develops naturally. For others, confronting an issue and resolving it can be difficult. Conflict resolution should be thought of as a series of positive steps taken toward understanding another individual and the situation at hand.

If conflict arises, consider the following steps:

Step 1. Don't simply react emotionally to the situation. Thoughtfully plan the best approach to the situation. Determine mutually what both parties hope to achieve by resolving the conflict.

Step 2. Approach the conflict with an attitude of trying to understand the other person, his or her perspective, and the situation.

Step 3. Assume that the person you are approaching has good intentions. Avoid jumping to conclusions. Ask questions to clarify the meaning of the person's words and his or her intentions.

Step 4. Use voice tones that are neither condoning nor condemning. Avoid raising your voice. Keep an open mind and be accepting of other ideas and perspectives.

Step 5. Be clear with the individual about your concerns. Share your thoughts as clearly and concisely as possible.

Step 6. Use "I" statements rather than "you" statements when expressing your thoughts. For example, state "I feel really upset" or "I am not sure I understand what to do." Pointing the finger by saying "you did this" and "you made me feel" may sound accusatory and is unlikely to facilitate effective communication.

Step 7. Find common ground on which you can agree.

Step 8. Accept that a difference of opinion can exist. Agree to disagree, but remain respectful of each other.

8

success steps for resolving conflict

- Remain objective and keep emotions under control.
- Try to understand the other person's perspective.
- Assume the other party has good intentions.
- Speak in a conversational tone of voice.
- State your concerns clearly and directly.
- Use "I" statements rather than "you" statements.
- Find common ground on which you both agree.
- Respect differences.
- If you are wrong, acknowledge it.
- Make necessary changes.

Step 9. If you are in the wrong, acknowledge this. Seek to implement changes that will be beneficial to all concerned.

Step 10. Make necessary changes. Learn from the conflict resolution process.

These steps can also be used when questioning a professor about grades. Often the conflict or misunderstanding about a grade or a situation in class can be resolved by using the steps as outlined. Depending on the situation, it may be hard to implement these steps. Although it may be difficult, approach the instructor first in an attempt to resolve the issue. If this is unsuccessful, then talking to a department chair, the assistant dean, or your advisor may be the next option. It is important to understand that instructors want to hear about students' concerns. Sometimes students are upset or unhappy, but the instructor is unaware of the situation. As much as possible, communicate directly with each instructor. Remember that approaching the individual with whom you have an issue is the preferred method of handling conflict before going to another party. Building relationships and trust is important. Remember too that simply because you state your stance appropriately, you may not get exactly what you want.

8

apply it

Find printable activities on the companion web site for this book, accessed through www.cengagebrain.com.

 Conflict Resolution

GOAL: To help develop skills in conflict resolution through role-playing.

Prior to this activity, the instructor should prepare a variety of scenarios in which conflict arises and resolution is achieved. Alternatively, pairs of students may write scenarios to be distributed to the class. Students may write a scenario that they personally experienced or describe a situation that they believe would be difficult for them to address.

STEP 1: Divide the class into the appropriate number of individuals for each scenario.

STEP 2: Hand out a scenario to each group. (If students have written the scenarios, they should not receive their own.)

STEP 3: Each group is to practice role-playing the scenario. Once the scenarios have been successfully acted out, have group members switch roles and replay the scenario.

STEP 4: Regroup as a class and discuss what students learned in the activity. What was difficult about resolving the conflict? What was learned through trying to resolve the conflict? What might have been improved during the conflict resolution?

CHAPTER SUMMARY

This chapter addressed issues related to legal and ethical concerns in the academic setting. You learned about various laws that affect you as a student, as well as your responsibilities for your conduct and honest behavior. Take notice of how methods of time management, note taking, and other techniques that have been discussed so far in *100% Student Success* can be used to contribute to other considerations such as academic honesty. In addition, topics such as understanding plagiarism will be critical to becoming information literate, as discussed in Chapter 7. The communication skills you learned in Chapter 5 will help you develop further conflict resolution skills.

POINTS TO KEEP IN MIND

In this chapter, a variety of main points were discussed in detail:

- Legal issues common in the academic environment include those dealing with sexual harassment and other various types of discrimination.
- Sexual harassment can be defined as unwanted attention of a sexual nature.
- Any type of harassment creates a hostile or intimidating environment.
- Title IX regulations require that all education institutions have a published grievance procedure that is adequate for dealing with sexual harassment complaints.
- Discrimination is defined in civil rights laws as unfavorable or unfair treatment of a person or class of persons in comparison to others who are not members of the protected class because of race, sex, color, religion, national origin, age, physical/mental disability, and sexual orientation.
- Title IX of the Education Amendments of 1972 prohibits sex discrimination.
- Section 504 of the Rehabilitation Act of 1973 prohibits discrimination based on an individual's disability.
- Title II of the Americans with Disabilities Act of 1990 prohibits disability discrimination by public entities, including educational institutions.
- Legal information contained in student education records is protected by the Family Educational Rights and Privacy Act (FERPA).
- Generally, schools are required to obtain written permission in order to release information from a student's education record.

8

▶ Schools are required to inform students on an annual basis of the rights students have through FERPA.

▶ Academic dishonesty occurs when a student cheats or engages in plagiarism.

▶ The acts of cheating and plagiarizing are harmful to the college, the student body, employers, and future graduates.

▶ Conflict resolution should be thought of as a series of positive steps taken toward understanding another individual.

CHECK YOUR UNDERSTANDING

Visit www.cengagebrain.com to see how well you have mastered the material in Chapter 8.

SUGGESTED ITEMS FOR LEARNING PORTFOLIO

▶ Ethical Issue Research
▶ Conflict Resolution
▶ Legal Research

REFERENCES

College of the Canyons, Student Services. (2001–2013). *Tips to avoid allegations of academic misconduct.* Retrieved February 7, 2013, from http://www.canyons.edu/offices/student_services/Academic_Info/Dean/AvoidCheatin.asp

Foothill College. (n.d.). *Student conduct academic honor code.* Retrieved February 7, 2013, from http://www.foothill.edu/services/honor.php

Howard, J. (2010). *A blended librarian talks information literacy.* In *The Chronicle of Higher Education—Wired Campus Newsletter.* Retrieved February 7, 2013, from http://chronicle.com/blogPost/A-Blended-Librarian-Talks/25938/?sid=pm&utm_source=pm&utm_medium=en

8

United States Department of Education. (2012). Family Educational Rights and Privacy Act (FERPA). Retrieved February 7, 2013, from http://www.ed.gov/policy/gen/guid/fpco/ferpa/index.html

United States Department of Education, Office for Civil Rights. (2007). Annual report to Congress fiscal year 2006. Retrieved February 7, 2013, from http://www2.ed.gov/about/reports/annual/ocr/annrpt2006/report_pg7.html

United States Department of Education, Office for Civil Rights. (2010). Title II Part 35 nondiscrimination on the basis of disability in state and local government services. Retrieved February 7, 2013, from http://www2.ed.gov/policy/rights/reg/ocr/edlite-28cfr35.html#S130

United States Department of Education, Office for Civil Rights (2011). Regulations enforced by the Office for Civil Rights. Retrieved February 7, 2013, from http://www2.ed.gov/policy/rights/reg/ocr/index.html

United States Department of Justice. (2009). A guide to disability rights laws. Retrieved February 7, 2013, from http://www.ada.gov/cguide.htm

8

part 4

Success Strategies for Personal Well-Being

Part IV of *100% Student Success* addresses two important issues in your personal life: understanding and managing finances and following proper nutrition and fitness schemes to maintain good health.

Chapter 9: Financial Considerations for School Success reviews options for effective management of finances to give you the freedom to pursue your goals and expand your ability to engage more opportunities.

Chapter 10: Nutrition and Fitness Strategies for the Successful Student focuses on the importance of physical considerations, such as nutrition, exercise, sleep, and posture, to your daily functioning. When considering meeting your needs (think back to Chapter 2), these basic health considerations are some of the foundations of success.

Financial Considerations for School Success

LEARNING OBJECTIVES

By the end of this chapter, you will achieve the following objectives:

▶ Describe general financial considerations that must be made during college attendance.

▶ Discuss management of credit.

▶ Discuss elements to consider when making major purchases.

▶ Define various forms of financial assistance and locate resources for each.

▶ Be able to determine a workable budget based on recommended budgeting principles.

▶ List ways to save for the future.

BE IN THE KNOW

How Much Do You Know about Managing Money?

Take the quiz below to see how much you know about managing your finances.

1. Perhaps the biggest mistake you can make with student loans is:

   a) Paying your loan(s) off too soon.

   b) Borrowing more than you can reasonably afford to repay after you graduate.

   c) Consolidating multiple student loans into a single loan.

2. Before going to the dealership to shop for a new car, if you have to borrow money for the purchase you should:

   a) Talk to several lenders and decide how much you can comfortably afford to spend on a car after factoring in monthly payments on a loan (such as for three years) and then stick to that maximum purchase price.

   b) Determine how much expensive car you can comfortably afford, but if you want a more expensive vehicle, find out if you can qualify for a larger loan when you get to the dealership.

   c) Check advertisements for "special" financing from the dealer (such as zero-percent interest) because that will always result in the lowest-cost deal.

3. The savings strategy called "paying yourself first" means:

   a) You arrange to put a certain portion of your income into savings before you are tempted to spend it.

   b) You set aside a certain amount of your income for fun—perhaps restaurant meals and entertainment—so that you do not feel deprived as you put other money into savings or investments.

4. Putting money into tax-advantaged retirement accounts as soon as you start earning income is a good idea because:

   a) The sooner you start, the sooner you can benefit from the compound growth of interest and dividends.

   b) With the potential tax savings, your take-home pay may not be reduced as much as you think.

   c) Both of the above.

9

d) None of the above. Young people shouldn't be concerned about saving for retirement because that's many years away.

5. Generally speaking, the financial product for managing your everyday transactions that has the best federal consumer protections and the lowest chance of unexpected fees is:

a) A low-cost checking account for which you agree ("opt in") to an overdraft program for debit card transactions that exceed your balance.

b) A low-cost checking account for which you do *not* agree to an overdraft program.

c) A prepaid card advertising no fees to get started (Federal Deposit Insurance Corporation, 2012).

6. It's always smart to send in the minimum payment due on a credit card bill each month and stretch out the card payments as long as possible instead of paying the bill in full. ***True or False?***

7. Your credit record (your history of paying debts and other bills) can be a factor when you apply for a loan or a credit card but cannot affect noncredit decisions such as applications for insurance or an apartment. ***True or False?***

8. While one or two late payments on bills may not damage your credit record, making a habit of it will count against you. ***True or False?***

9. There's no harm in having many different credit cards, especially when the card companies offer free T-shirts and other special giveaways as incentives. The number of cards you carry won't affect your ability to get a loan; what matters is that you use the cards responsibly. ***True or False?***

10. A debit card may be a good alternative to a credit card for a young person because the money to pay for purchases is automatically deducted from a bank account, thus avoiding interest charges or debt problems. ***True or False?***

11. It makes no sense for young adults to put money aside for their retirement many years away. People in their 20s should

continued

9

continued

focus entirely on meeting monthly expenses and saving for short-term goals (such as buying a home or starting a business) and not start saving for retirement until their 40s at the earliest. ***True or False?***

12. If you receive an e-mail from a company you've done business with asking you to update your records by reentering your Social Security number or bank account numbers, it's safe to provide this information as long as the e-mail explains the reason for the request and shows the company's official logo. ***True or False?***

13. The best way to avoid a "bounced" check—that is, a check that gets rejected by your financial institution because you've overdrawn your account—is to keep your checkbook up to date and closely monitor your balance. Institutions do offer "overdraft-protection" services, but these programs come with their own costs. ***True or False?***

14. All checking accounts are pretty much the same in terms of features, fees, interest rates, opening balance requirements, and so on. ***True or False?***

15. Let's say you put money in a savings account paying the same interest rate each month, and you don't take any money out. Even though your original deposit and the interest rate remain unchanged, the amount of money you will earn in interest each month will gradually increase. ***True or False?*** (Federal Deposit Insurance Corporation, 2005).

Note: Answer key to test is located on page 233.

● FINANCES AND COLLEGE

Financing college can be a challenge for anyone, although the type of challenge may be different depending on individual circumstances such as age, outside commitments, and other individual factors. Existing financial obligations and concerns can be complicated by emergencies and other unexpected events. Referring back to Chapter 2, consider the importance of financial stability to the foundational survival, shelter, and safety needs identified by Maslow. Managing your finances effectively can contribute significantly to your feelings of stability and security.

SEEKING FINANCIAL ADVICE

Ultimately, it is you who must take charge of your finances. Successfully managing one's financial situation can be a daunting task, with many risks (and rewards, it is hoped!) associated with it. The good news is that even though you hold final responsibility for your finances, there are people, companies, and government agencies that can help you in your financial decision making, now and well into your future.

People get their money advice from myriad sources. At your age, your main source of financial advice may come from your parents. Studies corroborate that most young adults today rely on their parents as the main source of financial knowledge (Shorb, n.d.). The good news is that parents are seen as a trusted source of information. The bad news is that if parents exhibit bad financial habits, those habits most likely are passed down to the next generation.

Here are some resources you can tap into to get financial advice:

▶ **FAMILY, FRIENDS, AND COWORKERS.** The caveat here is that while you trust and admire these people, they really might not be very financially literate themselves.

▶ **YOUR FINANCIAL INSTITUTION.** Every bank and credit union has people on staff who can give you advice on the services they offer that best meet your financial needs, including the merits of online banking. They can also provide you with written materials on a variety of topics that you can use for reference. Their web sites also contain useful information.

▶ **YOUR SCHOOL.** Check with the Financial Aid office for information on student loans, grants, scholarships, loan repayment information, exit counseling, and other

9

financial information. The Career Services office has both onsite and online resources available to you, including data on internships, job searches, networking, and other career counseling information.

▶ **GOVERNMENT AGENCIES.** Many federal and state government agencies are dedicated to financial information geared to consumers. Most of the information is available via agency web sites.

▶ **YOUR EMPLOYER.** Many employers, especially larger ones, offer investment opportunities through stock purchase plans, 401(k) programs, and the like. The Human Resources department generally has printed materials and might offer classes to help you make informed investment decisions.

▶ **THE MEDIA.** The Internet, newspapers and magazines, television, and radio are filled with information about financial matters. When accessing information via the Internet, bear in mind that anyone can put anything up on the World Wide Web, and not all sources are reliable or trustworthy. Generally, you can rely on the .gov and .edu web sites as being reliable and presenting relatively accurate information. The government or educational entity behind the site is usually bound by a code of ethics and is watched by many different individuals or agencies. Regardless, be sure to verify your source(s) before moving forward with any financial decisions or taking the information as truth.

▶ **EDUCATIONAL OPPORTUNITIES.** Consult your local library, schools, community college, and other educational resources for personal finance classes, seminars, and the like. Financial institutions and those in the "money business" (investment bankers, brokers, financial advisors, and so on) often sponsor discussions on different financial vehicles and investment opportunities.

▶ **FINANCIAL PLANNER.** A financial planner is an investment professional who helps individuals set and achieve their long-term financial goals. The role of a financial planner is to find ways to increase the client's net worth and

success steps for seeking financial advice

- Enlist the help of family, friends, and coworkers.
- Speak to staff members at your financial institution.
- Tap into resources at your school.
- Check the web sites of federal and state government agencies that provide financial guidance.
- Consult with your employer on retirement and investment opportunities.
- Use different media outlets to conduct research on financial issues.
- Take advantage of any financial educational opportunities in your area.
- Seek out the counsel of a financial planner.

help the client accomplish all of their financial objectives. As a college student, you might not need this level of financial advice, but you might want to seek the advice of such a person as you enter the workforce, purchase a home, start a family, and so on. Note that using a financial planner costs money.

PERSONAL FINANCES

Personal finances are influenced by several factors. Existing financial commitments, availability of financial support, and financial demands that occur during the course of school are some factors to consider. Housing and related expenses, food, and other costs in addition to the cost of school can put a significant strain on personal finances. Managing personal finances generally takes careful planning and discipline; this may be even more true with the added costs of college. Common sense dictates that having a spending plan or a budget in place will aid in managing your personal finances, along with the proper use of credit.

9

apply it

Find printable activities on the companion web site for this book, accessed through www.cengagebrain.com.

Budgeting Resources on the Web

GOAL: To become familiar with budgeting resources and strategies and select an effective approach to budgeting based on individual needs.

STEP 1: Conduct an Internet search using "budgeting tools" or "creating budgets" as your search term. There are many free options available.

STEP 2: Select a tool that fits your needs and that you will be comfortable using.

STEP 3: Use the tool for a month or two. Review your budgeting at the end of the time period to determine the tool's effectiveness. Make adjustments and changes as needed.

SELF-ASSESSMENT QUESTION

• What techniques and strategies do you use to manage your personal finances?

? CRITICAL THINKING QUESTION

▶ From whom do you seek financial advice?

A Spending Plan

A spending plan is similar to a budget. A spending plan allows you to determine the amount of money that you have available, track how your money is being spent, and make adjustments according to your needs. The article "Putting a Spending Plan Together" at Higher One, Inc. (2013) suggests the following steps:

success steps for creating a spending plan and budget

• Know your income and expenses. Collect all receipts, bank account records, invoices, income statements, and other documents related to spending and income. Create categories that fit your specific needs and spending patterns. Based on the documentation that you gathered, estimate the amount of money that you spend on each category per month.

• Determine your annual income from all sources. Divide that figure by 12 to arrive at your monthly income.

• Determine monthly amounts to spend on each category of expenses. Although these amounts may vary somewhat based on individual need, these percentages represent recommended proportions of total income that can be allocated to expense categories. Consider the following recommended guidelines:

- Housing: 23–33%
- Life/car insurance: 4–6%
- Food: 12–20%
- Charities: 5–10%
- Transportation: 7–10%
- Personal debt repayment: 8–18%
- Entertainment/recreation: 4–6%
- Clothing: 4–7%
- Savings: 5–10%
- Medical: 3–5%

- Remember that these are suggested amounts and should be used as guidelines. You may need to modify them by adding categories or adjusting the figures. Use your own best judgment and advice from your financial advisor to determine precise budgeting for your circumstances. The goal of this step is to gain perspective on your total income and determine the amount of money that you realistically have for each category of expenses.

- Understand your spending patterns. Keep receipts, check stubs or register, and other records of payments and purchases that you make. Use an expense tracking chart, plain notebook, or software program to track your expenses. Choose a method with which you are comfortable and that you will use consistently.

- Each month, compare your spending to the plan you have set. If there are major inconsistencies in your plan and actual spending patterns, assess where you can make adjustments. Determine whether long-term or short-term changes need to be made. You may need to make modifications to your overall spending habits or to accommodate a one-time expense, such as a car repair.

- Keep track of your spending and your plan. A monthly review of your spending compared to your plan will allow you to understand your spending habits and budget according to your needs.

- Build your monthly budget based on your spending plan and needs. Implement methods for staying within the budget that was determined by your spending plan.

9

apply it

Find printable activities on the companion web site for this book, accessed through www.cengagebrain.com.

Budget Activity

GOAL: To establish a monthly budget.

STEP 1: Prepare a ledger. The ledger should contain a column for bills, amounts due, and due dates. Include columns for listing categories such as entertainment, groceries, clothes, medical bills, and so on.

STEP 2: On the ledger, list the dates of incoming monies in one column.

STEP 3: Fill out each column correctly, indicating all bill amounts and amounts that are typically spent on a monthly basis.

STEP 4: Determine whether all areas have been covered and whether enough money is available on a monthly basis. If there is a lack of money for all the bills, analyze areas that might be consolidated. Call companies as needed to determine whether this is possible.

STEP 5: Readjust the ledger as decisions are made regarding due dates and consolidation.

STEP 6: If money is remaining after all bills have been paid, determine whether some bills such as credit cards can be paid off more quickly. Adjust these payments and payoff dates on the ledger as determined.

© RapidEye/istockphoto.com.

Part of your personal spending plan will include how you use credit wisely to establish a strong financial record for the future.

Limiting Credit

One of the recommended methods for staying within your spending plan is to limit your opportunities to use credit. Mapping Your Future (2011) suggests using only one credit card and requesting a low credit limit. Contact your credit card company to adjust your credit limit. If you have a balance on your card, you may also consider negotiating a lower interest rate. Interest charges on a balance add up, and credit card companies will sometimes reduce interest rates to keep your business. Research the current interest rates so that you can speak from an informed position.

apply it

Find printable activities on the companion web site for this book, accessed through www.cengagebrain.com.

Credit Research

GOAL: *To become aware of responsible credit use and the consequences of its abuse.*

STEP 1: Conduct an Internet search using "credit" or "use of credit cards" as your search term.

STEP 2: Look in the results for documents that explain the responsible use of credit and the consequences of abusing it.

STEP 3: Based on your findings, determine any changes to your credit practices that you believe to be important. Set goals and select methods for implementing these changes.

Online Banking

Online banking allows you to closely monitor your money by offering access to your financial records 24 hours a day, seven days a week. Online banking allows you to track debits and credits on a daily basis and may include features such as electronic bill paying, transfer of funds between accounts, and other additional services. If you choose to use features such as electronic bill payments, you can access the majority of your records in one place, which provides more efficient recordkeeping as well as greater convenience.

Check Registers and Ledgers

A paper check ledger, or a check register app, gives you immediate access to your account information when the Internet is not available. Keeping an accurate and current check register allows you to track your expenditures and know exactly where your spending was, as well as track the amount of your available funds. Recording and subtracting each check as it is written lets you know what checks have been written and the amount of money remaining in the account regardless of whether the check has cleared the bank.

9

Building a Strong Credit History

Manage your finances in a manner that builds a strong credit history. A strong credit history is created by paying credit card balances monthly. Furman (n.d.) suggests that you do not need to carry a balance or accumulate interest charges each month in order to establish a credit history—you only need to prove that you can use credit in a responsible manner. Experts also warn against the credit card offers that college students frequently receive and emphasize the importance of using credit responsibly. Use credit in accordance with your spending plan. The main concept to remember and put into practice is that establishing credit is important in today's world, but abusing it can lead to serious consequences. Using good judgment (and sometimes restraint!) is a key factor in achieving this balance.

CASE IN POINT: IN A FINANCIAL PICKLE

Read the scenario below. Then, in groups or as a class, discuss the questions at the end.

Paul McGuire is beginning his second semester of college. Paul's first semester was difficult for him financially. He never seemed to have enough money to purchase necessities such as food and rent, let alone extras such as entertainment and recreational activities. As a result, Paul has accumulated some credit card debt on several cards that he carries. He is looking forward to planning the remainder of his college education, but he is beginning to develop concerns about his finances. Paul receives some financial aid, but it appears that he may need additional funding. He works 25–30 hours per week in addition to attending classes.

▶ What strategies might Paul use in establishing a budget?

▶ What advice would you give to Paul regarding the use of credit cards?

▶ What might Paul do to supplement his financial aid? From what sources might he seek reliable information?

▶ How might Paul's employer be of assistance in Paul's financial planning?

9

SAVING WHILE IN COLLEGE

The phrase "saving while in college" may seem like an oxymoron to the average college student. College students are notoriously perceived as being broke or barely making it from semester to semester. This is not the case for all college students, obviously, but it is a fact of life for many students on campus.

As disheartening as that may sound, and as much as this reality may ring true for you, there *are* ways to save money while in college. This saving exercise has two approaches:

▶ Open some sort of savings account and put money aside each month.

▶ Find ways to cut back on your expenses so that you are not broke or fall short all the time. Let's take a look at both approaches.

▶ **PUTTING MONEY ASIDE EACH MONTH.** If you are living on a limited/fixed amount of income from your parents, putting money away each month in a savings account may not be feasible. But, if you are working full- or part-time, you should strongly consider this choice. There are several options for savings accounts, but one of the most attractive ones to college students is a student savings account. Major banks all vie for student accounts, whether checking, savings, or other types of accounts, and they tend to offer freebies as an incentive to choose their bank over a competitor's. Some possible benefits banks may offer to entice you to their student savings account services include the following:

• No minimum balance

• No monthly fee

• Online banking

• Competitive interest rates

• Available overdraft protection (fees often apply, however)

• Automatic transfers from your checking to your college savings account

• Easy transfers from parents' accounts to student savings accounts

As with any banking service, it's wise to shop around to get the best deal and find a program that best suits your

9

needs. If you already have a checking account at a financial institution, start there first. If nothing else, it will be a cinch to move funds from your checking account into your savings account automatically or through online banking services. Be sure to compare competitive interest rates among banks so that you will realize the greatest return on your money. It also doesn't hurt to keep tabs on your bank's competitors' interest rates, which, after a time, may be better than what you are currently getting on your account. Just be sure that you weigh the benefits that each bank offers and read the fine print to determine if there are any hidden costs or penalties.

▶ **CUTTING BACK ON EXPENSES.** This is easier said than done, of course. Many expenses are fixed, such as rent, car payments, insurance, and the like. If you have been diligent about tracking your expenses and creating a budget, you have identified the monies you absolutely need each month to make those payments. However, there are several flexible expense areas where you can make reasonable adjustments to cut back without really compromising your lifestyle. In fact, making some of these suggested adjustments can actually ease your stress levels because you are not sweating it out each month or semester.

Here are three major areas where you can make changes immediately that will positively affect your bottom line. This list is hardly exhaustive, but these areas generally impact college students the most and are among the easiest to change if you do not let peer pressure get the best of you. These areas include the following:

▶ **FOOD.** If you are on a meal plan, whether living on campus or not, use it to the fullest extent. It's been paid for, and if you don't use all the allotted meals, then you are throwing money away. Conversely, if you have gone through all your meals on a weekly basis and still need to supplement eating outside the plan, then you are routinely spending out-of-pocket money that you likely hadn't anticipated (nor budgeted). Evaluate your use of the plan prior to signing up for next semester's plan and adjust it accordingly.

Even if your meal plan is sufficient for your needs, the lure of pizza delivery, snacking at the student union, or the fast-food drive-through window is palpable. Peer pressure to participate in impromptu food activities can also be a mighty pull when

9

you know better. Sure, it's perfectly acceptable (and comforting) to have the occasional take-out or delivery, but making this action into a habit will wreak havoc on your wallet.

If you live in a dorm, one way to supplement your meal plan and to fuel your late-night study time is to stock up on nutritional snacks and drinks. Virtually all students have access to a refrigerator, either in their own room or in a common area, so take advantage of it. Stock items such as yogurt, string cheese, and cottage cheese, making sure you keep an eye on expiration dates. Store nonperishable items such as granola bars, bagels, and peanut butter in your room, and tap into those items when the munchies hit. If you (and perhaps a roommate or other friend) go to the grocery store even once a month to stock up on items, you will eat more nutritious food and save money at a really good pace. And just say no to the vending and soda machines in the lobby!

If you live in an apartment or off-campus housing, you have a distinct budgetary advantage: a kitchen. Even if it is small, a kitchen opens up a whole world to you. You need not be a gourmet cook or have myriad appliances to feed yourself (and perhaps a roommate or two) well on a consistent basis. If you're new to cooking and need ideas, literally hundreds of thousands of recipes are available online. The important thing is to keep staples around so that you can pull together even a simple meal every day. Here are some cost-saving ideas for when you grocery shop:

- **Go grocery shopping on a full stomach.** If you're hungry, it's harder to concentrate and you'll be more apt to buy things you hadn't planned on (or budgeted).

- **Always go with a list, and stick to it.** You will spend less on food if you shop with a list. It's amazing how quickly those impulse items can ruin your well-intentioned shopping plans.

- **Limit the number of trips to the store each month.** Try to keep your pantry stocked with the basics (which you should always buy on sale, if possible), and then fill in once every two weeks or so with perishable items. Frequent trips to the store for just a few things can be killer on your wallet.

- **Get a local grocery store saver card.** Grocery chains are highly competitive and their profit margins are remarkably slim. Because of this, stores like to reward their customers

9

for their loyalty by giving discounts on items when the card is used. You can also register at the chain's web site and download digital coupons directly to your card. When you purchase an item that has a coupon loaded on the card, you will receive the discounted price after you swipe your card at the checkout.

- **Cut coupons and check store sales flyers.** Despite our ever-growing online environment, 80 percent of all coupons *still* come from the Sunday paper. It is worth a dollar or two and a bit of your time each week to get the Sunday paper and cut out the coupons for items that you need. Couple that with weekly sales flyers and you can rack up substantial savings. Check your receipts to see how you are doing—your amount of savings will be indicated on the bottom. One note of caution, however. Do not buy a brand-name item simply because you have a coupon and can save a little coin. Store-brand items are always less expensive and the quality is often as good as the national brand names.

- **Purchase basic ingredients.** Keep household staples on hand at all times. Items like flour, sugar, rice, potatoes, and various canned and frozen goods will allow you to whip up a meal in no time. Avoid convenience foods if at all possible. Prepackaged components or ready-made items cost apprecia-bly more because you are paying a premium for somebody else doing the work. Plus, most of these items are full of processed ingredients that do not help your heart, your cholesterol, or your waistline.

▶ **TRANSPORTATION.** If you are living on campus, then using your feet, a bicycle, or perhaps a campus shuttle is the norm for you. But if you commute to class or live off campus, then here are some cost-saving options that you might consider:

- **Use public transportation.** Sure, it can be a headache to use it sometimes, but your city provides it because it's relatively inex-pensive, it gets you where you need to go, and it cuts down on congestion and pollution. Be sure to check for monthly passes or student passes that offer substantial discounts.

- **Limit the use of your car.** If you do own a car, owner beware. Not only are cars expensive to purchase, they can be a money pit to use and maintain. Consider your costs when

9

it comes to gas, parking, insurance, maintenance, and car payments. Investigate carpooling some days of the week and maybe using public transportation other days of the week instead of driving to work or class each day. Most metropolitan areas have some sort of carpooling program. Your city or state's official web site will have the details on how you can take advantage of this service. Many campuses also offer a ride-share program at no cost. Check with your Student Services office (or your school's intranet site) for information about how the program works.

- **Keep your vehicle in top shape.** Sometimes circumstances do not allow you to use public transportation, walk, or carpool. If that is the case and you must drive (whether to campus or to a job), then make a habit of keeping your car in the best shape possible.

▶ **ENTERTAINMENT.** Entertainment is one of the categories that can render you penniless without much effort. So many items come under this umbrella that you may not even realize they are wants instead of needs. For example, do you have cable TV? If so, how much do you pay each month for that service? And what about those premium channels (HBO, Showtime, Cinemax, and the like)? If you've subscribed to any of those, your monthly costs are even higher.

Some entertainment costs are obvious. Attending movies, concerts, and eating out are three of the most common areas where college students spend money. Other entertainment costs may not be as noticeable—items such as iTunes downloads, gamer subscriptions, video games, CDs, and renting movies all contribute to how much you have left over for the necessities (Caldwell, n.d. [a]). If you are putting your entertainment needs above what you really need, then you are breaking one of the tenets of being financially literate.

All is not lost, however. No one is saying that you shouldn't have fun and be entertained. Here are some ways to cut back on your entertainment costs and still have a great time:

- **Use your computer as both a television and a stereo.** If you already have access to cable (and the cost is not prohibitive), don't go to the expense of buying a TV. Use the

9

DVD/CD player in your computer to listen to music and watch movies. If you don't have cable, you can still stream many live events (such as sporting events) to stay current.

- **Rethink going to the movies.** Do you have to see the latest blockbuster as soon as it comes out? Consider going to a matinee instead of an evening show. Prices are lower during the day, and you'll get greater mileage out of your student discount card this way. Also, check campus postings for free movies on campus. There's a good chance that you can see classics, independents, student films, and film noir at no cost.

- **Rent; don't buy.** Rent DVDs as a group. Pass the disc along to your responsible friends before the due date. Everyone gets to watch at a fraction of the cost to rent individually. Subscribing to a DVD rental service is also a cost-savings measure. There is more and more competition out there in this arena, so comparison shop before you subscribe.

- **Take advantage of free local and campus events.** Many communities support free events such as concerts, arts and crafts fairs, indoor-outdoor theater, festivals, and free days at art galleries and museums. The vast majority of campuses also provide free or low-cost entertainment, especially on weekends (Collegescholarships.org, n.d.).

success steps for saving while in college

- Open some type of savings account.
- Cut back on expenses.
  - Food
    - Go grocery shopping on a full stomach.
    - Always go with a list and stick to it.
    - Limit the number of trips to the store each month.
    - Get a local grocery store saver card.
    - Cut coupons and use store sales flyers.
    - Purchase basic ingredients.

9

- Transportation
  - Use public transportation.
  - Limit the use of your car.
  - Keep your vehicle in top shape.
- Entertainment
  - Use your computer as both a television and a stereo.
  - Rethink going to the movies.
  - Rent; don't buy.
  - Take advantage of free local and campus events.

FINANCIAL RESOURCES FOR COLLEGE

There are many resources that students use to pay for college, including personal savings and income, parents' savings and income, and financial aid, such as loans, grants, scholarships, and work-study. The types of financing one can receive depend largely on individual situations.

Financial aid at your school and elsewhere can help you budget and finance your college education.

FINANCIAL AID

CollegeData.com (n.d. [c]) defines financial aid as "any form of assistance that helps you and your family cover the costs of attending college." There are numerous sources for financial aid, and the source that you use will depend again on your individual situation.

Qualifying and Applying for Financial Aid

Regardless of what you believe your financial situation to be, it is wise to apply for financial aid (CollegeData.com, n.d. [a]). Because of the many factors that are used to calculate eligibility for financial aid, you may qualify for some type of assistance, regardless of your financial circumstances. Be aware that financial aid is available for students already enrolled in college, as long as published application deadlines are met. Financial aid is not only for high school students applying to college for the first time.

Financial aid typically comes from the federal or state governments, the colleges themselves, or private sources such as banks and private organizations. To determine individual eligibility, sources of financial assistance use the Free Application for Federal Student Aid (FAFSA). The FAFSA is a tool used by the U.S. Department of Education to analyze individual financial need based on uniform standards. To learn more about financial aid and the FAFSA, go to www.ed.gov and click on the "Funding" tab. Further explore the web site to see numerous additional sources of information.

The following suggestions for completing the FAFSA and implementing the application process efficiently and effectively come from CollegeData.com's "Tips for your financial aid forms" (n.d. [b]):

1. **Read all instructions and review the form first.** The FAFSA instructions contain information that can influence how you complete the form and that may affect your eligibility for aid. For example, certain words are defined in specific ways, and using the wrong word may change the meaning of the information you provide.

2. The most convenient method of completing the FAFSA is to use the electronic option. This option provides calculation tools, methods for inserting tax information into the form, and the ability to access a saved FAFSA for updating in subsequent years. Visit www.fafsa.ed.gov to explore the options available to you.

3. **Plan ahead.** As you read through the instructions, note deadlines on your calendar. Be aware of details such as whether the deadline is a postmark date or the date the paperwork has to be received. You will need to plan accordingly and allow ample time for mailing if you are not completing the form electronically. (Even if you are using the electronic submission option, it is wise to allow extra time in case of transmission problems.)

4. **Write legibly and fill in all the blanks.** If you are not using the electronic option, you must ensure that the completed form is legible and clear. If you can type your application, do so. If not, write clearly in dark (preferably black) ink. It is wise to print an extra copy of the paperwork and complete a draft before completing the final copy for submission. If something does not apply to you, mark "N/A" to indicate that it is not applicable or indicate this as instructed on the

9

> ### success steps for completing financial aid forms
>
> - Read all instructions and review the form first.
> - Plan ahead. Note important deadlines on your calendar.
> - Complete the online form or write legibly and fill in all the blanks. Write "N/A" (not applicable) if the item does not apply to you.
> - Review the completed form.
> - Keep copies for reference.

form. Leaving the item blank could be interpreted as a missed item and could delay the processing of your application.

5. **Review the completed form.** Whether the form is completed in hard copy or electronically, read it over to ensure that you have answered questions thoroughly and provided complete information. Allow enough time in the planning process to let the completed form to sit for a day or two before submitting it. You may be more objective and focused when you return to the form after taking some time off.

6. **Keep copies for consistency.** Keep copies of all completed forms and correspondence related to the financial aid application process. Use your copies as a reference for completing future financial aid documentation. This will ensure that the information that you provide is consistent and eliminate the need to research the information a second time, except for necessary updates. The copy will also serve as a reference for you in the event you need to clarify or resubmit any information. Discard any draft copies and retain only the copy of the final version to eliminate confusion.

SELF-ASSESSMENT QUESTION

- How efficiently do you complete financial aid and related paperwork?

? CRITICAL THINKING QUESTION

▸ Where might you seek out additional help in filling out the FAFSA form?

Types of Financial Aid

Eligibility for financial aid is determined on the basis of need or merit. Need is determined by the difference between the cost of attending college less the amount that you are expected to contribute, based on analysis of the information on your FAFSA. Merit is determined by your performance and achievement record in academics and other areas. Some types of financial aid use a combination of these criteria to determine eligibility (CollegeData.com, n.d. [c]).

See Figure 9-1 for an overview of your financial aid options. Financial aid comes in the following types:

TYPES OF FINANCIAL AID

Type of Aid	Examples	General Parameters
Grants	▶ Pell grants	▶ Based on need.
	▶ Federal Supplemental Educational Opportunity Grants (FSEOG)	▶ Each grant has its own criteria for eligibility.
		▶ Each grant has its own maximum amount that can be awarded.
		▶ Does not have to be repaid.
Loans	▶ Government loans	▶ Based on need.
	▶ Private loans	▶ Each has its own eligibility requirements.
		▶ Each has its own criteria for repayment.
		▶ Must be repaid with interest.
		▶ Obtained by signing a legally binding agreement.
Scholarships	▶ Awarded by individual colleges	▶ Based on scholastic or other achievement.
	▶ Awarded by private sources	▶ Does not have to be repaid.
		▶ May be designated for particular groups or have other specific requirements.
Work-Study Programs	▶ Offer students an opportunity to work on or off campus while attending school	▶ Student earns a salary for specific job.
		▶ Usually based on need.
	▶ Federal government program that may be subsidized by states or private industry	▶ Earnings are not repaid.
Other Options	▶ Internships	▶ Less common than other forms of financial aid.
	▶ Education cooperatives	▶ Specifics depend on the program.
	▶ Other programs that provide an opportunity to work for wages while completing your education	

Figure 9-1   Having a working knowledge of financial aid options will help you to know what is available to you and guide you in asking appropriate questions of financial aid personnel.

Adapted from the U.S. Department of Education (2006) and CollegeData.com.

9

▶ **Grants.** Grants are given according to need and include Pell Grants, Federal Supplemental Educational Opportunity Grants (FSEOG), and others. Each type of grant has its own criteria for eligibility as well as maximum amounts that can be awarded. Grants are based on need and do not have to be repaid.

▶ **Loans.** Loans are also based on need and, as is the case with grants, there are several types, each with its own eligibility requirements and criteria for repayment. Loans can come from the government or from private lenders and must be repaid with interest. All loans are obtained by signing a legally binding agreement.

It is important to understand the difference between a subsidized and an unsubsidized loan. A subsidized loan is one that is awarded based on financial need, and interest on the loan does not accrue until loan repayment begins after graduation. The loan is subsidized in that the federal government pays interest while you are in school. Conversely, an unsubsidized loan requires that you pay interest on the loan from the time you first receive funds until the loan is fully repaid. Interest on unsubsidized loans is capitalized, so you are required to pay interest on any interest that accrues.

▶ **Scholarships.** Scholarships are generally awarded by individual colleges or private sources. They are traditionally based on scholastic achievement and do not have to be repaid. Some scholarships are designated for particular groups or have other specific requirements that must be met. For example, some agencies that provide scholarships require the recipient to work for the agency for a designated amount of time following graduation.

▶ **Work-study programs.** Work-study programs offer students an opportunity to work on or off campus while attending school. The government pays a part of the salary. Work-study programs are typically part of federal financial aid but may be subsidized by the state or college in some situations.

▶ **Other options.** Other possibilities for financial assistance include internships, education cooperatives, and other programs that provide an opportunity to work for wages while completing your education. Although these programs are less common than other forms of financial aid, they are available in some situations and can be viable options for some students.

9

- How knowledgeable are you about financial aid options?
- What additional information do you need to make informed decisions?

? CRITICAL THINKING QUESTION

▶ Have you sought out all forms of financial aid for which you might be eligible?

Finding Specific Resources

There are several resources for researching financial aid options. Financial aid information is available from your campus financial aid office, the federal government, your college or public library, or by conducting an Internet search (United States Department of Education, 2003). There are services that charge for searching for financial aid information. Free information is available, so if you do choose a service that charges a fee, get a clear indication of what the fee covers.

MAJOR PURCHASES AND BUYING INSURANCE

As an adult student, it is possible that you will make a major purchase during your college career. Major purchases such as automobiles, homes, and insurance require sound planning and wise choices.

RENTING A HOME

There are several elements to consider when preparing to rent a house or apartment. Both you and the landlord have rights that are often defined by local law and of which you should be aware before signing a lease or rental agreement. The following suggestions for renting a house or apartment are provided by Nolo (2013):

▶ **Understand the terms of your lease.** It is important that you know the terms of the lease and its stipulations. For example, will you be able to negotiate leaving before the lease expires? In addition, be clear on policies related to pets, guests, parking, and other concerns. What are the terms of a standard lease in your locale? Ask questions if you are unsure of any terms and maintain open communication lines with your landlord. Seek assistance from a knowledgeable person if you need additional advice.

▶ **Understand the finances.** An important part of the terms of the lease is knowing the date rent is due and the penalties for late payment. In addition, find out the amount of the security deposit and the conditions for its return. Know whether the first and last month's rent are required in addition to the security deposit.

▶ **Know your rights.** Know the legalities affecting rental properties in your area. Local laws affect your rights as a renter.

9

> ### success steps for renting a home
>
> - Understand the terms of your lease.
> - Understand the finances.
> - Know your rights.
> - Get it in writing.
> - Protect yourself.

For example, some locales have limits on rent increases. In addition, you have certain rights related to privacy and repairs. Contact your city government for information on housing regulations in your area.

▌ **Get it in writing.** Ensure that you obtain all terms, restrictions, and other expectations in writing. Doing so will minimize ambiguity and conflict should an issue arise. In addition, make requests and complete other communications in writing. If you conduct business by phone, document the conversation and outcome in some form of written communication such as e-mail or a letter.

▌ **Protect yourself.** Know and implement structures and processes for ensuring your safety. These include physical safety in terms of your neighborhood and living space as well as your financial safety by understanding the terms of your rental agreement.

PURCHASING A HOME

Purchasing a home can be an exciting yet somewhat intimidating process. Purchasing a home provides you with an investment and can be a tax benefit. It is important to understand the major considerations of purchasing a home and to know where to seek sound professional advice in the process. The U.S. Department of Housing and Urban Development (HUD) makes the following recommendations and suggestions for home buyers (2003, 2009):

▌ **Investigate your loan options.** There are many choices for obtaining a loan for the purchase of a home. HUD recommends shopping around as you would for any major purchase to find the best rate on loans. If you are in a situation such as having a poor credit history, needing a minimal amount for a down

9

payment, or other extenuating circumstances, contact the HUD offices, as options may be available for you.

▶ **Be a wise shopper.** Learn about the home purchasing process by taking a HUD course in home ownership. Know relative values and investigate the prices of homes in the neighborhood and surrounding areas to ensure that you are getting a comparable value. Follow HUD guidelines for completing loan applications to avoid loan fraud. Contact HUD for more detailed information on protecting yourself in the loan acquisition process.

▶ **Seek the assistance of professionals.** A professional real estate agent understands the intricacies of home buying and can advise you on elements such as financial issues, the area in which you plan to purchase your home, and other aspects of the transaction. The fees for the broker come from the home seller—not the buyer—so having a professional real estate broker does not add to your costs, yet is a valuable service. HUD recommends interviewing several professionals and checking their references before selecting the broker with whom you choose to work. Seek a certified home inspector to inspect any home that you are considering purchasing, to ensure that it is in good condition.

▶ **Know your expenses.** It is important to be aware of the costs, such as earnest money, down payments, and closing costs that are associated with home purchase. These costs can vary, depending on your situation. Again, a professional real estate broker can help you understand these fees and work with you to achieve a plan that fits your needs.

success steps for purchasing a home

- Investigate your loan options. Know which loan choice is best for you.
- Be a wise shopper. Consider taking a course in home buying, such as those offered by HUD (Housing and Urban Development).
- Seek the assistance of professionals, such as a knowledgeable real estate agent.
- Know your expenses. Be aware of the costs associated with purchasing a home.

9

Your best option is to work with knowledgeable professionals and agencies when making a major purchase such as a house.

PURCHASING AN AUTOMOBILE

Many of the considerations in purchasing an automobile are similar to those in buying a house. Consider the following guidelines when buying a vehicle:

▶ **Weigh leasing versus buying.** Although many people favor leasing over purchasing, leasing is not always the best option. Besides the fact that you will not actually own the vehicle, there may be additional fees associated with leasing. Check your options carefully and compare leasing to a variety of loan options.

▶ **Shop around for a loan.** Investigate several sources for loans to find the best rate possible. Possible sources for loans include banks, credit unions, and other lending institutions, as well as the car manufacturer itself. Having excellent credit can often qualify one for a low interest rate on a car.

▶ **Know the terms of the agreement.** Have a clear understanding of the terms and conditions of the loan or lease. Make sure that the agreement addresses issues such as prepayment options and penalties and the length of the loan or lease. Ensure that the amount of the loan is appropriate for the age of the vehicle.

Stockbyte/Getty Images.

Making a major purchase requires planning carefully, knowing your options, and understanding all related expenses.

success steps for purchasing an automobile

- Weigh the benefits and costs of buying versus leasing.
- Find the best loan—shop around.
- Know the terms of the lease or loan.
- Ensure that the terms of the loan are appropriate for the age of the car.

9

PURCHASING INSURANCE

There are many types of insurance, such as health, home, and automobile. Insurance regulations typically vary by state, and your best information regarding insurance purchases is likely to come from your state insurance commissioner's office. The following are general guidelines regarding different types of insurance. As with any major purchase, you are wise to educate yourself about your options and the reputation of the professional with whom you are dealing.

▶ **Health insurance.** Major medical insurance policies can protect you in the event of a major illness or medical need. General policies may include office visits, optical care, and other benefits. Your choice will depend on your needs. Schools sometimes offer insurance options to students at reasonable prices. Check your school to see whether this is a choice.

▶ **Homeowner's and renter's policies.** Homeowner's insurance is generally included in your mortgage payments, and you should be informed of its terms in the home purchasing process. Insurance is sometimes overlooked by renters, but it is a wise choice for protecting your belongings from theft and disasters such as fire. Insurance agencies typically offer some type of renter's insurance.

▶ **Vehicle insurance.** Automobile insurance includes several subcategories, including liability, collision, and comprehensive coverage. The amount and type of insurance that you purchase for your vehicle will depend on the age of your vehicle and the laws in your state. Know the types and amounts of coverage required by law in your location and, once again, shop for the best rates for the coverage that you are seeking.

▶ **Other insurance.** Other purchases might also warrant insurance. Items such as electronics and jewelry may require special policies or supplements (called riders) to your standard policy. It is often wise to insure items such as cell phones, smart phones, iPads, and laptop computers that are mobile and therefore more prone to loss and damage. Assess your situation

9

apply it

Find printable activities on the companion web site for this book, accessed through www.cengagebrain.com.

Insurance Inventory and Research

GOAL: To become familiar with your insurance needs and make appropriate insurance choices.

STEP 1: Review the insurances that you currently have. Compare what you currently have to your needs and the insurance requirements in your state. Assess your insurances for their adequacy in meeting your needs and legal requirements.

STEP 2: Note any discrepancies that you find and create a brief plan to address them.

STEP 3: Research your options for correcting discrepancies according to your state guidelines and the suggestions in this chapter.

and the items that you have and make wise decisions about your insurance policy.

SAVING FOR THE FUTURE

As an adult student, there are considerations that you will need to make about your future beyond college. If you have family members for whom you are responsible, there are factors specific to their well-being that you will need to take into account.

RETIREMENT PLANNING

For many (if not most) of us, saving for the future entails being able to retire at some point in our lives. Retirement may seem light years away if you are still in school and have barely or never entered the workforce. But that reality will be here sooner rather than later, so it

SELF-ASSESSMENT QUESTIONS

- Have you ever been in a difficult situation related to a rental or major purchase?
- What were the circumstances that resulted in the difficulty?
- How was the difficulty resolved?

? CRITICAL THINKING QUESTION

- Do you think it is wise to get all of your insurance needs from just one company? Why or why not?

9

truly is not too early to think about, and put into motion, ways that you can save for your golden years.

To be financially secure in your retirement, you must plan for it, commit to that plan, and use your money wisely. The U.S. Department of Labor cites the following statistics as they relate to retirement:

▶ Fewer than half of Americans have calculated how much they need to save for retirement.

▶ In 2009, 13 percent of private industry workers with access to a defined contribution plan, such as a 401(k), did not participate. A contribution plan is an employer-sponsored retirement plan that accepts employee as well as employer contributions.

▶ The average American spends 20 years in retirement (United States Department of Labor, 2010).

Don't be a part of these statistics! Consider the following retirement tips as you enter your postgraduate years:

▶ **MAKE SAVING FOR RETIREMENT A PRIORITY.** Devise a plan, stick to it, and set goals. Remember, it's never too early or too late to start saving.

▶ **KNOW YOUR RETIREMENT NEEDS.** Retirement is expensive. Experts estimate that you will need about 70 percent of your preretirement income to maintain your standard of living when you stop working.

▶ **CONTRIBUTE TO YOUR EMPLOYER'S RETIREMENT SAVINGS PLAN.** If your employer offers a retirement savings plan, such as a 401(k) plan, sign up and contribute all you can. Your taxes will be lower, your company may kick in more (called a matching contribution), and automatic payroll deductions make it easy. Over time, compound interest and tax deferrals make a big difference in the amount you will accumulate.

▶ **LEARN ABOUT YOUR EMPLOYER'S PENSION PLAN.** If your employer has a traditional pension plan, check to see if you are covered by the plan and learn how it works.

▶ **CONSIDER BASIC INVESTMENT PRINCIPLES.** How you save can be as important as how much you save. Inflation and the types of investments you make play important roles in how much you will have saved at retirement.

9

▶ **DON'T TOUCH YOUR RETIREMENT SAVINGS.** If you withdraw your retirement savings now, you'll lose principal and interest, and you may lose tax benefits or have to pay withdrawal penalties. If you change jobs, leave your savings invested in your current retirement plan, or roll them over to an Individual Retirement Account (IRA) or your new employer's plan.

▶ **PUT MONEY INTO AN INDIVIDUAL RETIREMENT ACCOUNT.** You can put up to $5,000 a year into an Individual Retirement Account (IRA); you can contribute even more if you are 50 or older. You can also start with much less. IRAs also provide tax advantages and can provide an easy way to save. You can set it up so that an amount is automatically deducted from your checking or savings account and deposited in the IRA.

▶ **FIND OUT ABOUT YOUR SOCIAL SECURITY BENEFITS.** Social Security pays benefits that are on average 40 percent of what you earned before retirement. You should receive a Social Security Statement each year that gives you an estimate of how much your benefit will be and when you can receive it.

▶ **ASK QUESTIONS.** While these tips are meant to point you in the right direction, you'll need more information. Talk to your employer, your bank, your union, or a financial advisor. Ask questions and make sure you understand the answers. Get practical advice and act now (United States Department of Labor, 2010).

success steps for retirement planning

- Make saving for retirement a priority.
- Know your retirement needs.
- Contribute to your employer's retirement savings plan.
- Learn about your employer's pension plan.
- Consider basic investment principles.
- Don't touch your retirement savings.
- Put money into an Individual Retirement Account.
- Find out about your Social Security benefits.
- Ask questions.

9

CHAPTER SUMMARY

The expenses associated with getting a college education in addition to the general cost of living can present challenges to students and their families. The goal of Chapter 9 was to review options for financing college and for managing personal finances as effectively as possible. In addition, you learned strategies for successfully completing major purchases and planning financially for your future.

Sound financial management is a foundation for completing other life tasks. Having peace of mind about finances also significantly reduces stress. Consider as well that effective financial management while in school lays the groundwork for financial success in later years and will reflect positively on you in the future.

POINTS TO KEEP IN MIND

In this chapter, the following main points were discussed in detail:

- Financial considerations of college students should include personal finances, the wise use of credit, and creation of a realistic spending plan.
- It is important to build a strong credit history by establishing a credit history, but not abusing credit.
- Finances are an individualized and often complex matter. Seek the advice of a qualified financial advisor.
- A spending plan can determine your current spending patterns and lead you to make necessary adjustments to your budget.
- Online banking provides convenient and current access to your financial information.
- When renting or purchasing a house or apartment, know the local laws, understand your lease or loan terms, and be aware of your rights.
- When purchasing a home, seek the services of a qualified real estate professional and home inspector.
- Know the legalities and agreement terms regarding any major product or insurance purchase.

9

▶ Know the types of insurance that are available and what each covers.

▶ Carefully research financial aid options and apply by completing the FAFSA. Many students qualify for aid because of the many factors that are considered.

▶ Complete financial aid forms thoroughly and carefully. Check them for errors and keep copies.

▶ Types of financial aid include loans, grants, scholarships, and work-study. The type for which you might qualify depends on numerous individual factors.

▶ Saving for the future is primarily about planning for one's retirement.

CHECK YOUR UNDERSTANDING

Visit www.cengagebrain.com to see how well you have mastered the material in Chapter 9.

SUGGESTED ITEMS FOR LEARNING PORTFOLIO

▶ Creating a Spending Plan
▶ Budgeting Resources on the Web
▶ Banking and Investment Research
▶ Credit Research

1. B
2. A
3. A
4. C
5. B
6. False
7. False

9

8. True

9. False

10. True

11. False

12. False

13. True

14. False

15. True

REFERENCES

Caldwell M. (n.d. [a]). *How to trim 3 common budget categories.* Retrieved February 7, 2013, from http://moneyfor20s.about.com /od/budgeting/a/trimbudgetcat_2.htm

CollegeData.com (n.d. [a]). *It starts with financial need.* A service of First Financial Bank. Retrieved February 8, 2013, from http:// www.collegedata.com/cs/content/content_payarticle_tmpl .jhtml?articleId=10079

CollegeData.com. (n.d. [b]). *Tips for your financial aid forms.* A service of First Financial Bank. Retrieved February 8, 2013, from http://www .collegedata.com/cs/content/content_payarticle_tmpl.jhtml?articleId =10091

CollegeData.com. (n.d. [c]). *What is financial aid?* A service of First Financial Bank. Retrieved February 8, 2013, from http://www.college data.com/cs/content/content_payarticle_tmpl.jhtml?articleId=10075

Collegescholarships.org (n.d.). *118 ways to save money in college.* Retrieved February 7, 2013, from http://www.collegescholarships.org /student-living/save-money.htm

Federal Deposit Insurance Corporation (Spring 2005). FDIC Consumer News. Special Guide for Young Adults. Retrieved February 11, 2013, from http://www.fdic.gov/consumers/consumer/news/cnspr05 /spring_05_bw.pdf

Federal Deposit Insurance Corporation (Fall 2012). FDIC Consumer News. For Young Adults and Teens: Quick Tips for Managing Your Money. Retrieved February 11, 2013, from http://www.fdic.gov /consumers/consumer/news/cnfall12/Fall2012B&W.pdf

9

Furman, J. (n.d.). *How to build a good credit history.* Retrieved February 8, 2013, from http://www.ehow.com/how_2400_build-credit-historybuild -credit-history.html

Higher One, Inc. (2013). *Putting a spending plan together.* Retrieved February 8, 2013, from https://swooponecard.higheroneaccount.com /info/marketing/spendingplan.jsp

Mapping Your Future (2011). *Use your credit cards wisely.* Retrieved February 8, 2013, from http://mappingyourfuture.org/money /creditcards.htm

Nolo: Legal Solutions for You, Your Family, and Your Business. (2013). *Ten tips for tenants.* Retrieved February 7, 2013, from http://www.nolo .com/legal-encyclopedia/ten-tips-tenants-29446.html

Shorb, V. (n.d.). National Financial Educators Council. *Financial literacy and the revival of the American dream.* Retrieved February 7, 2013, from http://www.financialeducatorscouncil.org/pdf/bonus/financial _literacy.pdf

United States Department of Education (2003). Looking for student aid: Federal, state, and other sources of information. Retrieved February 8, 2013, from http://www.gpo.gov/fdsys/pkg/ERIC-ED480475/pdf/ERIC -ED480475.pdf

United States Department of Housing and Urban Development. (2003). Don't be a victim of loan fraud. Retrieved February 8, 2013, from http://www.hud.gov/offices/hsg/sfh/buying/loanfraud.cfm

United States Department of Housing and Urban Development. (2009). *Common questions from first-time home buyers.* Retrieved February 8, 2013, from http://www.hud.gov/buying/comq.cfm

United States Department of Labor (2010). *Top 10 ways to prepare for retirement.* Retrieved February 7, 2013, from http://www.dol.gov/ebsa /publications/10_ways_to_prepare.html

9

Nutrition and Fitness Strategies for the Successful Student

LEARNING OBJECTIVES

By the end of this chapter, you will achieve the following objectives:

▶ Identify important components involved in achieving optimal health and energy.

▶ Explain the Dietary Guidelines for Americans and how they apply to personal health.

▶ Explain the major components of the MyPlate guide and identify related health practices to optimize health and energy.

▶ Demonstrate the ability to use food package labels to make healthy food choices.

▶ Explain the importance of sufficient sleep and identify strategies for getting a good night's sleep.

▶ Define *good posture* and describe correct ergonomic positions related to student activities.

▶ List the criteria for an effective exercise program.

BE IN THE KNOW

What Is Body Mass Index (BMI)?

Body Mass Index (BMI) is a number calculated from a person's weight and height. BMI provides a reliable indicator of body fatness for most people and is used to screen for weight categories that may lead to health problems.

BMI does not measure body fat directly, but it can be considered an alternative for direct measures of body fat. Additionally, BMI is an inexpensive and easy-to-perform method of screening for weight categories that may lead to health problems. However, BMI is not a diagnostic tool. For example, a person may have a high BMI. To determine if excess weight is a health risk, a healthcare provider would need to perform further assessments. These assessments might include skinfold thickness measurements, evaluations of diet, physical activity, family history, and other appropriate health screenings.

For adults 20 years old and older, BMI is interpreted using standard weight status categories that are the same for all ages and for both men and women.

The standard weight status categories associated with BMI ranges for adults are shown in the following table.

BMI	Weight Status
Below 18.5	Underweight
18.5–24.9	Normal
25.0–29.9	Overweight
30.0 and above	Obese

For example, here are the weight ranges, the corresponding BMI ranges, and the weight status categories for a sample height.

Height	Weight Range	BMI	Weight Status
5' 9"	124 lbs or less	Below 18.5	Underweight
	125 lbs to 168 lbs	18.5 to 24.9	Normal
	169 lbs to 202 lbs	25.0 to 29.9	Overweight
	203 lbs or more	30 or higher	Obese

10

The BMI ranges are based on the relationship between body weight and disease and death. Overweight and obese individuals are at increased risk for many diseases and health conditions, including the following:

- Hypertension
- Dyslipidemia (for example, high LDL cholesterol, low HDL cholesterol, or high levels of triglycerides)
- Type 2 diabetes
- Coronary heart disease
- Stroke
- Gallbladder disease
- Osteoarthritis
- Sleep apnea and respiratory problems
- Some cancers (endometrial, breast, and colon)

It's easy to calculate, and important to know your BMI. For an accurate measurement, simply conduct an Internet search using "BMI Calculator." Then enter your height and weight and press the "calculate" button. Your results will be immediately displayed, along with an interpretation of the numbers.

Do yourself a healthy favor and find out your BMI. If you are in the "normal" range, good for you. If your number falls into the "overweight" or "obese" categories, work to bring your BMI down. It is not too early to make positive lifestyle changes. (Centers for Disease Control and Prevention, 2011)

NUTRITION AND FITNESS: AN OVERVIEW

Positive health behaviors can significantly influence your success in school. Good nutrition can lead to better health, more energy, and higher levels of concentration. Optimal rest and sleep are important for optimal energy, reduction in fatigue, and the focus and attention required for effective and efficient learning. High levels of fitness and regular exercise can lead to positive health

10

SELF-ASSESSMENT QUESTIONS

- Before moving on, how would you rate your own nutrition? In what areas do you think you do well? In what areas do you already know you need improvement?

- How would you rate your sleep? Do you regularly get a good night's sleep? Do you get the appropriate rest from work, school, and other life stresses?

- How would you rate your current level of fitness? In what areas are you satisfied? In what areas do you think you need improvement?

- Do you often have problems (aches, pains, muscle soreness, fatigue) that might be related to poor posture?

? CRITICAL THINKING QUESTION

- Of the areas listed above (nutrition, sleep, exercise, posture), which area do you think will require the most time and effort on your part in order to see an improvement?

© Barbara Dudzinska/Shutterstock.

Choosing meals that represent a healthy and balanced diet will provide you with the nutrition and energy needed for success in school.

factors, a greater ability to relax and sleep well, and greater levels of attention. Good posture is an important part of fitness because it can help in alleviating the muscle soreness, aches and pains, and fatigue associated with long sessions of study, computer work, driving, or sitting in class. It is important for students to understand how to prioritize good nutrition, sleep, exercise, and posture for success in school.

NUTRITION: A KEY FACTOR IN HEALTH AND ENERGY LEVEL

Good nutrition is an essential element in good health, high energy, and focused attention. With the time and financial constraints facing students, practicing good nutrition behaviors can often seem impossible, yet a good diet may be a significant factor in school success and general health in the long run. A full discussion of nutrition is not possible in one chapter of a textbook. The goal here is to emphasize the importance of nutrition to school success, to highlight key elements of good nutrition, and to explain a few of the many tools available for helping you to make healthy food choices.

DIETARY GUIDELINES FOR AMERICANS

The *Dietary Guidelines for Americans,* published by the U.S. Department of Health and Human Services (HHS) and the U.S. Department of Agriculture (USDA) (2010), presents science-based dietary and physical activity behaviors designed to promote health and reduce the risk of chronic disease. The HHS and USDA work together to update these guidelines every five years based on the latest scientific findings. These suggestions recognize that good nutrition is essential for good health and that many of the leading causes of death and disease in Americans can be reduced or prevented entirely by practicing sound nutritional and physical fitness behaviors. Chronic diseases linked to poor diet or lack of physical activity include (but are not limited to) cardiovascular disease, hypertension, Type 2 diabetes, obesity, osteoporosis, diverticulitis, iron-deficiency anemia, oral disease, malnutrition, and some cancers.

MYPLATE

In June 2011, the United States Department of Agriculture (USDA) replaced MyPyramid with MyPlate as part of the Dietary Guidelines for Americans 2010, the federal food guidance system. The MyPlate logo divides a dinner plate into four sections for vegetables, fruits, grains, and proteins with a fifth smaller plate to one side for dairy. In conjunction with the logo, the USDA provides "10 tips to a great plate" to help Americans make smart food choices to help achieve and maintain a healthy lifestyle. These include:

Adhering to the USDA's recommendations for smart food choices will help you to achieve and maintain a healthy lifestyle.

- **Balance calories.** Find out how many calories you need for a day as a first step in managing your weight. Go to the MyPlate Web site (www.choosemyplate.gov) to find your calorie level. Being physically active also helps you balance calories.

- **Enjoy your food, but eat less.** Take the time to fully enjoy your food as you eat it. Eating too fast or when your attention is elsewhere may lead to eating too many calories. Pay attention to hunger and fullness cues before, during, and after meals. Use them to recognize when to eat and when you've had enough.

- **Avoid oversized portions.** Use a smaller plate, bowl, and glass. Portion out foods before you eat. When eating out, choose a smaller size option, share a dish, or take home part of your meal.

- **Foods to eat more often.** Eat more vegetables, fruits, whole grains, and fat-free or 1% milk and dairy products. These foods have the nutrients you need for health—including potassium, calcium, vitamin D, and fiber. Make them the basis for meals and snacks.

- **Make half your plate fruits and vegetables.** Choose red, orange, and dark-green vegetables like tomatoes, sweet potatoes, and broccoli, along with other vegetables for your meals. Add fruit to meals as part of main or side dishes or as dessert.

- **Switch to fat-free or low-fat (1%) milk.** They have the same amount of calcium and other essential nutrients as whole milk, but fewer calories and less saturated fat.

10

- **Make half your grains whole grains.** To eat more whole grains, substitute a whole-grain product for a refined product—such as eating whole-wheat bread instead of white bread or brown rice instead of white rice.

- **Foods to eat less often.** Cut back on foods high in solid fats, added sugars, and salt. They include cakes, cookies, ice cream, candies, sweetened drinks, pizza, and fatty meats like ribs, sausages, bacon, and hot dogs. Use these foods as occasional treats, not everyday foods.

- **Compare sodium in foods.** Use the Nutrition Facts label to choose lower sodium versions of foods like soup, bread, and frozen meals. Select canned foods labeled "low sodium," "reduced sodium," or "no salt added."

- **Drink water instead of sugary drinks.** Cut calories by drinking water or unsweetened beverages. Soda, energy drinks, and sports drinks are a major source of added sugar, and calories, in American diets (United States Department of Agriculture, 2011).

The MyPlate web site presents some basic messages for those desiring to improve their health through food choices and exercise. These basic messages are the same as those of the 2010 dietary guidelines. Along with basic messages, the MyPlate web site provides numerous tools to help in applying these messages. Review the site thoroughly to explore applying the information to your personal life.

FOOD PACKAGE LABELS: NUTRITION FACTS

The Nutrition Facts label found on food packages in the United States presents important information to help consumers determine healthy food choices. Read the entire package label to establish exactly what nutrients are contained in the food and how much of each nutrient is contained in each serving. Figure 10-1 explains each part of a Nutrition Facts label.

The following packaging elements provide various facts about the food products that you purchase:

- **Front panel.** The front panel of any food container must say whether any nutrient has been added or whether any claim is being made about the food benefiting health. There are very

10

Nutrition Facts

Start here →

Serving Size: 1/2 Cup
Servings Per Container: 4

Amount Per Serving

Check calories

Calories 100	Calories from Fat 30
	% Daily Value*

Total Fat 3g	5%
Saturated Fat 0g	0%
Cholesterol 0mg	0%

Limit these nutrients

Sodium 340mg	14%
Total Carbohydrate 15g	5%
Dietary Fiber 1g	4%
Sugars 0g	
Protein 2g	

Get enough of these nutrients

Vitamin A 0%	•	Vitamin C 0%
Calcium 0%	•	Iron 2%

*Percent Daily Values are based on a 2,000 calorie diet. Your daily values may be higher or lower depending on your calorie needs:

Footnote

	Calories	2,000	2,500
Total Fat	Less than	65g	80g
Sat Fat	Less than	20g	25g
Cholesterol	Less than	300mg	300mg
Sodium	Less than	2,400mg	2,400mg
Total Carbohydrate		300g	375g
Dietary Fiber		25g	30g

Calories per gram:
Fat 9 • Carbohydrate 4 • Protein 4

Ingredients:
Flour, Water, Yeast, Vegetable Oil, Salt, Artificial Flavor and Color.

Quick guide to % DV

• 5% or less is low

• 20% or more is high

Copyright © Cengage Learning®.

Figure 10-1   Knowing how to read and interpret nutrition labels will allow you to make wise food choices.

strict guidelines about what a food manufacturer can put on a food label. Only a few health claims are allowed. These claims must be backed by substantial research. It is wise to think critically about any health claims that are presented.

❱ **Ingredient list.** The ingredient list tells whether any substance has been added to the food in the package. Nutrients, fats, sugars, and other additives and preservatives are often added to foods to increase the nutritive value, to lengthen the shelf life, or to change the appearance or texture of the food. Ingredients are listed in descending order by weight. For example, if sugar is the first or second ingredient, it is a

10

main ingredient of the food and that food should probably not be consumed in large quantities.

▶ **Nutrition facts.** This box on a food package is designed to help consumers compare foods. There are several important elements on the Nutrition Facts label that nutrition-conscious consumers should understand.

- **Serving size:** Pay close attention to the serving size. All other values on the label are listed relative to this serving size. In other words, if the label says that there are five grams (g) of protein and the serving size is one cup, then for every cup of the food, there are 5 g of protein.

- **Servings per container:** This number says simply how many of the servings are in the entire container. Servings can be tricky. For example, if there are 220 calories per serving of juice and a bottle contains two servings, you are actually consuming 440 calories if you drink the entire bottle.

- **Percent daily value (% DV):** This section tells the amount of major nutrients contained in each serving. The % DV tells the percent of the recommended daily intake of that nutrient (not the percent of the nutrient) in the food. Remember that all values are based on one serving of the amount indicated in the serving size notation.

- **Other nutrients:** If the food contains more than 2% DV of specific vitamins and minerals, the label must state the amount on the label. Remember that all amounts are based on the serving size. For example, if the label says 10% DV of vitamin A and the serving size is 1 cup, you must consume 10 cups of the food to get 100% of the recommended amount of vitamin A, if this is the only food you are consuming.

- **Footnotes:** The footnotes provide reference information. Remember that each person is different. A highly active person might need to consume more than 2000 calories to maintain body weight. A very inactive person might need to consume fewer calories.

- **Calories and calories from fat:** This value tells how many calories there are in one serving. The label further states how many calories are specifically from fat.

10

- **Types of fat:** For foods containing fat, the amount of each kind of fat is listed. In general, monounsaturated fats are the best choice for good health. Many polyunsaturated fats are also good choices. Saturated fats are a poor choice for good health. They are known to be a factor in atherosclerosis, high cholesterol, and heart disease. Another type of unsaturated fat is trans fat. Nutritionally, trans fats are not essential, and they contribute specifically to the risk of coronary heart disease. Health officials worldwide recommend that consumption of trans fat be reduced to trace amounts.

- **Types of carbohydrate:** Carbohydrates are compounds including sugars, carbohydrates, and fiber. Carbohydrates and fiber are both important for good health. Foods high in sugars should be consumed on a limited basis.

apply it

Find printable activities on the companion web site for this book, accessed through www.cengagebrain.com.

Food Package Label Activity

GOAL: To understand the correct use of the food package labels

STEP 1: Organize into groups, if possible. Each person should collect five packages of foods or beverages. Choose different types of foods and beverages and try to represent all food groups.

STEP 2: For each package, decide whether the serving size on the package label represents the serving size typically eaten by a college student.

STEP 3: For each of the nutrients, determine which food/beverage has the greatest amount of the nutrient by weight and percent daily value.

STEP 4: Using as many different foods as needed from the group of packages, create a nutritionally sound menu for one day. Try to create a menu that includes 100 percent of as many nutrients as possible and that you consider reasonable in terms of your budget and appetite. Identify and discuss any deficiencies and solutions to repair these deficiencies.

SELF-ASSESSMENT QUESTION

- Review some food labels you have in your kitchen. What is your typical serving size for each food compared to the serving size used in food guides and package labels? Is there a difference, and, if so, how does it affect using these tools?

❓ CRITICAL THINKING QUESTION

▶ How much do you think reading and understanding food package labels for nutritional information will help you to achieve and maintain a healthy lifestyle?

10

> ## success steps for maintaining a healthy diet
>
> - Be aware of the nutritional value of the foods you eat.
> - Use scientifically based standards such as *Dietary Guidelines for Americans* and MyPlate to guide your food choices.
> - Know how to read food labels to understand a food's nutritional value.

CASE IN POINT: BURNING THE CANDLE AT BOTH ENDS

Read the scenario below. Then, in groups or as a class, discuss the questions at the end.

Alan is in his second year of college. He has a full-time job, family responsibilities, and difficult courses that require significant time spent studying. Alan often skips breakfast in order to get to his job, which starts at 7:30 A.M. He grabs a quick bite at one of the fast food places on his way from work to school. He often eats dinner out of the vending machine during the break between his 6:00 P.M. and 8:00 P.M. classes each evening. Alan works at a customer service call center during the day, sitting at the phone answering questions. When Alan gets home from his night classes, he spends at least two hours studying. He also studies for many hours on the weekends.

- Reflect on your own daily schedule and work, family, and school responsibilities. How do Alan's challenges compare with your own situation?

- What specific health behaviors do you think Alan should be concerned with? List as many as you can identify from this short scenario. Read between the lines.

- Alan often complains of very low energy, difficulty in falling asleep at night, problems concentrating in class, and inability to rid himself of a nagging cold. What specific recommendations can you suggest to Alan to improve his energy, alertness, and preparation for his challenging responsibilities?

10

SLEEP: AN ESSENTIAL ACTIVITY FOR THE SUCCESSFUL STUDENT

The stresses associated with college are many and often overwhelming. These stresses, combined with normal and situational stresses of other areas of life, can have a negative impact on regular, sound sleep, which in turn negatively affects health, focus and attention, and the energy required to be a successful learner. It is estimated that adults need between seven and eight hours of sound sleep each night. The inability to fall asleep or stay asleep is termed *insomnia*. Insomnia can occur in people of all ages at different levels of severity and can cause sleep difficulties ranging from a few nights to many months in duration. Transient insomnia is when individuals have sleep difficulty for less than four weeks and is seen with excitement, stress, unfamiliar environments, and so forth. Short-term insomnia is defined as sleep difficulty for four weeks to six months. This kind of insomnia can be caused by long-term stress, psychiatric issues, or medical conditions. Chronic insomnia lasts more than six months and may be caused by physical problems.

Insufficient sleep can result in the need for naps during the day, which can negatively affect school performance.

CAUSES AND CONSEQUENCES OF INSUFFICIENT SLEEP

According to the Nebraska Rural Health and Safety Coalition (2002), there can be multiple possible causes of difficulties in sleeping:

- An inadequate amount of time devoted to sleep
- Factors that lead to poor-quality sleep (e.g., poor mattress, noisy environment, or a restless partner)
- Sleep disorders
- Excessive worry and preoccupation with life concerns
- Psychological factors and conditions, such as depression
- Disruption of the sleep schedule, caused by factors such as working at night or extensive travel
- Medical conditions that cause pain or other symptoms that interfere with sound and continuous sleep

The consequences of poor-quality or insufficient sleep include decreased alertness and attention, an inability to think and recall

10

information clearly, and low energy, resulting in decreased performance and productivity in school. In addition, if you are working in a lab or shop, safety may be compromised. Most of the body can rest and recover during wakefulness in a relaxed state. However, the cerebral cortex part of the brain seems to need deep, nondreaming sleep. It is thought that the cerebral cortex requires the large, slow (delta) waves that occur during sleep. If deep sleep doesn't occur, skills are diminished. Studies by Harrison and Horne (1999, 2000) and Blagrove, Alexander, and Horne (1995) suggest that impairment of decision making, effective communication, innovation, and memory all result from sleep deprivation. With long-term sleep deprivation, individuals become irritable and experience problems with relationships, and the risk for serious psychological disorders increases.

STRATEGIES FOR GOOD SLEEP

According to the Western Washington University Counseling Center (2012), there are many things an individual can do to improve the likelihood of a good night's sleep or to overcome difficulties in falling asleep. Those who are struggling with falling asleep or not sleeping well can try any or all of the following recommendations to optimize sleep benefits:

▶ **Practice relaxation techniques before bedtime.** It is easier to fall asleep when one is relaxed. Relaxation helps relieve anxiety and tension that can hinder falling asleep quickly. Use relaxation techniques, play relaxing music, and avoid irritating interruptions to help in falling asleep.

▶ **Distract your mind before bedtime.** Consider reading a nonstressful book, watching nonstressful movies, or engaging in peaceful conversation before bedtime, to distract the mind from the day's stress and challenges.

▶ **Take a hot bath just before bedtime.** Sleep naturally follows a sharp drop in body temperature; therefore, increasing body temperature with a hot bath may lead to sleep as the body returns to room temperature.

▶ **Create a quiet and peaceful environment.** Ensure that the environment is conducive to sleep, free of bright lights and

10

sound (like the TV), and at the appropriate temperature (not too cold, hot, or stuffy).

▶ **Control the diet for sound sleep.** Avoid eating large meals right before bedtime, especially those high in fat. If a bedtime snack is necessary, choose foods higher in carbohydrates (i.e., breads, crackers, cereal). Avoid alcohol and caffeine right before bedtime. Caffeine is not only a stimulant, but it is also a diuretic. Consumption of caffeine within a few hours of bedtime will make it difficult to fall asleep, cause the sleep to be lighter, and increase the need to urinate, interrupting sound sleep. Though alcohol is classified as a depressant and may increase drowsiness, alcohol consumption before bedtime also leads to lighter sleep and waking up more frequently. Nicotine prior to bed can also hinder sound sleep.

▶ **Manage pain before bedtime.** Pain, even minor pain, can make it difficult to fall asleep and can wake a person often. Consider taking precautions to manage aches and pain before going to bed. Simple strategies include over-the-counter pain medication, heat, massage, and stretching. Obviously, those with serious or chronic pain should consult a physician.

▶ **Exercise daily.** Exercise early in the day (not close to bedtime) to help with falling asleep more easily and to support more sound sleep. Exercise right before bedtime can increase the metabolic rate, which makes falling asleep more difficult.

▶ **Keep the bedroom for sleeping.** Avoid working or watching TV in bed or using the bedroom for a study place or office, if possible. The brain might find it difficult to make the switch between work and rest. If falling asleep is difficult, consider moving to a different room and doing some quiet activity. Also, do not fall asleep outside of the bedroom (like on the couch in front of the TV).

▶ **Go to bed and get up at the same time each day.** Keeping a good sleep schedule can help train the body for regular, sound sleep.

▶ **Avoid napping in the daytime.** If drowsiness is preventing productive work, consider exercising. If a nap is unavoidable, sleep for no longer than a few minutes and do not nap late in the afternoon.

SELF-ASSESSMENT QUESTIONS

- What is your assessment of your sleep? Do you think you get sufficient sleep for optimal performance? How many hours of sleep do you get on average each night? What is the quality of your sleep?
- If your sleep is not optimal, what strategies do you think might work for you to improve the quantity and quality of your sleep?

? CRITICAL THINKING QUESTION

▶ What relaxation techniques do you or might you use before bedtime?

10

- Use relaxation techniques before bedtime.
- Distract your mind from stressful thoughts before bedtime.
- Take a hot bath.
- Create a peaceful and quiet environment for sleep.
- Choose a healthy diet, which contributes to sound sleep.
- Address aches and pains that can interfere with sleep.
- Get adequate exercise.
- Avoid working and doing other activities in your bedroom. Reserve the bedroom for sleeping.
- Keep a consistent sleep and waking schedule.
- Don't take naps during the day.

EXERCISE: STRATEGIES FOR AVOIDING FATIGUE AND OPTIMIZING ENERGY

In addition to good nutrition and sleep, you can use regular exercise to help to avoid fatigue, increase focus and attention, improve energy levels, reduce risk for some diseases, and maintain or improve overall health.

EXERCISE GUIDELINES

The American Academy of Family Physicians (2006) makes specific recommendations for physical activity:

- Engage in regular physical activity and reduce sedentary behavior to promote health, psychological well-being, and a healthy body weight.

10

▶ Achieve physical fitness by including cardiovascular conditioning, stretching exercises for flexibility, and resistance exercises or calisthenics for muscle strength and endurance.

▶ Specifically, be physically active for at least 30 minutes most days of the week.

▶ Consult your physician on exercising for weight loss or if you have any medical conditions.

The President's Council on Physical Fitness and Sports (2010) further suggests strategies for safe aerobic activity:

▶ Warm up for 5 to 10 minutes before engaging in aerobic activity.

▶ Maintain exercise intensity for 30 to 45 minutes.

▶ Gradually decrease the intensity of the workout, then stretch to cool down during the last 5 to 10 minutes.

COMPONENTS OF EXERCISE

There are five major components of effective and safe exercise. Figure 10-2 shows examples of activities that can improve physical fitness.

▶ **Cardiorespiratory endurance.** Cardiorespiratory endurance describes how well the body brings in oxygen to the body,

Regular exercise contributes to overall health by maintaining cardiovascular fitness, increasing muscle tone and flexibility, and relieving stress.

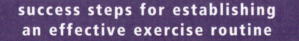

success steps for establishing an effective exercise routine

- Select an exercise routine that you like and that you will engage in regularly.
- Include exercises for both flexibility and cardiovascular fitness.
- Engage in your exercise routine most days of the week.
- Warm up before engaging in aerobic activity.
- Sustain aerobic activity for 30 to 45 minutes.
- Decrease intensity gradually and stretch to cool down.

10

FITNESS ACTIVITY BOX	
Activity Intensity	**Activities**
Light Intensity	Walking slowly
	Golf, powered cart
	Swimming, slow treading
	Gardening or pruning
	Bicycling, very light effort
	Dusting or vacuuming
	Conditioning exercise, light stretching or warm-up
Moderate Intensity	Walking briskly
	Golf, pulling or carrying clubs
	Swimming, recreational
	Mowing lawn, power motor
	Tennis, doubles
	Bicycling 5 to 9 mph, level terrain or with a few hills
	Scrubbing floors or washing windows
	Weight lifting, resistance machines or free weights
Vigorous Intensity	Race walking, jogging, or running
	Swimming laps
	Mowing lawn, hand mower
	Tennis, singles
	Bicycling more than 10 mph, or on steep uphill terrain
	Moving or pushing furniture
	Circuit training

Figure 10-2   Select the activity of appropriate intensity based on your individual needs.

moves it to the blood for circulation throughout the body, and then distributes it among the body's cells for fuel utilization. The more active a person is, the greater his or her cardiorespiratory endurance must be. Improving cardiorespiratory endurance is accomplished by aerobic or endurance exercises such as biking, swimming, walking, running, and so forth.

▶ **Muscle strength.** Muscle strength describes how well the muscles exert force during activity. Improving muscular strength requires resistance exercises such as weight lifting.

10

▶ **Muscle endurance.** Muscle endurance describes how well muscles perform without fatiguing over a long period of activity. Some of the same activities that improve cardiorespiratory endurance also improve muscular endurance including running, biking, and swimming.

▶ **Body composition.** Body composition describes the relative amounts of bone, muscle, fat, and organs making up the body. This is often referred to as Body Mass Index, or BMI. A high level of body fat has been shown to increase the risk for many diseases, including heart disease, hypertension, joint disorders, and some cancers. Weight only describes one factor of body composition. Because muscle weighs more than fat, a person with well-developed muscles and low fat might weigh more and have a smaller size than a person with higher body fat. Lowering body fat can be accomplished by regular aerobic exercise and sound nutritional practices.

▶ **Flexibility.** Flexibility describes the range of motion of a joint. Flexible joints resist injury. Increasing the flexibility of joints is accomplished by safe stretching exercises (Losefree.com, 2009).

SELF-ASSESSMENT QUESTIONS

- How much do you currently exercise? In what areas do you think you might need to improve?
- Do you think you are at risk for any disease that might be prevented by increasing your exercise level? Describe these diseases and how exercise might lower the risk.

? CRITICAL THINKING QUESTION

▶ Do you know your body's Body Mass Index (BMI)?

apply it

Find printable activities on the companion web site for this book, accessed through www.cengagebrain.com.

Exercise Program Research and Development

GOAL: To develop a safe and effective exercise program that can be utilized by a busy college student.

STEP 1: Connect to the Internet and search for aerobic, strength, and stretching exercises. Consider using these topics as your search terms.

STEP 2: Make a list of safety considerations you find in your research.

continued

10

continued

STEP 3: Design an exercise program that you personally will enjoy and that will fit into your student lifestyle. Include goals you have (e.g., weight loss, strength building, overall health maintenance, and so on). Use the examples in Figure 10-3 to help organize your program.

POSTURE

In addition to exercise, posture is an essential component in good health. Poor posture can drain energy, cause fatigue, and increase the stress on the body. Good posture is defined as the position in which the bones are properly aligned so that joints, ligaments, and muscles can work in the way they were designed to work. Good posture allows the body's organs to rest in the proper position so that they can function normally. It also helps to strengthen the back muscles that maintain the natural curve of the spinal column, which helps to prevent or relieve lower back pain. Poor posture requires the muscles to work harder just to perform normal tasks and puts unnecessary and imbalanced stress on joints.

Poor posture can result from several factors:

- Injuries
- Poor sleep support (a poor-quality mattress)
- Excessive weight
- Visual deficiencies

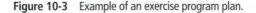

Time of day	Exercise details (Describe specifically the exercise you will do)	Number of repetitions or length of time dedicated to this exercise	Designated days in the week
6:00 am	Ride bike	25 minutes	M,W,F

Figure 10-3 Example of an exercise program plan.

Copyright © Cengage Learning®.

10

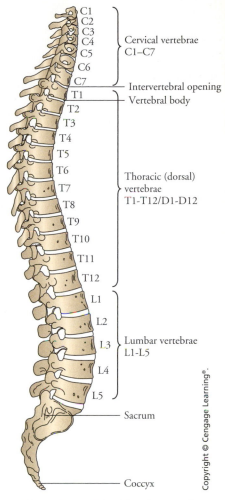

Figure 10-4   Maintaining the natural curves of the spinal column contributes to good posture and health.

success steps for assessing your posture

- Stand in a relaxed position facing a mirror and wearing as few clothes as possible.

- Imagine a vertical line running down the body that goes exactly between the eyes and through the middle of the chin, collarbones, sternum, pubic bones, and midpoint between the ankles. This line should be vertical and straight from head to toe.

- Turn sideways to the mirror. Assess the curves made by your spinal column. You should see three natural curves: the cervical curve, the thoracic curve, and the lumbar curve. See Figure 10-4 for proper curvature.

- Face the mirror again. Imagine a horizontal line through each of the following pairs of joints: the shoulders, the hips, and the knees. Each horizontal line should be perfectly straight and parallel to the ground.

- Assess the head while relaxed. It should be perfectly straight, as though it were floating on top of the spinal column, not tilting to either side.

- Solicit help from a friend, camera, or video recording. From the back, assess the vertebrae. The spinous processes of the vertebral column forming the bumps down the center of the back should be straight and even down the entire spinal column.

 Foot problems and improper shoes

 Weak muscles and muscle imbalance

 Careless sitting, standing, and sleeping habits

 Occupational stress (including working on a computer)

 Poorly designed workspace

Poor posture can cause and contribute to health difficulties as well as general fatigue. Consider the following possible consequences of poor posture:

 **Reduced oxygen intake and compromised circulation.** In order to function optimally, the lungs must be able to

inflate and deflate adequately. Slumped posture impedes the lungs' ability to expand and contract, resulting in shallow breathing. Consequently, the amount of oxygen available to body tissues via normal circulation is reduced, resulting in fatigue and less than optimal function of body systems.

▶ **Joint and muscular pain.** Poor posture can cause misalignment of joints, placing unnatural pull and pressure on muscles. The result can be chronic muscular pain, such as in the low back.

▶ **Nerve dysfunction.** The nerves that supply the body exit the spinal cord through the vertebrae, the small bones that make up the spinal column. Nerves travel throughout the body to muscles and tissues, and control movement as well as organ function. A misaligned spinal column or pressure on a muscle or organ due to poor posture can compress nerves and impair their function.

▶ **Improper digestive and bowel function.** The digestive and excretory systems rely on wave-like movements to propel food and waste through the respective systems. Poor posture inhibits the natural movements of these systems and can interfere with healthy digestion and elimination.

▶ **Serious medical conditions.** Poor posture that causes chronic compression of muscles, nerves, or other systems can result in serious medical conditions. Many people are familiar with carpal tunnel syndrome (CTS), which causes compression of the nerves in the wrist, resulting in pain, tingling, and numbness of the hands. In severe cases, surgery is required to correct the problem. In many cases, attention to posture and ergonomics can prevent CTS.

Maintaining good posture requires paying attention to how you sit, walk, lift and carry items, and sleep. Consider the following suggestions for improving your posture:

▶ Keep body weight within normal ranges.

▶ Sleep on a firm mattress of high quality.

▶ Get regular eye exams and resolve vision problems.

▶ Create a work environment conducive to good posture.

▶ Be aware of ergonomic principles and apply them to your daily activities.

▶ Focus on good posture until it becomes an unconscious habit.

▶ When standing, hold head high with chin forward, shoulders back, chest out, and stomach tucked in.

▶ When sitting, use a chair with a firm seat and low back support, keep table top at elbow height, and keep knees at about 90 degrees.

▶ Maintain good posture by incorporating sound ergonomic principles into the design of your work space. Figure 10-5 illustrates an ergonomically designed work space.

• Top of monitor just below eye level. This supports keeping the head over the shoulders. Comfortable viewing is generally 5 to 30 degrees below horizontal. Place in front of the body to prevent sitting in a twisted posture or turning the head.

• Head over the shoulders to allow the skeleton to carry the weight of the head, relieving overuse of neck, shoulder, and back muscles.

• Monitor distance so that chin doesn't jut forward while the trunk is against the chair back.

• Seat back should support curve in lower (lumbar) spine. Higher seat backs are recommended to relieve spinal pressures. A slight backward angle is preferred to allow the chair to take some load off the spine. Allow the chair to carry a share of the body weight.

• Keyboard height should allow for relaxed shoulders, flat wrists, and at least 90 degrees at the inside of elbow. Sit directly in front, close enough not to have to reach forward. Rest palms on rest only when fingers can remain relaxed.

• Armrests, if used, soft and wide. There should be no contact during keying. Close enough to not force extension of elbows, and low enough for shoulders to be relaxed without slumping or leaning.

• Thighs level with or just above knees to promote a neutral spine. Apply the "90-90-90" rule: hips, knees, and ankles should be flexed at 90 degrees.

• Seat pan not so deep that comfortable contact with chair back is prevented. Contact behind the knees must be avoided. Optimal contact with thighs provides greatest degree of effortless support.

• Feet in firm contact with the floor to distribute load through the whole body. Use a footrest only if necessary. Leave space under desk free of any obstruction to legs.

Figure 10-5 Ergonomics is the study of effective positioning of work-related tasks. Ergonomic workstations position tools and equipment so that good posture and body alignment are maintained.

SELF-ASSESSMENT QUESTIONS

- Do you often feel sore spots anywhere on your body?
- How often do you take breaks from studying to move around, stretch, and rest your eyes?
- What is your typical position when sitting, standing, working on a computer, and walking? (Take a look at your posture critically and in the mirror and describe specifically what you see. Start with your head and assess each joint, the alignment and evenness of joint pairs, and each segment of your body as a unit.)

? CRITICAL THINKING QUESTION

- Do you think that your posture is negatively impacted if you use a laptop or a tablet for schoolwork?

success steps for improving your posture

- Set an alarm to go off every 20 or 30 minutes during long study sessions as a reminder to take a quick break and stretch.
- Using a search tool such as Google, search the Internet for stretching exercises. Select ones you like and incorporate them into your study sessions.
- If you have problems with posture, try to develop the habit of checking your posture several times throughout the day while walking, sitting, driving, and so forth.

▶ When studying or working at a desk, stand up, move around, rest the eyes, and do stretches every 20 minutes or so.

▶ When sleeping, sleep on your side with knees bent and head supported by a pillow or on your back with a small pillow supporting neck. Avoid sleeping on your back.

CHAPTER SUMMARY

This chapter focused on the importance of physical considerations, such as nutrition, exercise, sleep, and posture, to your daily functioning. If you compare how well you function when you are feeling your best to when you are ill or fatigued, the significance of maintaining your health may become more apparent.

The demands of school, which are typically in addition to other life responsibilities, require endurance, clear thinking, and energy. Sound health practices, such as those described in this chapter, become the foundation for success in carrying out all of your responsibilities effectively. Good health lays the foundation for success in all of the areas discussed in *100% Student Success*.

10

POINTS TO KEEP IN MIND

In this chapter, several main points were discussed in detail:

> ▶ Nutrition and fitness are critical to good health, high energy, and the focus and attention needed to be a successful student.

> ▶ The *Dietary Guidelines for Americans* and the MyPlate guide serve as excellent guides for good food choices.

> ▶ Knowing how to read food package labels also helps in making good food choices and in comparing foods for purchase.

> ▶ Sleep is an essential part of good health and success as a student. There are several strategies that can be used to increase the quality and quantity of sleep and to avoid the problems associated with poor or insufficient sleep.

> ▶ Exercise is essential for good health, and the benefits of regular exercise are important for the successful student.

> ▶ Posture is an important component of fitness and good health. Good posture can help students avoid aches, pains, and fatigue associated with long study sessions.

CHECK YOUR UNDERSTANDING

Visit www.cengagebrain.com to see how well you have mastered the material in Chapter 10.

SUGGESTED ITEMS FOR LEARNING PORTFOLIO

> ▶ Food Package Label Activity
> ▶ Exercise Program Research and Development

10

REFERENCES

American Academy of Family Physicians. (2006). Exercise: A healthy habit to start and keep. Retrieved February 11, 2013, from http://www .aafp.org/afp/2006/1215/p2097.html

Blagrove, M., Alexander, C., & Horne, J. (1995). The effects of chronic sleep reduction on the performance of cognitive tasks sensitive to sleep deprivation. *Applied Cognitive Psychology, 9*(1), 21–40.

Centers for Disease Control and Prevention (2011). About BMI for Adults. Retrieved April 2, 2013, from http://www.cdc.gov/healthyweight /assessing/bmi/adult_bmi/index.html

Department of Health and Human Services and the U.S. Department of Agriculture. (2010). Dietary Guidelines for Americans 2010. Retrieved February 11, 2013, from http://www.healthierus.gov/dietaryguidelines

Harrison, Y., & Horne, J. (1999). One night of sleep loss impairs innovative thinking and flexible decision making. *Organizational Behavior and Human Decision Processes, 78*(2), 128–145.

Harrison, Y., & Horne, J. (2000). The impact of sleep deprivation on decision making: A review. *Journal of Experimental Psychology—Applied, 6*(3), 236–249.

Losefree.com (2009). *5 basic components of physical fitness.* Retrieved February 12, 2013, from http://losefree.com/2009/03/5-basic-components-of-physical-fitness/

Nebraska Rural Health and Safety Coalition. (2002). Sleep deprivation: Causes and consequences. Retrieved February 11, 2013, from the Centers for Disease Control and Prevention, National Ag Safety Database web site: http://nasdonline.org/document/871/d000705/sleep -deprivation-causes-and-consequences.html

President's Council on Physical Fitness and Sports. (2010). Fitness fundamentals: Guidelines for personal exercise programs. Retrieved February 11, 2013, from http://www.rd.com/health/fitness/fitness-fundamentals-begin-and-maintain-an-exercise-program/5/

United States Department of Agriculture (2011). *10 tips to a great plate.* Retrieved February 11, 2013, from http://www.choosemyplate. gov/food-groups/downloads/TenTips/DGTipsheet1ChooseMyPlate-BlkAndWht.pdf

Western Washington University Counseling Center (2012). Sound sleep strategies. Retrieved February 11, 2013, from http://www.wwu.edu /counseling/sleep.shtml

10

Index